The Complete Book of
Anchoring and Mooring

BY EARL R. HINZ

Sail Before Sunset, 1979

Understanding Sea Anchors and Drogues, 1986

The Offshore Log, 1991

Pacific Wanderer, 1991

Landfalls of Paradise: The Guide to Pacific Islands, Third Edition, 1993

The Complete Book of Anchoring and Mooring, Second Edition, 1994

The Complete Book of
Anchoring and Mooring
Second Edition

BY EARL R. HINZ

With drawings by RICHARD R. RHODES

Cornell Maritime Press

CENTREVILLE, MARYLAND

Library of Congress Cataloging-in-Publication Data

Hinz, Earl R.

The complete book of anchoring and mooring / by Earl R. Hinz ; with drawings by Richard R. Rhodes. — 2nd ed.

p. cm.

Includes bibliographical references (p.) and index.

ISBN 0-87033-452-2

1. Mooring of ships. 2. Anchors. I. Title.

VK361.H56   1993

623.8′62—dc20

93-41799

Manufactured in the United States of America

First edition, 1986. Second edition, 1994

Contents

Acknowledgments

This book is the product of many people's experiences. I am particularly grateful to all the skippers of boats on which I have crewed for passing along valuable bits of their anchoring knowledge to me. To my own crews over the years who have put up with experimental anchoring systems on *Horizon*, I say thank you. And a hearty thanks is due the hundreds of sailors who weathered storms at anchor around the world over past years and made available the knowledge of how they survived. A similar vote of gratitude is owed to those whose boats didn't weather the storms, but were still generous enough to pass along the reasons for their failures.

Many manufacturers of ground tackle supplied information for this book. I want to recognize, in particular, the Campbell Chain Co., Washington Chain and Supply Co., R. C. Plath, Simpson-Lawrence, and Aeroquip Corporations. And then there were several trade associations like the Cordage Institute, the National Association of Chain Manufacturers, and the American Boat and Yacht Council who willingly shared technical data from their files in the interests of making boating safer through this book.

A significant amount of technical data on anchors and moorings was received through the good offices of R. J. Taylor of the U. S. Navy Civil Engineering Laboratories. I am certain that all recreational boaters will appreciate that these data have been made available for public use.

Both *Motor Boating & Sailing* and *Sea* magazines are to be thanked for allowing me to use technical information generated under their aegis.

Lastly, personal thanks are due specific individuals without whose help this volume could not have been produced with such completeness— Jack Ronalter who went through the hell and high water of hurricane Veena in Tahiti in order, I would like to believe, to give us a firsthand account of how to do it; "Monk" Farnham, a veteran boatman and writer himself, who did the first carving on this manuscript and helped to make sense out of its immensity; Joe Brown, free-lance boating writer, past editor of *Oceans* and a wooden boat enthusiast who smoothed the way editorially for the reader. And last in this lineup of assisting talent is Bob

Sharp, a lifelong boating friend with whom I have cruised and raced thousands of miles and whose engineering background was helpful in clarifying the quantitative aspects of the book.

My illustrator, Dick Rhodes, a man of varied talents who has been associated with the Hokule'a (Hawaiian Voyaging Canoe), redrew the lines of the square-rigged *Falls of Clyde,* and made the drawings for many Polynesian canoe books and stories. I was hesitant to ask him to join me in a subject as mundane as anchoring and mooring, but the subject needed enlightened graphics and Dick, thankfully, supplied his talents.

While most of the photographs are my own, I gratefully acknowledge the courtesies of the other photographers whose work I have been able to include.

The reason for crafting this second edition is to provide the reader with the latest in anchoring and mooring technology—advances which have been made over the past seven years. For much of this new information I have to thank the people at NAV-X Corporation who sponsored (and inspired) numerous new anchor test programs as part of the introduction of their Fortress anchor to the boating public. Many organizations participated in those tests and, in the end, were responsible for producing a wealth of new knowledge on boat anchoring. Among them were *Cruising World* magazine, BOAT/US, and West Marine Products. Numerous persons (too many to list), but whose names are synonymous with the world of recreational boating, contributed to the conduct and verification of the several test programs.

A new emphasis on preserving the marine environment has taken hold in recent years and it is a pleasure to recognize those on the front lines of the effort to preserve one of nature's most amazing living objects—the coral reef. I recognize with thanks the work done by the Key Largo National Marine Sanctuary in Florida and the University of Hawaii Sea Grant Program for their development efforts in coral moorings which allow boaters to enjoy the wonders of coral reefs without needlessly destroying them at the same time.

The anchoring and mooring of boats has taken on its own high-tech look. No longer do we simply throw the hook in the water. Now the hook has been scientifically designed, the ground tackle has been made into a complete boat system, and the once hidden element of the system, the seabed, is considered a partner to be respected in boating operations.

Although I appear as author of this book, it is really the entire boating community that has made it possible. May all readers benefit in some small way from it.

The Complete Book of
Anchoring and Mooring

CHAPTER ONE

Introduction

> An experienced and careful master mariner who
> never made a call upon underwriters for any loss.
>
> —*Epitaph of Captain Augustus N. Littlefield who died in 1878,
> aged 75. Located in the Common Burying Ground, Newport, Rhode
> Island**

There is no aspect of boating that is less glamorous or more critical to the
well-being of a boat and crew than anchoring. It requires an inordinate
amount of work, heavy gear, some hazard to crew, and it usually is a wet
and dirty job. Furthermore, anchoring is the last event in a passage, and
the crew is eager to get ashore. As a result there is a sense of urgency that
may result in carelessness.

To minimize potential problems under these circumstances, it is
important for your boat to be properly equipped with good ground tackle
and for the crew to know how to use it. Then, and only then, can you toast
a successful day at sea and sleep well at anchor.

You may expect a book on anchoring to begin with anchors and
immediately launch into a debate on which is the best anchor. I have
chosen not to do that because the anchor is no more important than any
other component of the ground tackle system.

Some months after the Tahiti hurricanes of 1982 and 1983, I had the
opportunity to have a round table talk with four skippers who had
survived one or more of these storms—three whose boats finally went on
the beach, but were later salvaged, and one whose boat survived at anchor.
All four skippers emphasized that anchors were not the problem—all
anchors of adequate size did their jobs. What failed were rodes, bow
rollers, windlasses, and people. The fetish of concentrating solely on the

---

*Quoted in Robert Hendrickson, *The Ocean Almanac*. (Garden City, N. Y.: Doubleday & Co.,
1984).

anchor obscures the real issues, which are the total ground tackle system and how to use it.

This *Complete Book of Anchoring and Mooring* addresses the needs of recreational and workboats in the 12- to 80-foot range. It covers monohulls, multihulls, light displacement sailboats, cruisers, sportfishers, passagemakers, and workboats. For the convenience of the reader it is divided into three parts:

Part I—*The Technology of Ground Tackle* utilizes a systems approach to determine loads at anchor and translate them into ground tackle design criteria. What was formerly considered strength through size (big anchors and heavy rodes) has been refined in order to reduce weight and loads on the boat, and to ease the difficulties the crew has in handling the total ground tackle system.

Part II—*The Art of Anchoring* brings into play the human factors which not only help design the ground tackle but determine its limitations and application. Techniques are presented that make use of your head rather than your back to make the most of an anchoring situation.

Part III—*Permanent Moorings* is a treatise of its own on how to design and fabricate permanent moorings for harbors and other sheltered areas. Available mooring space (including local political restrictions) and your mode of use of the boat are critical to the decision to put in a mooring and what kind to use.

But, before you can delve into the principles of modern day anchoring and mooring, everyone must speak the same language. The jargon of the sea has always been a puzzle to landlubbers. You'll find in *The Ingoldsby Legends* the statement: "It's very odd that Sailor-men should talk so very queer." But it really isn't so odd when you consider that sea transportation evolved during a period of history when education was a rarity—schools for sailors did not exist, and seamen, in general, were a polyglot of the lowest classes of society. Officers came from "midships" or bought a commission with money gained from land-bound enterprises. Those who served on ships found it necessary to create their own language (actually it evolved) because that of the land did not fit their needs.

Today, those of you who take to the sea like to think you are following the venerable traditions of the sea right down to the salty terms employed around boats. At least in the ground tackle department, you can improve your salty talk by using nautical terminology correctly.

THE JARGON OF GROUND TACKLE

Anchoring, mooring, and docking are distinctly different actions. A boat is "anchored" when it "rides" or "lays" to a single anchor "rode," although it is conceivable to have two anchors in tandem on that rode. A boat is "moored" after it "picks up a mooring buoy" or has set a multiple-anchor moor of its own. "Docking" means to "tie up to a dock," which is a land-bound structure. If the boat is simply "docked," then it is in "drydock"—a subtle but traditionally important difference.

You speak of the anchors of a boat as "hooks," the hook being a colloquial expression based on the desired action of the anchor. In today's

A stone anchor, used by the early Polynesians in the Cook Islands, is on display at the Cook Islands Museum on the island of Rarotonga. The rode is made of sennit, a product of the fibrous husk of the coconut.

boating world there are lunch hooks, working anchors, and storm anchors, which haven't always been known by those names.

In the seventeenth century, Captain John Smith described "proper tearmes" [*sic*] for anchors in his *A Sea Grammar,* published in 1627, as follows:

> The proper tearmes belonging to Anchors are many. The least are called *Kedgers,* to use in calms weather in a slow streame, or to kedge up and downe a narrow River, which is when they feare the winde or tide may drive them on shore. They row by her with an Anchor in a boat, and in the middest of the streame or where they finde most fit [drop anchor] if the Ship come too neere the shore, and so by a Hawser winde her head about, then weigh it againe till the like occasion; and this is *kedging.*
>
> There is also a *streame Anchor,* not much bigger, to stemme an easie streame or tide. Then there is the *first, second,* and *third Anchor,* yet all such as a Ship in faire weather may ride by, and are called *bow Anchors.*
>
> The greatest is the *sheat Anchor,* and never used but in great necessity.

Carrying a variety of anchor types and sizes has been general practice since the days of Caesar when extensive seafaring covered the Mediterranean Sea and the eastern Atlantic Ocean. For routine anchoring offshore, Caesar's galleys carried several anchors ready, fore and aft. One of these would be larger than the rest, and in a severe blow the captain of the galley would give the order to "lower the last anchor," the "sacred one," as seafarers called it. The sacred anchor later came to be known in merchantmen and men-of-war as the sheet anchor.

Some traditional anchor terms are still used, for example, the bow anchor (or bower) is found in the hawsepipes of practically every ship and is used for all anchoring purposes. Most ships today do not carry a sheet anchor depending instead on two bow anchors and propulsion to handle severe weather at anchor. Sailing vessels that lack propulsion-assist may still carry the "greatest" of all anchors—the "sacred one."

The much misinterpreted kedge anchor is also standard gear on sailing vessels and small boats. Many persons call the old-fashioned (also known as the Admiralty pattern, fisherman, and yachtsman) anchor a kedge anchor. This is incorrect unless an old-fashioned anchor is, indeed, being used in the act of kedging. Any anchor that you take out from your vessel for the purpose of kedging is really a kedge anchor while serving in that role. In comparison to today's patent lightweight anchors, an old-fashioned anchor would be unnecessarily awkward and heavy to handle as a kedge.

Small boat anchor terminology has departed somewhat from Captain John Smith's *Sea Grammar*. What was the *sheat Anchor* is now the storm anchor. His *bow Anchor* has become the working anchor. His *streame Anchor* is now known as the stern anchor. And, as for the modern lunch hook, traditional sailors knew better than to risk their boats to an undersized piece of gear. But the *kedge Anchor* remains the same—any small anchor that is used for kedging.

The word anchor comes from the Latin word *anchora* meaning bend or bent which certainly suggests the shape of an anchor. But you also "bend a line" to the anchor "ring" which then becomes the "anchor line" or "rode." At the other end of that line you "make fast" or "belay" it to a "Samson post" (named after an Israelite judge of great strength) using a "hitch." If the line is not long enough, you "bend" two lines together.

The tail of the line beyond the Samson post is called the "bitter end." The meaning of this term is varied, and you can take your choice. It is the end of the anchor line that sees the least wear; therefore, it is the "better end." Or, it is the end of the anchor line that is made fast to foredeck "bitts" and is, therefore, the "bitter end." But the meaning that will stay with you the longest comes from the "bitter" feeling you get after having "let go the anchor" only to see the tail of the anchor line follow the anchor itself into the briny deep. More than one boater has suffered the embarrassment of losing an anchor and line this way.

You speak of "line" on a boat, such as an "anchor line," to differentiate it from plain rope which is the bulk material from which any number of lines can be made for the boat. There are only a few legitimate "ropes" on a boat such as the "bell rope," "bolt rope," and "tiller rope," among others. To "know the ropes" is a landlubberly expression since it identifies only with the few ropes aboard a sailing vessel—nine, in fact, on a square-rigger—and does not address the dozens of "lines" that constitute the working gear of boats or ships.

Even the general term "anchor line" has its variations. Traditionally, it was called a "cable," and it was 120 fathoms (720 feet) long. Ships continue to use the term "anchor cable," but the length is no longer a unique 120 fathoms. A ship's small boats—cutters, launches, pinnaces, etc.—ride at anchor to a line called a "rode," a term commonly used in the United States. In European boating circles, the term "cable" is still used.

You would "take out a line" when the line is transported away from the boat by dinghy as in kedging. You "haul in" a line hand over hand or by a windlass. "Slack off" means to ease up or let out a line. "Set the

An old-fashioned anchor of the admiralty pattern found in the lagoon at Abemama atoll in the Gilbert Islands (now Kiribati).

anchor" means to snub up gradually on the rode so that the anchor bill digs into the seabed.

Anchor terminology has carried over into the everyday jargon of the sailor. A ship is said to "slip her cable" when the "Old Man" orders that the cable be cut and the anchor abandoned. Seamen have adopted the phrase, "He slipped his cable," to explain a death. If a wife or mistress has run off with someone else, it is said, "She slipped her cable." A sailor who has permanently left the sea is said to have "swallowed the anchor."

Although the romance and superstitions of sailing days of yore have been replaced with more scientific and technical nomenclature, there is every reason to retain the jargon of the sea as it pertains to anchoring. This is a language used in all parts of the world, and it is an important facet of the anchoring game.

SETTING A REAL ANCHOR TO WINDWARD

Long ago I lost track of the number of times I anchored a boat, completing yet another day of boating or another blue water passage. I have anchored in good anchorages and in bad, in anchorages surrounded by vicious coral reefs and volcanic bluffs, in bottoms that "shoaled" to 15 fathoms, in seabeds of slippery mud, and with winds up to 50 knots. In all of these anchorages (and I am very generous to call some of them anchorages at all) a good set of the anchor provided the kind of satisfaction that is the equal of the finest after-dinner cigar.

Good ground tackle is the unheralded security blanket for a boat. Anchors throughout history have been the symbol of steadfastness and an emblem of hope. When things seemingly are at their worst, a firmly embedded anchor offers a ray of hope.

Anchoring is such an integral part of boating that it is often taken for granted—if you can make a boat go, you can also make it stop. Wrong. Watching "anchor drills" in a harbor can be a source of great amusement at someone else's expense until someone anchors too close and then your amusement turns to dismay.

With the increasing numbers of recreational and commercial boats on the water, competition for anchorages is becoming more severe. It can only get worse since the number of natural harbors and bights suitable for anchoring is virtually fixed for eternity, while the boating population continues to grow. There is no choice but to make better use of good anchorages and safer use of less desirable anchorages. You can grouse about it all you want, but it will be better for all if everyone learns more about proper anchoring to get along in our gregarious and ever-increasing boating society.

Recreational and working boats should have nothing less than complete ground tackle on board, and the crew should know how to use it. Being able to hold a boat relatively still and off the rocks while a clogged fuel filter is replaced or a torn sail is changed is a far better mark of seamanship than being able to call a proper Mayday on the radiotelephone.

When the winds begin to howl through the anchorage, it is too late to shop for ground tackle and train your crew. The die is cast and you have to place the security of your boat on whatever ground tackle sits on the foredeck and whatever knowledge your crew has. Before that happens, however, you can design a proper ground tackle system and train your crew in the proper art of anchoring. Then you will be ready to stake the safety of your boat on its anchor system in any weather.

In making a passage at sea, it matters little if you violate some of the fundamental precepts of steering or sailing. If your passage takes a little longer than planned, so be it. But at the end of the passage, setting your anchor must be done in a proper manner for your boat is now near its mortal enemy—land.

Most of my blue water cruising has been done without conventional marine hull insurance because of the prohibitively high cost of premiums.

Among the later developments of the old-fashioned anchor was the Trotman anchor (about 1846) which embodied a contemporary stock and upper shank but had a pivoting arm and flukes to minimize the chances of the lazy arm fouling the rode. There was a tripping palm on the backside of the arm which positioned the lower fluke to bite into the bottom. The Trotman shown here was reportedly carried by the U. S. battleship *Maine* when it was blown up in Havana harbor in 1898. The anchor was re-covered from the bottom in 1912 and taken up the Atlantic coast where it and many other relics were lost in a winter storm of 1912 in Ipswich Bay just north of Gloucester, Massachusetts. The anchor was resalvaged in 1975 and is now on display at the Seven Seas Restaurant Wharf in Gloucester. Photo: Jim McNitt.

Since most serious boating casualties occur in the vicinity of land, I have paid particular attention to the adequacy of my ground tackle and the process of setting the anchor. I know of no better insurance for a boat than a properly set anchor and a reliable anchor watch.

Nowhere in boating is the old saw "a chain is only as strong as its weakest link" more appropriate than in the boat-anchoring game. Few boaters realize how many links there are in the chain of equipment and events that constitute successful anchoring. The way to insure your boat is to provide capable links in the anchor system.

There is an interesting trade-off that you can make with insurance premiums. On the one hand, you can buy a paper policy that will reimburse your heirs for the price of the boat. On the other, you can make a similar investment in the boat to make it more seaworthy and your crew more capable. In the latter case, the payoff is the successful completion of your voyage. Further, not only has the boat survived, but your personal belongings aboard and maybe even your life have been spared to sail another day. Don't skimp on ground tackle and expect paper insurance to

The Bay of Islands, Suva, Fiji, has good holding ground and sufficient room for visiting cruising boats to anchor with a single hook. This is not a hurricane anchorage.

make up for it. Remember, a boat afloat is far more valuable to you than one on the rocks covered by paper insurance.

There is no moral to this story, only hard personal choices. If your budget can stand blue water insurance as well as good ground tackle, go for both. But remember, budget your own safety ahead of insurance.

For reader and author alike, it is now time to get on with the vital business of boat security at anchor.

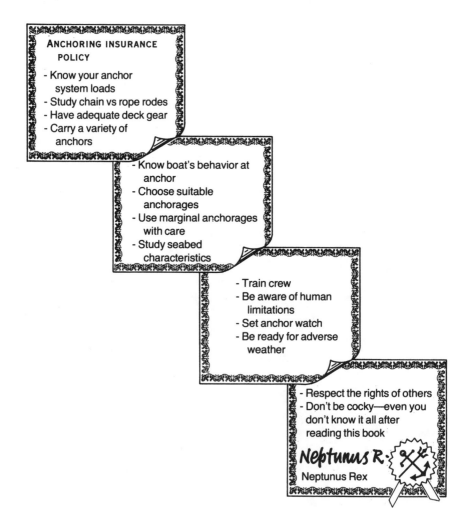

ANCHORING INSURANCE POLICY

- Know your anchor system loads
- Study chain vs rope rodes
- Have adequate deck gear
- Carry a variety of anchors

- Know boat's behavior at anchor
- Choose suitable anchorages
- Use marginal anchorages with care
- Study seabed characteristics

- Train crew
- Be aware of human limitations
- Set anchor watch
- Be ready for adverse weather

- Respect the rights of others
- Don't be cocky—even you don't know it all after reading this book

Neptunus R.

Neptunus Rex

PART I

THE TECHNOLOGY OF GROUND TACKLE

A comprehensive guide to requirements for ground tackle on boats and technical advice on the proper design, installation, and use of it.

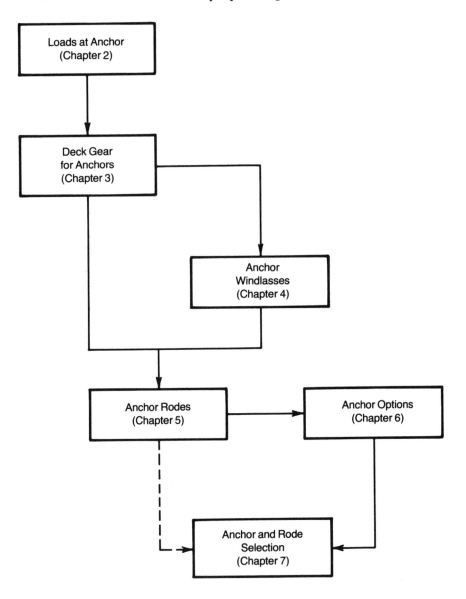

CHAPTER TWO

Loads at Anchor

Good seamanship calls for anchoring your boat in an area sheltered from wind and seas and with a seabed that will provide adequate holding power. But neither the elements nor the seabed are always found in suitable combinations to implement idealized seamanship. You must instead make the most of the situation which calls for equipping your boat with ground tackle that can take the fury of the wind and seas and survive. To do that, you first need to have some idea what the loads are that your boat will have to face.

All boats should be designed and equipped with ground tackle to survive winds of 30 knots (Beaufort 7) (see Fig. 2-1) with some shelter from the seas. There are many boats that by virtue of their use in fishing, cruising, or chartering, may find it necessary to anchor in much heavier winds. Any boat of substance can ride out 60 knots of wind (Beaufort 11) on the high seas and away from land and rocky shorelines. But it takes a well-equipped boat and an experienced crew to ride out the same winds and accompanying seas at anchor. The loads on a boat from a wind of 60 knots are four times as great as those from a wind of 30 knots and the seas have changed from rough to mountainous.

Wind by itself is not your principal adversary when anchoring, but it sets the stage for it. Actually, the sea is your adversary. Most ground tackle can handle a steady tug from the wind on the boat well. But throw into the fray simultaneous pitching, surging, and yawing of the boat, and you have every reason to be concerned about the integrity of your ground tackle system.

A boat in a seaway is considered to have "six degrees of freedom" or movement—three in linear motion and three in rotational motion (Fig. 2-2). These six motions are never seen or felt independently, generally they occur simultaneously although one or two of them may appear to be the dominant motion at a particular moment. A good example of this in a boat at anchor is the apparent dominance of pitch and heave when there is any wave motion.

Beaufort number	Wind speed knots	Seaman's term	Estimating wind speed / Effects observed at sea	Term and height of wave - ft. *	Sea state code
0	under 1	Calm	Sea like mirror.	Calm, glassy, 0	0
1	1-3	Light air	Ripples with appearance of scales; no foam crests.		
2	4-6	Light breeze	Small wavelets; crests of glassy appearance, not breaking.	Rippled, 0-1	1
3	7-10	Gentle breeze	Large wavelets; crests begin to break; scattered whitecaps.	Wavelets, 1-2	2
4	11-16	Moderate breeze	Small waves, becoming longer; numerous whitecaps.	Slight, 2-4	3
5	17-21	Fresh breeze	Moderate waves, taking longer form; many whitecaps; some spray.	Moderate, 4-8	4
6	22-27	Strong breeze	Larger waves forming; whitecaps everywhere; more spray.	Rough, 8-13	5
7	28-33	Moderate gale	Sea heaps up; white foam from breaking waves begins to be blown in streaks.		
8	34-40	Fresh gale	Moderately high waves of greater length; edges of crests begin to break into spindrift; foam is blown in well-marked streaks.	Very rough, 13-20	6
9	41-47	Strong gale	High waves; sea begins to roll; dense streaks of foam; spray may reduce visibility.		
10	48-55	Whole gale	Very high waves with overhanging crests; sea takes white appearance as foam is blown in very dense streaks; rolling is heavy and visibility reduced.	High, 20-30	7
11	56-63	Storm	Exceptionally high waves; sea covered with white foam patches; visibility still more reduced.	Very high, 30-45	8
12	64-71	Hurricane	Air filled with foam; sea completely white with driving spray; visibility greatly reduced.	Phenomenal, over 45	9

*Fully developed sea

(margin left: Working anchor — Storm anchor)

Fig. 2-1. Wind speed by the Beaufort scale with corresponding sea states, reproduced from *American Practical Navigator (Bowditch)*.

The three linear motions—surging, swaying, and heaving—are non-oscillatory, and the boat does not return to its original position of equilibrium unless the directions of the applied forces are reversed. The three rotational motions—yawing, rolling, and pitching—are all oscillatory, and the boat will tend to return to its equilibrium position when the disturbing forces are removed.

All six motions are experienced by a boat at anchor. The wind tends to create yawing and swaying. The waves tend to create pitching and

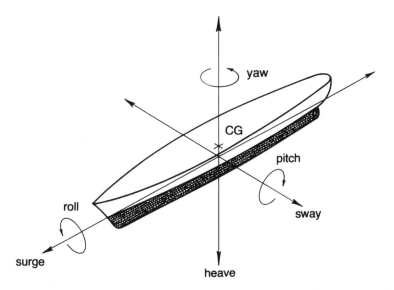

Surge—motion forward and backward in the direction of boat travel along the longitudinal axis.

Sway—athwartship motion of the boat along the transverse axis.

Heave—motion up and down in the vertical axis.

Roll—angular motion about the longitudinal axis. When the boat rolls, it lists alternately from starboard to port and back again.

Pitch—angular motion about the transverse axis. When the boat pitches, it trims alternately by the bow and stern.

Yaw—angular motion about the vertical axis. When the boat yaws, the bow and stern swing from side to side.

Fig. 2-2. The six degrees of freedom of a boat, derived from the Mariners Weather Log. Courtesy: National Oceanic and Atmospheric Administration.

heaving while the anchor restraint is involved with surging depending on its elasticity. Wind and wave combine to create roll but that is the least important of the six motions of the boat at anchor. A properly designed and set anchor system under normal circumstances is able to react to all of these motions without undue attention by the crew. In storm conditions, however, the unpredictability of wind and wave loadings and the possible wear and failure of ground tackle elements require constant vigilance on the part of the crew.

AMERICAN BOAT AND YACHT COUNCIL GROUND TACKLE DESIGN LOADS

The American Boat and Yacht Council (ABYC) has prepared a table of Typical Design Horizontal Loads (see Table 2-1) for use of designers and builders of boats and boat hardware. The table applies to both power and sail monohull boats and is simplified in that discrete boat lengths and beams are used assuming more or less conventional designs. Ground tackle loads are given for "working" and "storm" anchoring conditions as well as for "lunch" hooks. The anchored boat is assumed to have freedom to oscillate and to have moderate shelter from seas proportionate to its hull size.

To use the ABYC table, enter with your boat's length (LOA) and beam (separate columns for power and sail) using that parameter which gives you the larger load. The horizontal loads on the boat's ground tackle are then taken from the succeeding three columns identified as "Lunch hook," "Working anchor," or "Storm anchor." The approximate wind speeds that go with these three columns are 15 knots, 30 knots, and 42 knots, respectively.

If you ever expect to anchor in force 9 winds or greater, you should design your ground tackle for 60 knots of wind. The ABYC table can be

Table 2-1. Typical Ground Tackle Design Horizontal Loads

Critical dimension[a]			Horizontal load on boat—lbs[b]		
LOA	Beam—ft		Lunch	Working	Storm
feet	power	sail	hook	anchor	anchor
10	5	4	40	160	320
15	6	5	60	250	500
20	8	7	90	360	720
25	9	8	125	490	980
30	11	9	175	700	1,400
35	13	10	225	900	1,800
40	14	11	300	1,200	2,400
50	16	13	400	1,600	3,200
60	18	15	500	2,000	4,000
c 70	20	17	675	2,700	5,400
80	22	19	900	3,600	7,200

Source: American Boat and Yacht Council (ABYC), Inc., P. O. Box 806, Amityville, NY 11701.
[a]Use LOA or beam of your boat, whichever produces the larger load. Houseboats should use the load for the next larger powerboat size
[b]Assumes freedom to oscillate, and moderate shelter from seas proportionate to hull size.
[c]Extrapolated by author.

adjusted to 60 knots by multiplying the loads given in the Working anchor column by 4.

As an example of how to use the ABYC table, consider finding the ground tackle horizontal loads for a Uniflite Coastal Cruiser with a flying bridge (Table 2-2). The values for ground tackle loads are simply interpolated on the basis of LOA or beam and the larger set is the one used. In this case they are seen to be quite close in magnitude which is what you would expect for a conventionally proportioned boat.

The general run of sportfishing and cruising power boats should have ground tackle designed to withstand 42 knots of wind which is a common gale condition on either coast of the United States as well as in the Great Lakes. Powerboats that are based in hurricane-prone areas, such as the Caribbean, should be designed to withstand 60-knot wind speeds.

The ABYC table can be adjusted to 60-knot wind conditions by multiplying the loads given in the "Working anchor" column by four. In the case of the Uniflite Coastal Cruiser, 60 knots of wind would produce horizontal ground tackle loads of approximately 4,240 pounds (4 × 1,060).

CALCULATING GROUND TACKLE LOADS

If your boat is atypical, that is, if it is beamier, has higher or lower freeboard, has more rigging, or is a multihull, you must take time to calculate the wind loads making suitable corrections for surge loading at the same time.

The aerodynamicist has given us various tools to estimate the wind loads on a boat at anchor. One method is to measure them in a wind tunnel, which few of us can afford to do. Another way is to estimate wind loads mathematically based on test data for other boats, for other vehicles,

Table 2-2. Example of Ground Tackle Design Horizontal Loads by American Boat and Yacht Council Method

Boat: Uniflite Coastal Cruiser	Ground tackle design horizontal loads—lbs		
LOA: 37 ft 9 in	Lunch hook	Working anchor	Storm anchor
Beam: 12 ft 9 in			
Equivalent steady state wind speed—knots	15	30	42
Loads as a function of length	265	1,060	2,120	Use
Loads as a function of beam	220	880	1,760

such as automobiles and airplanes, and on a whole variety of components which make up a vehicle. The latter method will be described here as it can be done for most boat shapes using a simple hand calculator and the drawings of the boat.

In addition to the static aerodynamic drag loads on a boat at anchor, there are also dynamic loads caused by the surging of the boat in the seas and, sometimes, there may also be current drag loads. These are all factored into the final answer.

The equation for the aerodynamic drag of an object in a wind stream is:

$$d = q \cdot C_d \cdot A \qquad \textit{[Equation 2-1]}$$

where d = drag force—lbs

q = dynamic pressure—lb per ft^2

C_d = drag coefficient—dimensionless

A = characteristic area—ft^2

The dynamic pressure, q, is determined from the equation:

$$q = \frac{\rho}{2} \cdot V^2$$

where ρ = .002378 slugs per ft^3 at standard sea level conditions

V = wind speed in ft per second

Values of dynamic pressure, q, for a range of wind speeds at sea level are:

V—knots	Beaufort number	(q) lbs per ft^2
10	3	0.33
20	5	1.3
30	7	3
40	8	5
50	10	8
60	11	12
70	12	17
80	13	22
90	15	28
100	16	34

Be sure to note one very important characteristic of the dynamic pressure which is that it increases as the square of the wind speed. The dynamic pressure acting against a boat at wind speeds of 60 knots is four times that acting against a boat at 30 knots.

The drag coefficient, C_d, comes from wind tunnel test data and is applicable to similar body shapes at different wind speeds as long as the flow is incompressible which is the case for wind speeds of interest here (Table 2-3). These drag coefficients are for a 0° angle of attack and a 0° angle of yaw. The drag coefficients for boats include a nominal allowance for rigging, lifelines, and antennas.

The author calculated a number of additional drag coefficients for monohull sailboats of differing displacement-length ratios.

$$\frac{D}{L} = \frac{\text{displacement (long tons)}}{(.01\ LWL)^3} \qquad [Equation\ 2\text{-}2]$$

where LWL = water line length—ft

These correlated well with the displacement-length ratio of the hulls (Fig. 2-3).

The characteristic area, A, is the area of the body measured perpendicular to the wind. The drag of a body, d, is proportional to the area of the body allowing scaling of drag forces for bodies of different size but the same shape. Boats, however, have been observed to veer as much as 30° from side to side when at anchor. Therefore, the characteristic area to be used for wind drag load calculations is the yawed area presented to the wind when the angle of yaw reaches 30° (Fig. 2-4). One could also make a correction for the drag coefficient at an angle of attack but this becomes of secondary importance if the characteristic yawed area has been used.

Table 2-3. Typical Vehicle Wind Drag Coefficients

Vehicle	C_d with wind ahead
Angular tramp steamer	1.2
Cabin cruiser	1.0
Long liner	0.9
Oil tanker	0.85
Modern ocean liner	0.7
Cruising trimaran	0.6
Cruising catamaran	0.55
Modern automobile (sedan)	0.52
Racing trimaran	0.45
Modern automobile (fastback)	0.34
Ultrastreamlined playboat	0.2
Racing automobile	0.17
Airplane	0.09

Source: T. Baumeister, ed. *Mark's Standard Handbook for Mechanical Engineers*, 8th ed. (New York: McGraw-Hill Co., 1978) and William F. Durand, ed., *Aerodynamic Theory*, Vol. 4 (Gloucester, Mass.: Peter Smith, 1976).

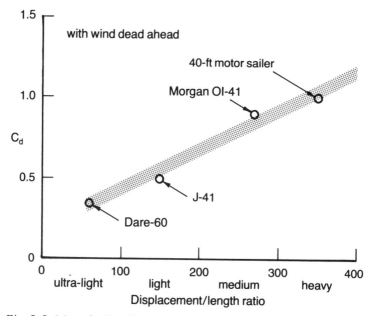

Fig. 2-3. Monohull sailboat wind drag coefficients.

The wind drag load on a boat yawed at 30° to the wind becomes:

$$d = q \cdot C_d \cdot A_{30°} \text{ lbs} \qquad [Equation\ 2-3]$$

CURRENT DRAG LOAD

Current drag load is not a major contributor to ground tackle loads. Test data on a 40-foot boat showed that current drag amounts only to about 300 pounds in a 5-knot stream. For a 60-foot boat, the equivalent current would add only 750 pounds of drag. Currents of 5 knots rarely occur in an anchorage, generally they are found in rivers, streams, and passes. Wind-driven ocean currents are of even lesser importance. Data in Bowditch indicate that the maximum surface current expected from a 60-knot wind with an unlimited fetch is 1.2 knots.

SURGE LOADING

Reports from boats that have faced whole gale to hurricane winds at anchor say that it is not the winds that break anchor gear and upset anchors, but the accompanying wave action which causes the boats to pitch, surge, heave, and yaw. Surge is the worst of these motions as the boat rides over the waves alternately stretching and relaxing the anchor

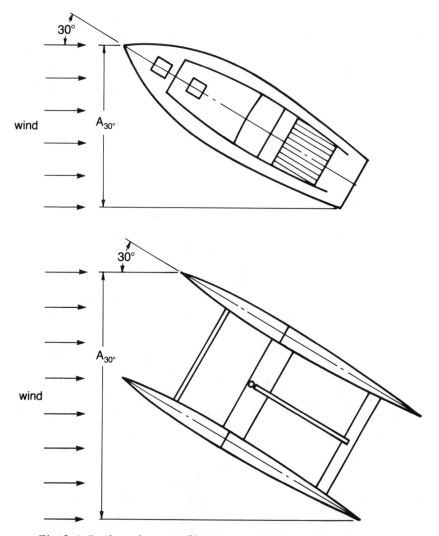

Fig. 2-4. Projected areas of boats yawed 30° to the wind.

rode like a horizontal yo-yo. But one cannot separate surge from the other motions so what is said here relative to surge takes into account the other motions as well.

There is neither theoretical nor experimental data available on the subject of surge loading on anchor rodes; therefore, we have to resort to judgment and experience. There are many qualitative accounts in the literature of boats riding out storms of various levels while at anchor. The common denominator seemed to be that surging of the boat sometimes as much as "doubled" the loads felt from wind drag alone. Van Dorn, in his fine book, *Oceanography and Seamanship* (see Bibliography), calculated storm loads on a small boat's elastic anchoring system, and although his approach was different, the end result appeared to confirm that surge could as much as double the wind loading on the boat.

You can rationalize that the total loading on an anchor rode is made up of the wind drag and some factor representing the dynamics of the wind-induced surge motion:

$$\text{Ground tackle load} = d \cdot SF \text{ lbs} \qquad [Equation\ 2\text{-}4]$$
$$\text{where } SF = \text{surge factor}$$

Using your intuition, you can quantify the surge factor, SF. Quite obvious is the fact that it should be proportional to the weight (displacement) of the boat. Heavy boats have higher surge forces than lighter boats. This fact was clearly brought home to me when my medium displacement fiberglass ketch replaced a heavy displacement wood schooner at a San Pedro, California, marina dock. Whereas the management had to replace dock cleats regularly for the schooner because of the unwelcome surge in the harbor, no dock cleats were ever loosened by my lighter boat. The same would appear to hold true for boats at anchor; therefore, the surge factor can be proportioned to the boat's displacement.

Likewise, you would expect the surge factor to be related to the length of the boat. A long boat has a lower pitch-up angle for a given wave height, and, therefore, exerts a smaller transient pitching load on the ground tackle.

Using displacement and length as arguments, you have the familiar displacement-length ratio as the dominant parameter to describe the surge factor for monohull boats at anchor (Fig. 2-5).

Multihull boats, on the other hand, are faced with an additional phenomenon, and that is the increased "wing" area presented to both wind and wave crest as the boat is pitched to a high angle of attack when riding over the crest of the wave. It is estimated that the added frontal impact forces of wind and water can result in a surge factor for multihull boats from 15 to 20 percent higher than for monohulls.

GROUND TACKLE LOAD CALCULATIONS

The author has calculated ground tackle loads for four popular recreational boats using Equation 2-3. The characteristic yawed drag area, $A_{30°}$, was calculated for each component of the boat—hull(s), cabin, other superstructure, masts, lifelines, life raft, rigging, etc. This

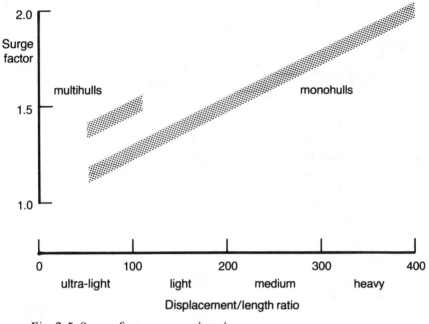

Fig. 2-5. Surge factor approximations.

Table 2-4. Examples of Calculated Ground Tackle Loads

	Morgan OI-41 monohull	Polynesian Concept catamaran	Brown Searunner trimaran	Uniflite Coastal Cruiser
LOA—ft	41.3	35.5	37.3	37.7
Displacement-length ratio	305	100	100	200
Drag coefficient C_d	0.9	0.55	0.6	1.0
Dynamic pressure q (psf)	3	3	3	3
Characteristic area $A_{30°}$ ft^2	237	302	255	226
Wind drag at 30 knots lb	640	450	460	680
Surge factor	1.8	1.5	1.5	1.5
Total ground tackle load:				
30-knot wind—lb	1,150	675	690	1,020
60-knot wind—lb	4,610	2,700	2,760	4,080

Sources: Earl Hinz, "Morgan Out Island 41 Sea Trial," *Sea*, January, 1981; Buddy Ebsen, *Polynesian Concept* (Englewood Cliffs, N. J.: Prentice-Hall, Inc., 1972); Jim Brown, *Searunner Trimarans* (P. O. Box 14, North, VA 23128: author's publication, 1973); and Earl Hinz, "Uniflite Coastal Cruiser Sea Trial," *Sea*, April, 1979.

was the most laborious part of the exercise. Once done, however, the remaining work was trivial. Drag coefficients, C_d, dynamic pressure, q, and surge factors were taken from appropriate tables. The results are reproduced in Table 2-4.

It is interesting to note that even the light displacement multihulls can generate substantial ground tackle loads. These boats, without deep steadying keels and heavy ballast, are much livelier at anchor than comparable size monohulls. An owner of a trimaran that rode out Hurricane Iwa in Hawaii in November 1982 stated that it felt like the boat was flying through wave crests as it was partially airborne most of the time.

For boats that are of a nominal design, such as the Uniflite Coastal Cruiser, the calculated ground tackle loads are comparable to those determined by using the ABYC table. For instance, the 30-knot wind load as just calculated is 1,020 pounds. This compares with a value of 1,060 derived by the ABYC method (Table 2-2).

The author's Morgan Out Island 41 ketch, *Horizon*, at anchor in Tarawa lagoon. Forty years earlier the atoll had been racked by days of ship and airplane bombardment prior to being captured from the Japanese in a violent 72-hour battle by the U. S. Marines. The bottom is good holding ground of coral sand, but you first have to get inside the barrier reef to enjoy it.

CHAPTER THREE

Deck Gear for Anchors

Several years ago I read a magazine article entitled *"Anchoring* 'How Do Porcupines Make Love?'" by Larry Haupt (in *The Ensign,* January 1979). The answer to the amorous porcupine question is, of course, "very carefully," and Haupt artfully applied the same answer to the problems of anchor handling, pointing out that there simply is no easy way. Good equipment and care are essential. Taking an anchor aboard and stowing it is, at best, hard work and, at worst, a dangerous task.

It is necessary that an anchor be stowed properly, for if it gets loose at sea, it is a lethal weapon. And, if it is stored anyplace but in the bilge, it seems to have an affinity for fouling sheets and dock lines at the worst possible times. As attractive as the bilge is, though, an anchor stored there is not a ready anchor, and every boat should have a ready anchor. During boat races sailors may want to remove their anchors temporarily from the bow and stow them below, but when they approach land, whether racing or not, anchors should be made ready.

When square-rigged ships made their multimonth-long passages, they often removed the heavy old-fashioned anchor from the cathead and put it inside the bulwarks on the deck where there was less chance of losing it to wild seas. Some blue water cruisers still do this but mostly for weight distribution. The trend today is for cruising and working boats to stow their bow anchor on a multipurpose bow roller leaving the anchor ready all of the time. It may appear to be a lazy approach to the problem, but it is usually shallow water and land that get boats into trouble and not the high seas. My own boat, which has seen many blue water miles, carries two CQR anchors ready on the bow, one semiready Danforth on the aft cabin top, and a fourth Luke old-fashioned take-apart anchor in a cabin locker. Readiness and flexibility of ground tackle is the key to survival when in the vicinity of land.

STEMHEAD ANCHOR ROLLER

The most useful anchoring accessory to come forth in recent years is the stemhead anchor roller which not only forms a good stowage

27

place for the anchor but makes the whole job of anchoring simple, safe, and nondamaging to the boat hull. The concept is simplicity itself, but the implementation of it is not so simple because of differences in bow designs, types of anchors, and the high loads encountered in storm anchoring.

The roller is the key to the stemhead anchor fitting (Fig. 3-1), and it should be made as large in diameter as is practical but never less than about three inches diameter at its center. The roller should have a concave surface to center the rode as it rolls back and forth. The center of the roller should be grooved to support a rope rode or slotted to accept alternate chain links edgewise. If the chain can be prevented from turning, it will be less apt to kink in the chain locker.

Roller material can be metal or hard plastic. Marine aluminum or brass are very good materials, but tough plastics like Delrin or Teflon work equally well and provide a measure of quiet when bringing in the chain. The roller axle should be a loose fitting, stainless steel bolt that will help hold the sides of the trough together under extreme side loads. Either a safety lock nut or a substantial cotter pin should be used to secure the nut on the bolt.

The trough of the roller should be viewed as a major structural element of the boat and should be fabricated to take extreme loads encountered in storm anchoring. The trough cannot be built too strong nor attached too securely. In *Sail* magazine (June 1983) Lin and Larry Pardey, writing on the disaster at Cabo San Lucas, noted:

> Without a doubt, bow rollers were one of the weakest links in the anchoring systems, not only of the boats that hit the beach but also of those that escaped to sea or were actually able to ride out the gale at anchor. A few minutes after we arrived at Cabo, we saw a man walking toward town carrying a stainless steel bow roller fabrication that had been twisted almost 180 degrees.

One thinks of the anchor rode as pulling forward on the boat which is an idealized situation. Actually, when the boat pitches there is also a vertical or downward loading put on the trough. The angle of pull can reach 45° in heavy seas resulting in a downward loading, F_v, of 70 percent of the load in the anchor rode. The total fulcrum load at the very stem is, then, $F_v + F_r$.

Side loads on the bow roller trough can be just as easily visualized coming from the sheering of the boat and/or steady side loads from wind

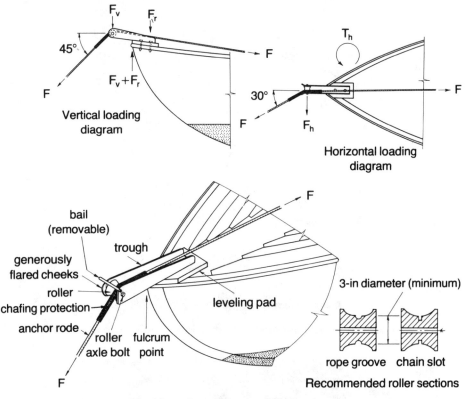

Fig. 3-1. Stemhead anchor roller installation loads.

or current if the boat is anchored bow and stern. At 30° of sheer the side load, F_h, on the trough is approximately 50 percent of the load in the anchor rode. The side load, F_h, creates a significant horizontal torque, T_h, which must be countered with substantial through-bolting.

Chafe is the number one enemy of nylon rodes and can be especially critical in a bow roller installation when sheering of the boat takes place. There should be no sharp edges on the trough to cause chafe. Generously flare the cheeks of the trough to make a smooth, rounded surface for the nylon rope to rub against. Even then, chafing protection should be added to the rope anchor line.

Lastly, the bow roller trough should be fitted with a bail or keeper pin to prevent the rode from jumping out of the trough when the bow of the boat pitches down (Fig. 3-2). A removable bail is recommended in case you have to change your anchor rode configuration.

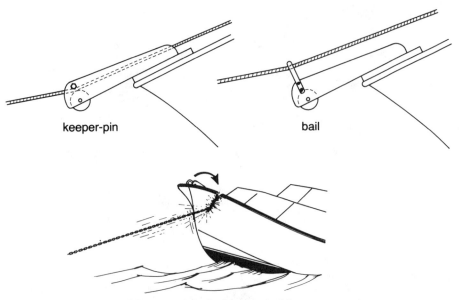

keeper-pin   bail

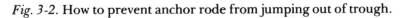

A keeper-pin or bail prevents this

Fig. 3-2. How to prevent anchor rode from jumping out of trough.

The heavy-duty bow roller on the author's Morgan Out Island 41 has been fitted with a keeper-pin to restrain the anchor rode from jumping out of the trough when the boat pitches down. The small radius cheeks

ANCHOR PLATFORMS

A natural extension of the stemhead anchor storage is the installation of an anchor platform on the bow. The platform can serve a variety of purposes: making dock line handling easier; allowing for a lookout spot when in bad weather, or in areas of reefs; and providing for a location to stow two anchors as well as a structure to support the anchor roller. Anchor platforms are very popular on powerboats, some being molded into the foredeck structure.

A good anchor platform is one that extends far enough forward to assure that the anchor will not strike the hull if it should swing during weighing. Another valuable feature is to have substantial braces under the platform to enable it to take the vertical and side loads from the anchor rode during storm anchoring. Remember, of course, that the longer the platform is, the greater the side loads are.

An anchor platform and bow roller have been integrated into the deck mold on this Ocean 40 powerboat. Factory attention to the needs of ground tackle on a boat can be an attractive feature to the potential buyer.

---

can cause excessive wear when a rope rode is used; so a short length of chain is used as a riding stopper through the bow roller trough (see Fig. 5-23.).

All of the platforms I have seen or used were admirably smooth with well-rounded corners on the upper side but loaded with sharp edges underneath and to the sides where the rode would ride when the vessel sheers. Out of sight is not out of mind as far as anchoring is concerned, and maximum protection should be given the nylon rode on the underside of the anchor platform.

BOWSPRIT ANCHOR STOWAGE

Sailboats with bowsprits have a natural mounting location for anchors keeping them away from the hull and allowing two anchors to be comfortably carried. Rollers can be installed on both sides of the bowsprit, and the anchors either two-blocked on the roller or lashed to the hull below the sprit. The latter, however, creates the danger of a loose anchor banging the hull in a seaway.

Square-rigged ships would hoist their anchors to the catheads and then lash them in place across the rail much to the detriment of the rail,

A stainless steel tubing bowsprit makes an excellent mounting for a bow anchor roller trough. The cheeks of the trough are well flared, and a bail is welded to the cheeks. The long trough takes up chain wear on the sprit deck. Note how the chain passes through a small fairlead in the bulwark preventing shackling on additional lengths.

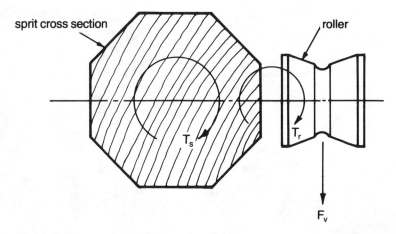

Fig. 3-3. Torques on a bowsprit roller.

topsides, and bulwark cosmetics. This method of stowing an anchor is, however, far better than to hook the anchor flukes around the bobstay as is so commonly done.

While the preferred way to stow an anchor on the bowsprit is with the use of a roller, there are some necessary design features to be considered. Besides all of the problems of a stemhead roller, the bowsprit also has to handle unsymmetrical loads (Fig. 3-3). The vertical rode load, F_v, produces two torques which must be counteracted—T_r which tends to bend the anchor roller axle and T_s which tends to twist the sprit.

If the axle bends, there is binding in the roller's bearing, and it will not operate freely. If the sprit twists (assuming that it is strong enough not to twist off), the lead of the anchor rode will be at an angle to the side such that it will want to run off the outboard side of the roller.

What it gets down to is making a very simple engineering load and stress analysis of the design before anything is built. The techniques for analysis are covered in elementary mechanics books and could well save an expensive boat from going on the rocks.

THE CATAMARAN BOW ROLLER

Cruising catamarans generally utilize a spreader tube between hull stems to support an anchor rode bow roller (Fig. 3-4). Chain is rarely, if ever, used as an anchor rode for a multihull boat so adequate size plastic rollers can be used in the fairlead. These must have some kind of a bail over them to prevent the rode from jumping out of the rollers when the boat pitches down.

An all-too-common sight—an anchor wedged against the bobstay for stowage. The anchor not only mars the bobstay cable, hastening its fatigue failure, but the lateral shaking of the anchor in a seaway will loosen the bobstay assembly.

The spreader tube must be of sufficient cross section to withstand vertical bending loads occurring when the bow pitches up over a wave. These loads, as noted previously, can amount to 70 percent of the anchor

Fig. 3-4. A modest-size bow roller mounted on the forward hull spreader tube of a catamaran. The spreader tube must have adequate bending strength to resist the vertical load applied by the anchor rode when the boat is pitching.

rode loading. Similarly, side loads on the rollers can amount to 50 percent of the anchor rode loading. The rode is not belayed to the spreader tube but is led aft to conventional deck gear.

Racing catamarans often do not have a spreader tube between the bows of the hulls; so they must use a bridled anchor rode as discussed later (Chapter 9).

ON-DECK STOWAGE

Anchors need to be stowed where they are readily available, partly because they are heavy and awkward to handle and also because they may be needed quickly, and should be ready. The most important criterion for stowing an anchor on deck is to make it so secure, it cannot break loose in the most severe storm. A heavy anchor can become a lethal weapon if allowed to get loose in a seaway. Heavy anchors are difficult enough to handle under normal conditions, but trying to corral a loose anchor on the foredeck while the boat is pitching and rolling on a storm-tossed sea is tantamount to suicide.

An anchor that stows well on the deck is the Danforth lightweight. In this anchor the stock and flukes are essentially parallel allowing the anchor to lie flat on the deck. The trick is to cover all ends of the anchor to prevent lines from catching on them, as well as to avoid skinned ankles should you carelessly step near one.

There are two versions of brackets or chocks for the lightweight anchor shown in Fig. 3-5. One consists of cast brass fittings which can be purchased from chandleries, and the other is a homemade set of saddles. When using the cast brackets there is the ever-present danger of a crew person skinning his ankle on the tips of the stock. This can be prevented to an extent by removing the extended ends of the stock as shown in (B) of the illustration.

The plow anchor is difficult to stow on deck and the Bruce is impossible. They should be carried on a bow roller if at all feasible. On *Horizon* I have carried my 60-pound CQR bow anchor on a roller and a smaller CQR bower over the edge of the foredeck always ready (Fig. 3-6). A teak chafing strip at deck edge and a small saddle block protect the gelcoat.

Another way to carry a CQR anchor on deck is to lay it on its side in specially carved chocks (Fig. 3-7). This installation seen on a powerboat looked very practical for a moderate size CQR.

The versatile old-fashioned anchor with a removable stock can also be deck-mounted using wood saddles (Fig. 3-8). The blocks have to be properly notched to fit the anchor and must be well secured in place.

A very well designed mounting for twin Danforth anchors on the house of a Hinckley SW-50 sailboat.

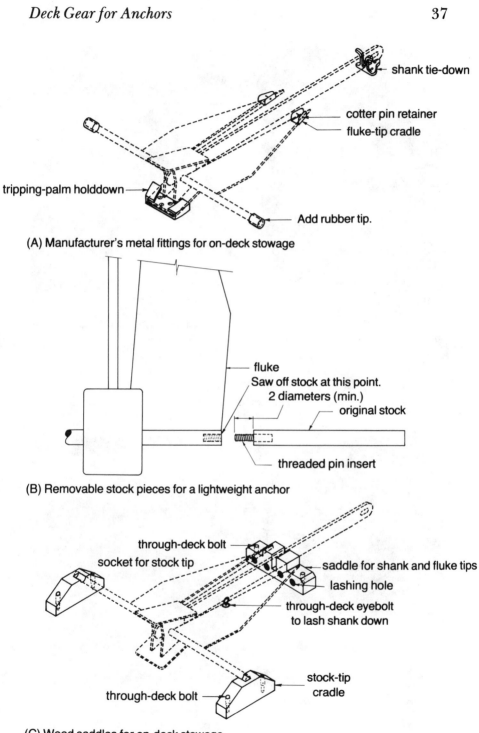

(A) Manufacturer's metal fittings for on-deck stowage

(B) Removable stock pieces for a lightweight anchor

(C) Wood saddles for on-deck stowage

Fig. 3-5. On-deck stowage of lightweight anchor.

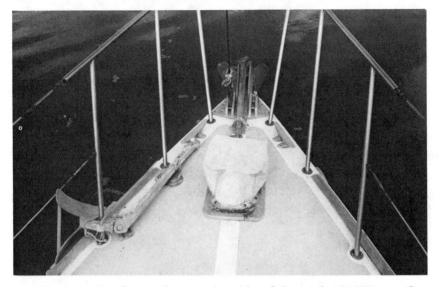

Fig. 3-6. The forward ground tackle of the author's Morgan Out Island 41: a 60-pound CQR on the bow roller with ⅜-inch chain and a Simpson-Lawrence two-speed manual horizontal windlass (covered); a 35-pound CQR stowed over the toe rail on a billboard to prevent damage to the fiberglass hull and attached to ⅜-inch chain and ⅝-inch nylon rope; and bow cleats located at the sheer line eliminating need for chocks.

Fig. 3-7. Custom-carved mounting pads restrain a CQR anchor on the stern deck of a harbor tuglet.

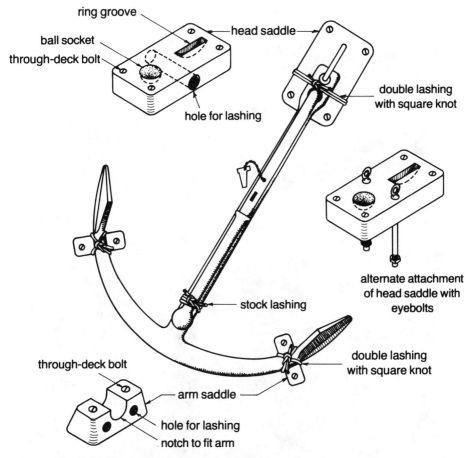

Fig. 3-8. On-deck stowage of old-fashioned anchor.

HANGING LIGHTWEIGHT ANCHORS

It is entirely practical to hang lightweight anchors on pulpits using special brackets purchased from the chandlery (Fig. 3-9). The brackets are clamp-on devices requiring no drilling of the pulpits. However, in both cases the anchors should also be lashed in place assuring no damage to the boat should extra heavy seas release them from their brackets.

ANCHOR WELLS

The advent of fiberglass boat construction made practical the consideration of stowing anchor and other ground tackle in a well molded into the foredeck. Such a concept, however, involves a preselection of an

Fig. 3-9. Above, the Danforth anchor can be neatly carried on brackets suspended from a pulpit. Recommended only for local cruising. *Facing page,* another way to carry the Danforth anchor for local cruising is on a bracket which grasps the tripping palm of the anchor. Note on this installation the angled stern roller trough.

anchor so that the well can be tailored to fit it. The very successful Cal-39 Sloop has an anchor well molded into its foredeck for a Danforth light-weight anchor (Fig. 3-10). A Simpson-Lawrence manual windlass is also contained in the well, and a metal bolster is placed at the forward end of the well to prevent chain chafe to the fiberglass deck edge. The windlass is mounted on the reinforced aft bulkhead of the well, and the chain and rope rode drops randomly into the bottom of the well. The Danforth lightweight anchor simply lies on top of the windlass and rode.

While the concept is great, the implementation of the foredeck well is difficult. The foul lead of the chain offers increased loading on the windlass. The hatch is vulnerable to being knocked off its hinges if it should accidentally come open in a seaway. Keeping water out of the well is not attempted, hence a drain is placed at the lowest point leading to the outside—usually through the stem. Plugging this drain will trap a large weight of water in the bow which is highly undesirable. Lastly, if the top

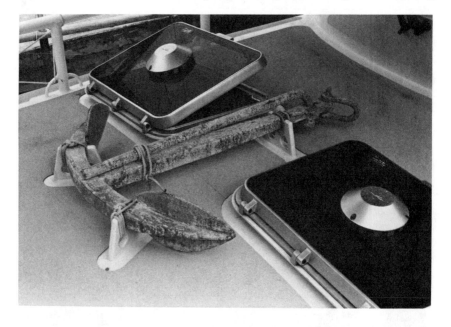

An old-fashioned anchor with Nicholson flukes mounted on saddles on the Dutch aluminum around-the-world motor cruiser *Bylgia.*

fits properly, the well has almost zero ventilation, and the contents of the anchor well will be exposed to constant moisture, producing rust, corrosion, and general deterioration of the ground tackle.

A variation to the foredeck anchor well is the side deck anchor well built into the J-36 light displacement sailboat (Fig. 3-11). The well has room for the chain lead but not the nylon rode. The philosophy of the side deck installation is to get the weight out of the bow and amidships where it belongs.

THE DISASSEMBLED ANCHOR

Obvious problems with stowing an old-fashioned anchor have led to the development of a take-apart anchor by Paul Luke. This anchor can be taken apart into three pieces which can be easily stowed below decks. A dry bilge is a favorite place to store the disassembled anchor. The bottom of a deep locker can also be used as long as other gear is not piled on top, making it inaccessible when needed in a hurry. The parts of the anchor should be secured in place in such a way that they cannot get loose in case of a knockdown or other disastrous movement of the vessel at sea.

Fig. 3-10. Many fiberglass boats come with an anchor well molded into the foredeck. Shown is the Cal-39 whose anchor well contains a manual windlass and stows both rode and Danforth anchor. A metal bolster at the forward edge of the well acts as a fairlead over the hump to the bow roller. Anchor wells must have drain holes which are usually located in the stem just above the waterline. The lightly secured lid to the well may be vulnerable to waves breaking over the bow. Courtesy: *Sea* magazine.

Two lightweight anchors which can be disassembled for stowage are the Fortress aluminum and the Pekny stainless steel. Optional fitted carrying bags for the disassembled anchors are available. Both anchor designs are excellent candidates for light displacement monohulls and all multihulls.

RODE STOWAGE

Like the anchor itself, the rode for the anchor must be stowed out of the way when not in use so that there is no interference with the operation of the boat under power or sail. At least one set of ground tackle

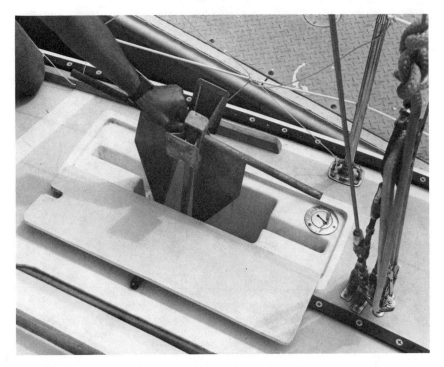

Fig. 3-11. A side deck anchor well on the light displacement J-36 provides stowage for a Danforth anchor and a chain lead. Anchor wells generally limit the owner to anchor designs and sizes selected by the manufacturer. Courtesy: *Sea* magazine.

should be made up at all times when you are operating your boat near land.

Anchor rodes also need protection from the elements. Even though chain looks almost indestructible and the rope on your rode is hefty, salt water and sunlight can play havoc with them. Even galvanized chain rusts after a period of use and nylon rope absorbs ultraviolet rays from the sun which deteriorate its fibers. Both should be stowed under cover to be out of the way and to preserve them.

Several proven concepts for anchor rode stowage have developed over the years. Small vessels usually stow their rodes below decks on reels, in coils, or in baskets. Larger boats will use the same technique for their stern or kedge anchors. Light displacement monohulls and multihulls prefer to stow their anchors in the bilges and the rodes below decks in coils or baskets or on reels. Large vessels, cruising boats in particular, like to leave their bow anchor rode attached to the anchor in place and ready for use. In this case the forepeak is designed as a chain locker, and chain and rope rodes are led through a foredeck navel pipe into the locker when the anchor is weighed.

REEL RODE STOWAGE

A simple way to stow a rope anchor rode is to rewind it on the original reel (spool). Usually these reels are durable enough to withstand many years of use, and the price is right. An axle and stand can be made out of wood to support the reel on the foredeck when in use. For very small boats (under 25 feet LOA) it is possible simply to put a mop handle through the reel center and have a crew member hold it while the rode is being deployed or retrieved.

For larger boats where the weight of the rode becomes significant, a free-standing reel should be employed (Fig. 3-12). It is low to the deck for stability, can be made large enough to accommodate 400 feet of ¾-inch nylon, and can be carried below decks for enroute stowage.

Fig. 3-12. A portable reel for carrying about 300 feet of ¾-inch nylon rope for the stern anchor rode of a 56-foot ketch.

To coil a rope anchor rode, fake it down in a large figure eight pattern and tie it with short pieces of small stuff to hold its shape as shown above. Then double one of the loops over the other and tie the two together with the bitter end of the rode as indicated below.

COILED RODE STOWAGE

Rope anchor rodes up to about ½ inch in diameter can be coiled up when not in use making a simple package to stow below in the bottom of a locker or under sails, but never the bilge. To prevent kinks forming in the line, coil the line in a figure 8 when the anchor is being weighed, wash it off, and then let it dry in this position. When dry, secure the coils tightly with short lengths of marline and then fold one part of the figure 8 coil back on the other for compactness and take it below decks for enroute stowage. The marline ties will hold the coils together even if the whole coil becomes a pillow for a tired crew member.

The new ventilated milk bottle carriers made of sturdy plastic are ideal baskets for stowing rope anchor rodes. The bitter end of the rode should be tied to the basket and to the boat so the whole assembly is not lost overboard while deploying or weighing the anchor. A standard milk bottle basket can conveniently take up to 250 feet of ½-inch diameter nylon rope. Of all rode stowage methods, this one probably ventilates and dries the rope the best and gives it the most protection without sacrificing

Two hundred and fifty feet of one-half-inch diameter nylon line can be conveniently stowed in a plastic milk bottle carrier. The first thing to do when getting ready to use the basket line is to secure the bitter end to the boat by bringing it out near the bottom of the basket.

portability. Other types of baskets can be used, but avoid metal or wooden ones with iron fasteners.

CHAIN LOCKERS

In a general sense, a chain locker is simply a space set aside in the boat, usually in the bow, where the anchor rode(s), whether chain or rope, can be permanently stowed and kept separate from other gear. Although the bow is not a good place for needless weight, a proper anchor system cannot be called needless, and properly designed cruising boats have adequate bow buoyancy to support the system. Designers should not minimize the possible weight of essential anchor gear that needs to be carried in the bow. On a 40-foot boat this could mean about 50 pounds of anchor, 450 pounds of chain, 75 pounds of windlass plus miscellaneous fittings. This adds up to 600 pounds or more.

Although one is constrained in the nature of a forepeak anchor locker to the shape of the hull, there are some guidelines in designing a chain locker that should be kept in mind. The locker should be deep and narrow so that gravity can play its part in automatically "faking down" the chain or rope as the anchor is weighed. Hull sides should be provided with ceiling strips to keep the chain and metal rode fittings off of the hull and well ventilated. A grate should be installed at the bottom of the locker to allow drainage and ventilation. Generous limbers should be made in the bulkheads fore and aft of the locker. Access doors need to be made into the locker so that rode snags can be quickly cleared. A visual inspection of the chain locker interior before anchoring will ascertain that the rode is free to run, which may save embarrassment during an anchoring exercise.

The location of a single chain locker in the forepeak is relatively simple. It should be along the centerline, as deep as possible, but not at the expense of taking up good berthing space in the forecastle. Two chain lockers can be fitted into the bow of a boat (Fig. 3-13). Narrow lockers, as opposed to wide ones, present less possibility of the chain or rope tipping over when the boat heels thereby upsetting the natural faking arrangement of the rode. An upset pile could very well lead to snags when deploying an anchor.

Chain lockers should not be made too small, and they should be designed for rope or chain because there is about a 2 to 1 difference in volume requirements (Table 3-1).

ANCHOR CHAIN CHUTE

Occasionally a boat owner will want to shift the center of gravity of the stowed anchor chain as far aft as possible to save forecastle room and

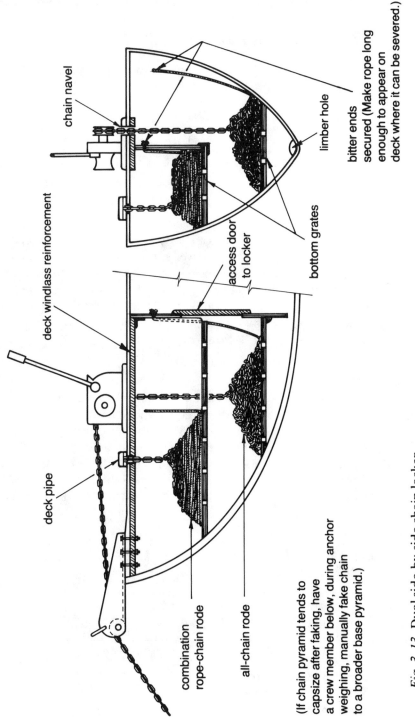

chain navel

deck windlass reinforcement

deck pipe

access door to locker

bottom grates

limber hole

bitter ends secured (Make rope long enough to appear on deck where it can be severed.)

combination rope-chain rode

all-chain rode

(If chain pyramid tends to capsize after faking, have a crew member below, during anchor weighing, manually fake chain to a broader base pyramid.)

Fig. 3-13. Dual side-by-side chain locker.

Table 3-1. Minimum Chain Locker Volume

Proof Coil chain		Twisted 3-strand nylon rope	
size— in	volume per 100 feet—ft³	diameter— in	volume per 100 feet—ft³
5/16	1.5	1/2	3
3/8	2	5/8	4
7/16	2.7	3/4	5
1/2	3.5	7/8	7
5/8	5.5	1	11

to improve weight distribution. This can be done with an angled chain pipe or chute (Fig. 3-14). The pipe has to be well supported in all directions.

The size of any navel pipe—angled or straight—needs to be large enough to accommodate the anchor shackle of a chain rode or the thimbled eye splice of a rope rode in a vertical pipe (Table 3-2). Smaller sizes than these will only lead to frustrating hang-ups when deploying or retrieving the anchor rodes (unless shackles are removed).

DECK PIPES

If you stow your rode in a chain locker, it becomes necessary to put one more hole (the navel) in the foredeck and fit it with a deck pipe to absorb chain wear on the deck, to help keep water out of your chain locker, and to hang the end of the chain on when not in use.

Deck pipes come in a variety of styles, being made for rope rodes with large thimbled eye splices and all-chain rodes where shackles are removed and only the chain enters the deck pipe (Fig. 3-15). Both hinged and

Table 3-2. Minimum Deck Pipe Sizes (in inches)

Proof Coil chain with anchor shackle		Chain attached to thimbled eye splice in twisted 3-strand nylon rope	
Chain size	Recommended I. D. of pipe	Rope size	Recommended I. D. of pipe
5/16	2-1/2	1/2	3-3/4
3/8	3	5/8	4-1/2
7/16	3-1/2	3/4	5-1/4
1/2	4	7/8	6
5/8	5	1	7-1/2

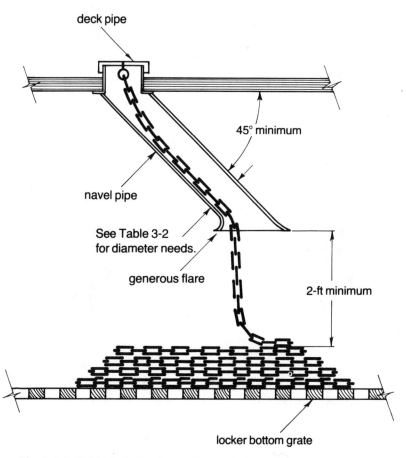

deck pipe

45° minimum

navel pipe

See Table 3-2
for diameter needs.

generous flare

2-ft minimum

locker bottom grate

Fig. 3-14. Critical chain chute dimensions.

free-cap models are available, but if you get the free-cap model, replace the delicate ball-chain lanyard with a heavier chain or a cable lanyard. Deck pipes should have extensions (spigots) that protrude through the deck. If there are no extensions, epoxy the edges of the deck cutout to protect them.

To overcome the problem of persistent water leakage through the deck pipe, Abeking and Rasmussen (boat builders in Bremerhaven, West Germany) have designed a screw-in concept which uses a threaded plug to fill the pipe when not in use.

The importance of having leak-proof deck pipes cannot be overemphasized. On a presumed short 200-mile passage between Palmyra and

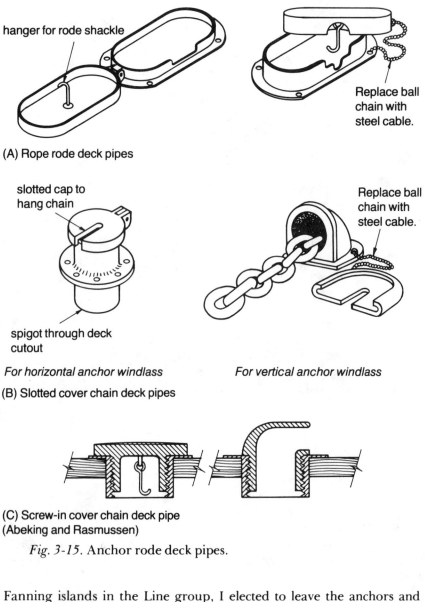

hanger for rode shackle

Replace ball chain with steel cable.

(A) Rope rode deck pipes

slotted cap to hang chain

Replace ball chain with steel cable.

spigot through deck cutout

For horizontal anchor windlass   *For vertical anchor windlass*

(B) Slotted cover chain deck pipes

(C) Screw-in cover chain deck pipe
(Abeking and Rasmussen)

Fig. 3-15. Anchor rode deck pipes.

Fanning islands in the Line group, I elected to leave the anchors and rodes assembled, leading them through the deck pipes to the chain lockers. The 2-day passage turned into a 4-day thrash to weather with the bow of the boat looking more like a submarine than a sailboat. Things were a sorry, wet mess in the forecastle by the time we arrived at Fanning Island.

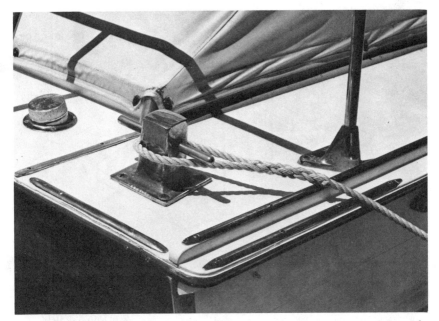

A bolt-on bitt makes an excellent dock line and stern anchor rode attachment for a powerboat. Note the generous use of rub strakes to minimize line wear and deck-edge damage.

An excellent dual bow anchor installation on a Hans Christian 43. The twin bitts are fitted with a common Norman pin. Note the horned hawsepipes in the bulwarks for dock lines.

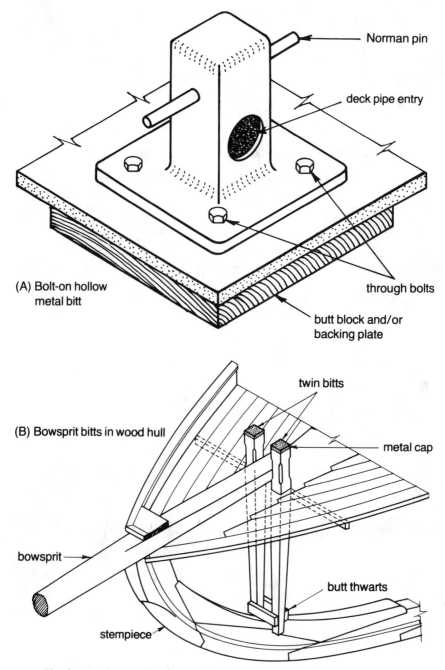

Fig. 3-16. Bitts and Samson post.

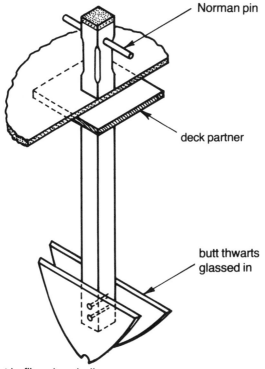

Norman pin

deck partner

butt thwarts
glassed in

(C) Samson post in fiberglass hull

OTHER DECK GEAR

The variety of deck gear put on boats is only limited by the imagination of the designers of boats and gear. But when you really get down to it, there are only a few fundamental pieces required to anchor, moor, or dock your boat. Needed is a place to secure the lines on deck, guides which can lead the lines over the deck edge in a fair manner, and some specialized pieces of gear to help in handling chain. And then there is the ever-present problem of handling chafe regardless of the hardware you choose to use. The latter is more dependent on the ingenuity of the user than that of the builder.

Deck gear, like all ground tackle, must be strong, functional, and resistant to corrosion. Most attempts to make deck fittings look pretty have failed in the hard operating environment of ground tackle. Diecast fittings wearing a shiny coat of chrome pose a latent danger to the boat.

Deck fittings need to be installed when the boat is built to get the proper location and the necessary backup strength. Many builders, however, try to keep the base price of the boat low so that necessary deck fittings are either omitted or included in options to be put on later. The valuable Samson post is very difficult to add, and deck-edge cleats are almost impossible to add after the boat is built. The buyer of a new boat must, when he places his order with the yard, specify the essential deck gear so that it can be put on as the boat is assembled.

BITTS AND SAMSON POSTS

The terms bitt, bollard, and Samson post are used interchangeably in many instances when, indeed, they are quite different. A bitt is a short, sturdy metal or wooden post located on the foredeck on which to belay an anchor rode, mooring, or dock line. A bollard is a short, sturdy metal or wooden post located on a wharf or pier on which to belay dock lines from a vessel. A Samson post is the upper end of a timber on the foredeck of a vessel which is used in the same manner as a bitt. The lower end of the Samson post attaches to the stempiece of the hull. What may appear to be a pair of Samson posts, that is, two parallel posts that penetrate the deck down to the stempiece of the hull, are actually knight-heads, but in small boats they are simply referred to as twin bitts (Fig. 3-16B).

Boats with bowsprits are naturals for twin bitts. The sprit, deck beams, and longitudinals are all bolted together to make a very strong installation. Whether bitt or Samson post, the tops of these timbers should be covered with a brass or copper cap well bedded and tacked in place to prevent weather splitting of the wood.

When mounting metal bitts, reinforce the deck underneath with hardwood plus a metal plate with a predrilled bolt pattern identical with the bitt base.

Since cosmetics and the desire for a clear foredeck seem to be the real reason for not having bitts or Samson posts on modern boats, how about making a disappearing bitt as in Fig. 3-17A or a disappearing Samson post as in Fig. 3-18A? These would be natural choices on steel or aluminum boats, and with proper support fittings, they would serve equally well on fiberglass boats.

A combined bitt and chain stopper (Fig. 3-17B) was first seen on an English boat and it could also be used as a bitt for rope provided that the corners were generously rounded.

Foredeck bitts and Samson posts are sometimes referred to as towing posts, which is a tribute to their sturdiness. But lacking either (as most modern boats do!) a useful substitute can be made on sailboats with

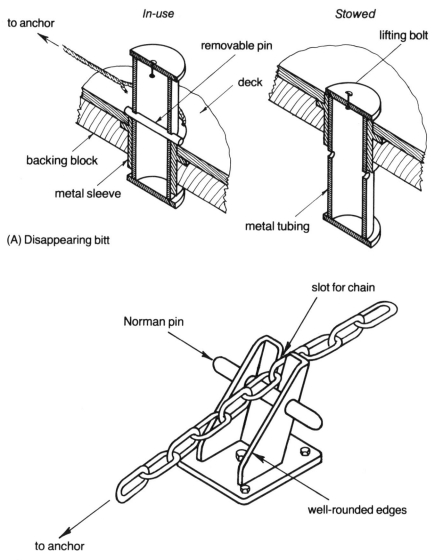

In-use

to anchor

removable pin

deck

backing block

metal sleeve

(A) Disappearing bitt

Stowed

lifting bolt

metal tubing

slot for chain

Norman pin

well-rounded edges

to anchor

(B) Bitt with chain stopper

Fig. 3-17. Special metal bitts.

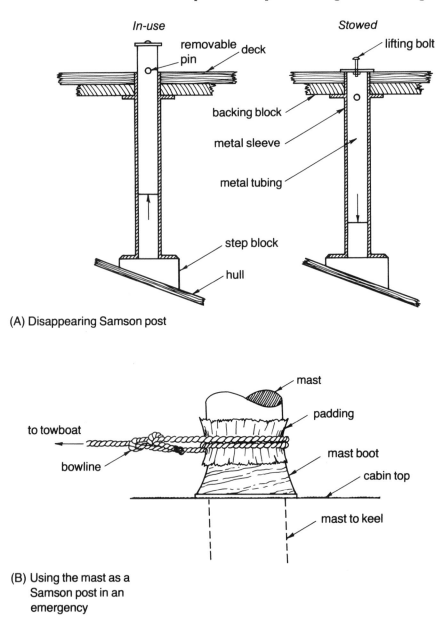

(A) Disappearing Samson post

(B) Using the mast as a
    Samson post in an
    emergency

Fig. 3-18. Alternate Samson post concepts.

keel-stepped masts (Fig. 3-18B). You should also look to your keel-stepped mast as a supplementary attachment point for securing multiple mooring lines should you have to ride out a hurricane at anchor (Chapter 12).

DECK CLEATS

Cleats are the primary means of securing anchor rodes and dock and mooring lines on modern boats. They range in style from the substantial hollow base horn cleat to the less substantial, but aesthetically more pleasing, Herreshoff cleat to the small, artfully formed cleats used on runabouts. The sole function of a cleat is to belay a line and not to stub toes which may appear to be the case at least for landlubbers aboard.

Cleats take a significant load when in use. The surging of the boat brings up the line in short jerks, wanting to tear them from their mountings. For that reason, cleats must be through-bolted with backing plates to a reinforced portion of the deck.

Proper deck cleats are made of bronze or stainless steel and provided with a broad, four-bolt base to prevent tipping when under side load. Unlike running rigging cleats which get loaded from one end only, deck cleats can get loaded from any direction. You should not depend on cleats made of die castings for ground tackle use as they have little strength.

The Herreshoff cleat with its widely spaced feet has one real advantage to its design (besides being cosmetically more attractive) and that is the ease with which you can lock a dock line to it (Fig. 3-20). It is, however, not as sturdy as a horn cleat and its smaller diameter parts cause more wear on lines. It is not recommended for ground tackle use.

There is a proper way to belay a line to a horn cleat and that is shown in Fig. 3-21. The procedure is one round turn, one crossover turn, and then one locking turn. A good seaman will learn to do that in the dark.

Cleats must be of a proper size to fit the lines they are to hold (Table 3-3). Inadequate size cleats not only are weaker, but they will crowd the line so much that it is not possible to get a proper hitch put on them. From my observation I would say that most boats have deck cleats too small for their intended use.

It is common practice to belay rope anchor rodes to deck cleats since few boats have bitts or Samson posts. Unfortunately, the deck cleats of most contemporary boats follow the "traditional" method of placement, and they end up well inboard of the gunwale requiring a fairlead (chock) at the toe rail. This is not only a needless piece of hardware but causes unnecessary wear on the rode or dock line passing through the chock.

(A) Twin bitt hitch

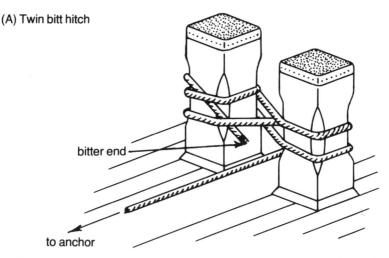

bitter end

to anchor

- To belay a line to a twin bitt, take a turn around the nearest bitt and follow that with a series of figure 8 turns between the bitts. End the hitch with a half-hitch around one of the bitts.

(B) Pinned Samson post hitch

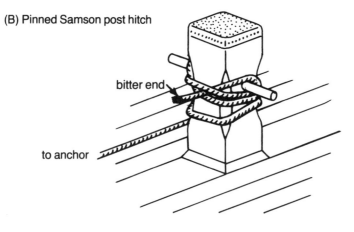

bitter end

to anchor

- To belay a line to a single bitt or a Samson post, take two turns around the post and then end with consecutive half-hitches around opposite ends of the Norman pin.

Fig. 3-19. Hitches for bitts and Samson posts *above* and on *facing page.*

(C) Plain Samson post hitch

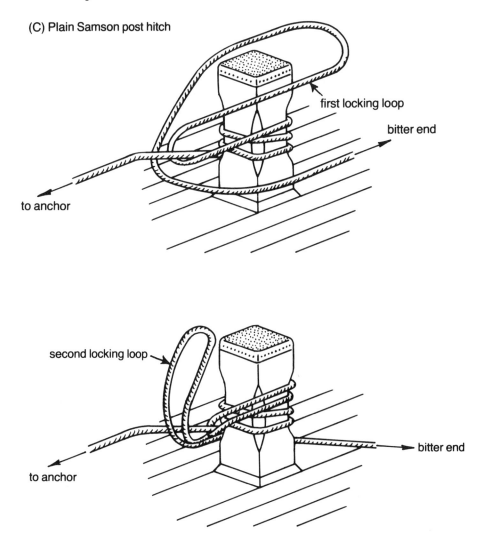

- To belay a line to a Samson post without a Norman pin, take two turns around the post first. Then take a bight of line from the inboard part, pass it under the standing part ahead of the post and bring it over the top of the post. Take another bight of the inboard part and pass it under the standing part in the opposite direction to the first and likewise drop it over the post. Draw up on the bitter end to remove the slack.

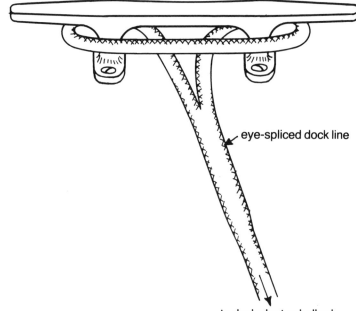

Fig. 3-20. Herreshoff cleat for dock line.

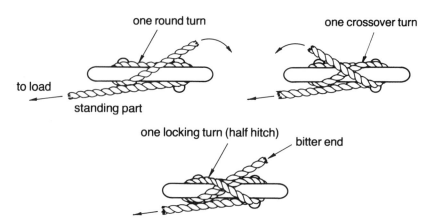

- Do not load the cleat horns with the excess line. If the boat is to be left unattended, drop a second locking turn over the opposite horn and then neatly coil the excess line and lay it to the side.
- Never put a locking hitch on the standing part of any anchor or dock line as attractive as it may be to quickly tauten up the line.

Fig. 3-21. Horn cleat hitch.

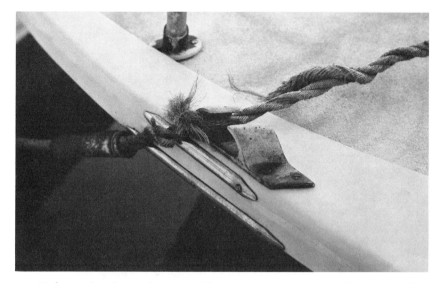

Rub strakes have done nothing to prevent serious damage to this dock line by the fairlead chock. A horn cleat mounted in its place at the sheer line could have prevented the line damage. Such a condition would be catastrophic if it were the anchor rode being abraded.

Table 3-3. Recommended Horn Cleat Sizes (in inches)

Rope diameter	Horn cleat length
3/8	6
7/16	7
1/2	8
5/8	10
3/4	12
7/8	14
1	16

The use of chocks and inboard cleats is justified on wooden boats because it is impractical to through-bolt a cleat at the deck edge. But on fiberglass, steel, and aluminum boats, this is not true. By putting the cleats right at the deck edge, you eliminate the need for chocks as well as the wear on the line running through the throat of the chock (Fig. 3-22).

DECK CHAIN STOPPERS

All chain anchor rodes must have some means of stopping off the chain on deck in order to hold it while the crew prepares the anchor

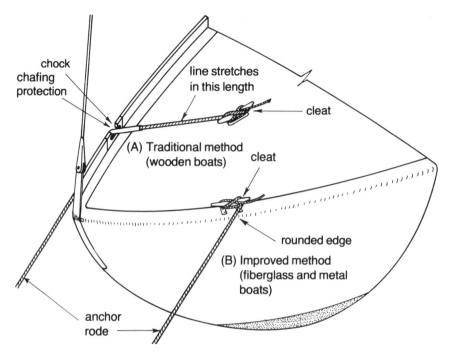

chock
chafing
protection

line stretches
in this length

cleat

(A) Traditional method
(wooden boats)

cleat

rounded edge

(B) Improved method
(fiberglass and metal
boats)

anchor
rode

Fig. 3-22. Positioning cleats to minimize line abrasion.

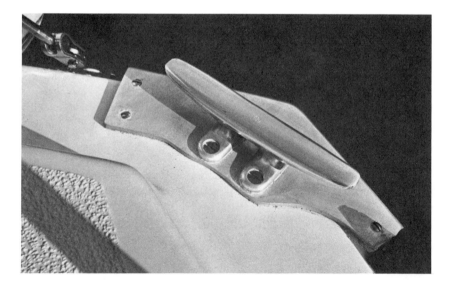

A substantial quarter horn cleat mounting on a Tartan 33 sailboat. Mounting the cleat right at the sheer line eliminates the need for a fairlead. The aluminum corner casting could do with a larger outer radius to further minimize line wear.

windlass or adds another shot of chain. This chain stopper also acts as a backup to the windlass brake and secures the anchor in the bow roller or hawsepipe.

The most common type of chain stopper is the pawl (Fig. 3-23A). The simple, gravity-activated pawl drops down on the chain between vertical links and stops the chain run. The chain trough is designed with a slot in

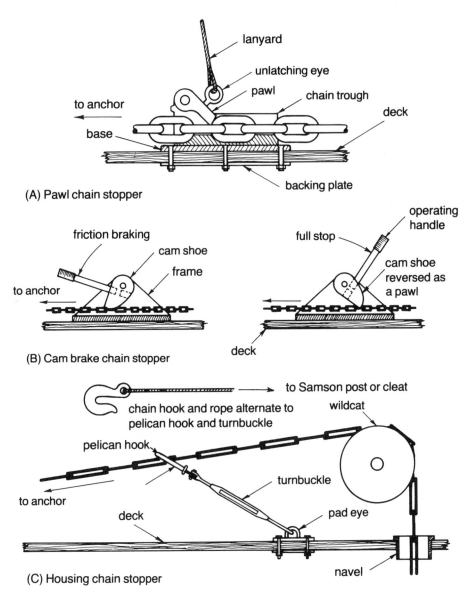

(A) Pawl chain stopper

(B) Cam brake chain stopper

(C) Housing chain stopper

Fig. 3-23. Deck chain stoppers.

its base so that alternate links stand upright in the trough. Care should be exercised in releasing the pawl because the chain will rattle out very fast and may be hard to stop again.

To slow the movement of the exiting chain, a special cam-brake chain stopper can be used (Fig. 3-23B). The reversible cam-shoe stops the chain in one direction and eases it out in the other. When changing from the full-stop position to the friction-braking position, it is necessary to temporarily belay the chain with a line while reversing the operating handle.

The housing chain stopper (Fig. 3-23C) is used to secure the chain and anchor when the vessel is underway. The anchor is drawn snug into the bow roller or hawsepipe and the pelican hook secured across a link of chain. The turnbuckle is then drawn up tightly bringing the anchor securely into its mount. As an alternative to the turnbuckle-pelican hook arrangement, you can use a chain grab hook with line secured to another deck fitting.

Great care must be used when employing a deck chain stopper. A sudden release can result in a wild deployment of the chain eventually coming up hard on the bitter end attachment. Dropping the pawl down on the chain when it is running wild can snap the chain, break the stopper, or damage chain links. Hands and feet should be kept a judicious distance from chain and stopper when handling this gear.

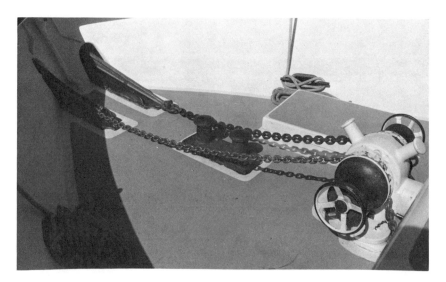

The ground tackle setup on the 52-foot passagemaker, *Teka III* from Coos Bay, Oregon. The windlass has two wildcats and two warping drums. Note the substantial bitts.

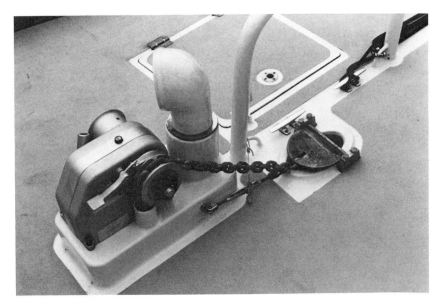

The anchor windlass installation on the Dutch aluminum around-the-world motor cruiser *Bylgia*. Note the housing chain stopper with a turnbuckle and the slotted hawsepipe cover to hold the chain and take the load off of the windlass wildcat.

HAWSEPIPES

The problem of stowing the old-fashioned anchor with its awkward stock and arms led to the development of the stockless anchor and hawsepipe stowage. This allowed the anchor to be weighed and stowed without so much as one sailor having to manually work the anchor in place. Today many boats 50 feet and over in length use hawsepipes to stow either the Navy stockless or the Danforth lightweight anchor (Fig. 3-24).

The length of the hawsepipe has to be sufficient to contain the entire length of the anchor shank to give a proper lead of the chain through the deck flange and over the bolster. The hawsepipe must be securely fastened to hull and deck so that no water can enter under any conditions.

Normally, a stockless anchor is carried in the hawsepipe at all times, but should it be removed for any reason, a hawse plug must be inserted into the hawse eye to reduce the chances of taking on water. The hawse plug is inserted from the outside but a pendant is run through the pipe to snug up on the plug after insertion.

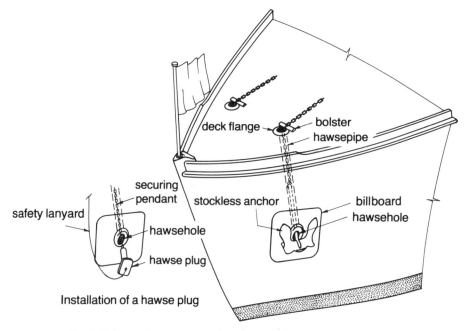

Fig. 3-24. Anchor stowage in a hawsepipe.

A stockless Hall anchor stowed in a centerline hawsepipe.

When the anchor is snugged up against the hull, there is considerable opportunity for it to chafe the surface of the hull. To prevent this, billboards are affixed to the hull covering the area where the anchor will contact it when stowed. Billboards attached to a wood hull must be well bedded in a rot-preventing compound and removed every few years to ascertain whether any hull rot is developing. Metal boards can be welded on metal hulls, but if stainless steel boards are put on carbon steel hulls, they must be insulated to eliminate galvanic action. Billboards on fiberglass hulls can be screwed or bolted in place and should also be bedded.

ANCHOR DAVIT

Most recreational boats have anchors light enough to handle by hand or at least they can be drawn into a bow roller with a windlass. But boats over 50 feet in length—both workboats and recreational boats—will have anchors of such weight that they will need special handling to hoist

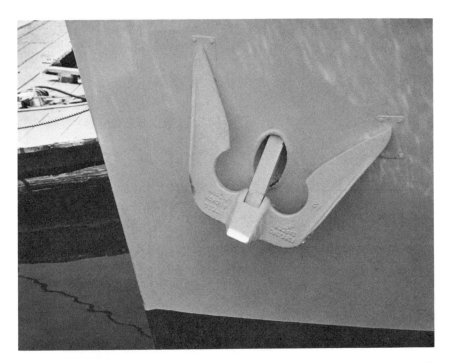

A Forfjord anchor is nestled in the hawsepipe of a steel-hulled vessel. Small individual billboards have been provided to save the hull plating from abrasion by the anchor bills.

aboard (if they are not stockless hawsepipe-stowed anchors). An anchor davit is the prescribed piece of equipment for this job (Fig. 3-25).

An anchor davit is essentially a small crane that can be extended over the side of the deck to hoist the anchor out of the water and swing it onto the deck without marring topsides, bulwarks, and handrails. Depending on the weight of the anchor to be hoisted, a multiple purchase block and tackle may be used to allow one person to hoist the anchor. The davit arm pivots in the deck support socket allowing the anchor to be swung inboard and lowered, preferably, right into its chocks. When not in use, the davit is removed from its socket and lashed to the deck out of the way.

The anchor davit can be used in many ways on a large boat. For example, it can be used for hoisting provisions and gear aboard; with

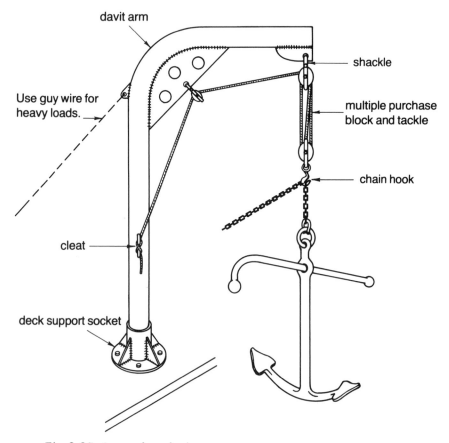

Fig. 3-25. An anchor davit.

The ground tackle deck of the very elegant power cruiser *Taurus* from Oyster Harbor, New York. The anchor davit is mounted on the centerline of the king plank so that it can handle both Danforth anchors. Note that each anchor has been equipped with a balancing band and eye for hoisting.

other support sockets, it can be used to lift heavy gear in other parts of the vessel; and it can be employed in hoisting heavy dinghies and outboard motors aboard. For extremely heavy loads, guy wires or braces may be needed to keep the strain on the deck socket at a reasonable level.

CHAPTER FOUR

Anchor Windlass

The first time you haul up an all-chain anchor rode without the services of an anchor windlass, you will realize the value of this piece of foredeck machinery. If you have a small boat with rope rodes you don't need to worry about it. But when the boat length exceeds 40 feet or so, the advantages of an anchor windlass become apparent even for a rope rode with a proper chain lead. Handling chain by hand, exclusive of its weight, can be very damaging to the hands and should be avoided.

Anchor windlasses driven by manual means are adequate for boats up to about 45 feet in length using up to 60-pound anchors and 3/8-inch chain. Larger boats and heavier anchoring gear require not only the mechanical advantage of a windlass but an energy source that will not wear down quite as easily as that of an individual's. Electricity is currently favored, but hydraulic power is becoming very popular.

Once you experience the ease of hauling anchors with power, you probably will not do without a powered anchor windlass again. While the convenience of the powered anchor windlass cannot be overstated, the horrors of having one fail cannot be overstated either. The chances of powered anchor windlass failure are, unfortunately, high because it resides in the worst of locations—on the foredeck—and it is designed only for intermittent service which is usually ignored when the departure schedule says go and the hook stays hooked.

Anchor windlasses properly installed as a system and operated and maintained according to manufacturer's instruction should perform satisfactorily for many years.

CAPSTAN OR WINDLASS?

Before chain found its way into ground tackle, rope rodes were used, and large ships were equipped with a mechanical device called a capstan to assist in weighing anchors. Initially, the capstan was manually operated by sailors pushing on the capstan bars (Fig. 4-1). With the arrival of steam, the sailors were, I am certain, happily replaced by the steam

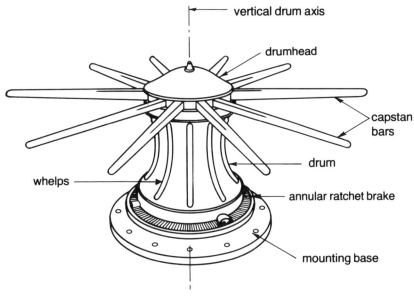

Fig. 4-1. The capstan.

A steam-driven horizontal windlass from a four-masted lumber schooner of 867 tons built in 1918 in Portland, Oregon. In the mid-1930s, the ship was renamed the *Seth Parker* and used by Phillips Lord in producing live radio broadcasts as the ship sailed to many foreign ports. On exhibit at the Hawaii Maritime Center, Honolulu.

engine. But the vertical capstan was retained as a means of handling all sorts of lines on the ship.

The windlass had its origin on land as a hoisting device for the castle portcullis, as a bucket lift in wells, and in general hoisting by rope in construction work. The feature of the windlass that sets it apart from the capstan is the use of a horizontal rather than a vertical drum.

Windlasses and capstans are both used on today's recreational craft to haul rope anchor rodes. They may be manually, electrically, or hydraulically powered, but they have one thing in common and that is the use of a warping drum (formerly called a gypsy) to handle the rope. Technically, they are not anchor windlasses but capstans and plain windlasses. Capstans and windlasses become anchor windlasses with the addition of wildcats to handle chain.

There are advantages and disadvantages to both types. The vertical windlass warping drum can be used omnidirectionally which is an advantage for general deck work. When electrically powered, the motor and most of the mechanism can be conveniently placed below the deck out of the elements. Placing the bulk of the anchor-weighing device below the deck leaves the foredeck much cleaner and lowers the center of gravity of the device. The big disadvantage of the vertical anchor windlass is that the hand crank (when fitted) is operated in a horizontal plane close to the deck which is very awkward at best.

It is probably that latter disadvantage of the vertical anchor windlass that has made the horizontal anchor windlass the more popular for handling anchor rodes. With the horizontal orientation of the wildcat and warping drum, it is simple to manually actuate it through a set of gears using a vertical rocking lever that can be operated by a crew member from the standing position.

COMMON DESIGN FEATURES OF ANCHOR WINDLASSES

Whether it be a vertical or a horizontal anchor windlass and regardless of how powered, there are several common design features that set the anchor windlass apart from other applications of the same principals (Fig. 4-2). One is the warping drum. It has a concave surface to keep the turns of rope centered and it usually is smooth although some have whelps and others are roughened by knurling or sandblasting. The drum is "engaged" by taking a couple of turns of rope around it and then snubbing up on the bitter end.

If the anchor windlass is to handle chain, a special sprocket fitted with link pockets to grasp the chain links is used. This sprocket is called a wildcat and it is fitted to the same shaft as the warping drum. The positive grip of the wildcat on the chain, however, prevents it from letting the chain run out unless a freeing clutch is provided so that the wildcat can spin backwards. This clutch is usually a cone or band brake that can be tightened to haul in on the chain or can be loosened to let the chain run freely.

The wildcat is appropriately named because, if carelessly tended, it can behave like one. For instance, if you inadvertently release the brake with a heavy weight of anchor and chain over the bow roller, the wildcat will start unwinding letting the chain run out in a blur of untamed links. The chain may even jump out of the wildcat and create havoc to chain pipe, deck, and human limbs. Conversely, when taking in on the chain rode, the chain can wedge in the pockets and the anchor windlass will come to a snarling halt. To avoid this, every wildcat on an anchor windlass must be fitted with a chain stripper to forcibly separate the chain from the sprocket and lead it smoothly into the chain pipe.

It is important that the wildcat be matched to the chain it is to drive. Small differences in chain link diameter, width, length, or shape need to be taken into account in the shape of the wildcat pockets. Failure to do this will cause links to jump pockets or wedge in them so tightly that even the chain stripper cannot separate them.

Although the anchor windlass has the power to haul on an anchor rode with hundreds or even thousands of pounds of force, it is not intended to break the anchor loose nor to carry constant anchor loads on the warping drum or wildcat while the boat is at anchor. Anchor loads and, especially, breakout loads should be taken by a deck chain stopper (Fig. 3-23) instead of carrying them through the complex of gears and levers that make up an anchor windlass. (see Breaking Out the Stubborn Anchor in Chapter 10 for techniques that neither damage the windlass nor strain a back.)

A proper anchor windlass installation will incorporate metal beams under the deck to transfer the windlass loads over a wide expanse of deck and into bulkheads and hull. Fiberglass decks also need a wood base under the anchor windlass to prevent crushing the fiberglass composite. Wood decks need substantial underdeck reinforcing with metal plates or angles. Metal decks will distort under load if load-spreading angles are not incorporated. In the Cabo San Lucas (Baja California, Mexico) anchoring disaster of 1982, at least two vertical anchor windlasses pulled right through the deck because of inadequate deck reinforcement.

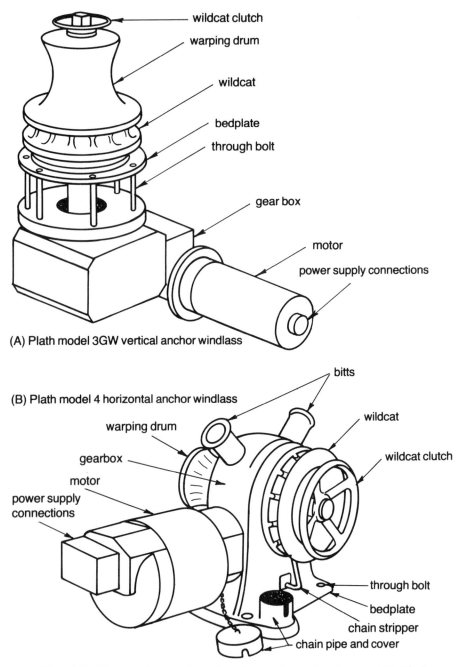

wildcat clutch

warping drum

wildcat

bedplate

through bolt

gear box

motor

power supply connections

(A) Plath model 3GW vertical anchor windlass

(B) Plath model 4 horizontal anchor windlass

bitts

wildcat

wildcat clutch

warping drum

gearbox

motor

power supply connections

through bolt

bedplate

chain stripper

chain pipe and cover

Fig. 4-2. Nomenclature for electric anchor windlasses: (A) Plath model 3GW vertical anchor windlass; (B) Plath model 4 horizontal anchor

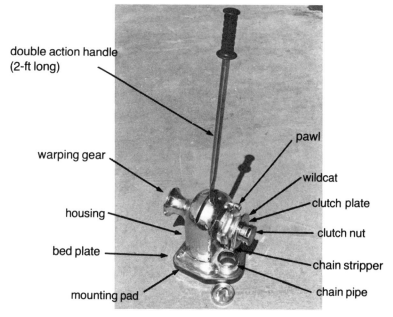

double action handle
(2-ft long)

pawl

warping gear

wildcat

clutch plate

housing

clutch nut

bed plate

chain stripper

mounting pad

chain pipe

(C) The ABI model 1000

Positioning of the anchor windlass on the foredeck requires consideration of the underdeck structure, the location of the chain locker, and the angle of rode lead from the bow roller (Fig. 4-3). Cosmetically, the anchor windlass should be centered on the king plank (centerline) of the foredeck. But if the anchor windlass is quite wide, which most horizontal models are, both the warping drum and the wildcat will end up with a bad rode lead from the bow roller. It is best to pick the warping drum or the wildcat as your primary drive and center that on the king plank. Or else, move the anchor windlass aft as far as is possible so that the lead angle to the bow roller from both drum and wildcat is made a tolerable minimum.

MANUAL ANCHOR WINDLASSES

When the chips are really down, the mechanical anchor windlass driven by muscle and determination is unsurpassed for reliability. It is simple, dependable, and with a good hand at the lever can take in chain as fast as an electric motor but, unfortunately, the drive gets tired.

----

windlass; and, in (C), above, the ABI model 1000 manual anchor windlass for boats to about 40 feet in length.

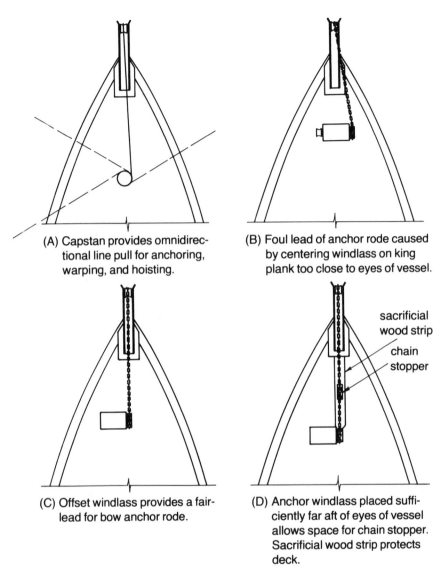

(A) Capstan provides omnidirectional line pull for anchoring, warping, and hoisting.

(B) Foul lead of anchor rode caused by centering windlass on king plank too close to eyes of vessel.

(C) Offset windlass provides a fairlead for bow anchor rode.

(D) Anchor windlass placed sufficiently far aft of eyes of vessel allows space for chain stopper. Sacrificial wood strip protects deck.

Fig. 4-3. Criteria for positioning an anchor windlass.

The manual anchor windlass may be operated with either a lever or a crank. The lever is, by far, the easier to operate because the crew member can stand up and rock it back and forth whereas with either a horizontal or vertical crank, the crew member must bend over in an awkward stance.

The lever has the additional advantage of greater leverage for a given internal gear ratio. It should be remembered, though, that the speed at which the rode is hauled in is the reciprocal of the line pull for a given force applied to lever or crank. Therefore, if you want to make a hard pull, you need a high gear ratio which yields a strong line pull but at a low hauling speed. Conversely, if you want to get your anchor up fast (and the load is not too great), then you want a low gear ratio. Most small anchor windlasses (boats 30 to 35 feet overall) use only a single gear ratio whereas larger anchor windlasses will incorporate two sets of gears for high speed and low power or low speed and high power.

There are still some old anchor windlasses in use that have a single-acting lever which tends to be unnecessarily slow in hauling. New models are usually double-acting, that is, you haul in on the rode with both fore and aft strokes of the lever. The length of an anchor windlass handle is proportioned to the strength of an average person pushing (or pulling) with 30 to 50 pounds of force. Two persons can double the force and by putting on an extension lever you can get just about any force you want. But you must remember that the total anchor windlass structure has design limits of its own and exceeding the design line pull on it may result in breakage while still not bringing home your anchor.

A cursory examination of manual windlass performance figures in Table 4-1 shows that they fall into two approximate classes—one for boats 30 to 35 feet LOA with a line pull of about 500 pounds and the other for larger boats to 45 feet LOA with a line pull of about 1,100 pounds. Chain sizes for the former run between ¼ inch and ⅜ inch in diameter and for the latter from ⅜ to ½ inch in diameter.

ELECTRIC ANCHOR WINDLASSES

Electricity has become the servant of sailor and landlubber alike because it has a greater flexibility of use than any other known power source. An electric windlass in place of a manual windlass can be a real blessing in cruising but may not be quite as attractive for racing boats because of the added weight and bulk. (Electric windlasses weigh up to twice as much as an equal line pull manual windlass.)

Basically, the electric windlass has the same mechanism in its gear case as the manual windlass. The difference comes in the substitution of an electric motor for the manual lever or crank. The performance then becomes less operator dependent and can be quantified for analysis.

Fig. 4-4 illustrates the performance of a typical electric anchor windlass. The first conclusion that you draw from this curve is that the hauling

Table 4-1. Manual Anchor Windlass Performance

Manufacturer and model	Chain size in	Unit weight lbs	Handle type	Mechanical advantage	Line pull lbs	For boat sizes— to approximate ft
Plath 7	1/4—3/8	45	Lever	NA[a]	NA	35
Plath 1	1/4—1/2	80	Crank	24:1	400	40
Finderwinch Handy	1/4—5/16	20	Lever	NA	550	30
Finderwinch Maxi-Handy	5/16—1/2	66	Lever (2 speed)	NA	1,350	45
Ideal HWCM	1/4—5/16	42	Lever	10:1	NA	30
Simpson-Lawrence Hyspeed	1/4—3/8	21	Lever	12:1	550	35
Simpson-Lawrence 555	3/8—1/2	42	Lever (2 speed)	14:1 40:1	1,100	45
Nilsson H400m	1/4—3/8	31	Lever (2 speed)	7:1 20:1	600	35
Nilsson H700m	3/8—1/2	94	Crank (2 speed)	5:1 15:1	1,000	45

[a] NA = Not available.

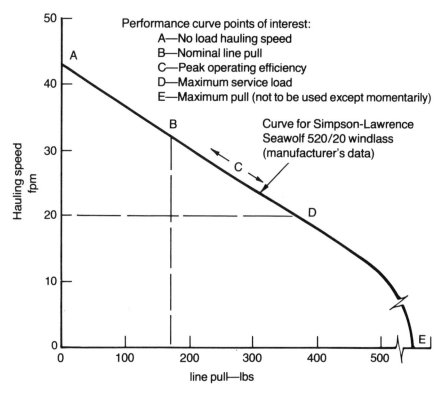

Fig. 4-4. Electric anchor windlass performance.

speed of the line is the inverse of the pull on the line. That is, a fast hauling speed is attained only at the sacrifice of line pull. The drop-off in hauling speed is almost linear with the buildup in line pull until some point D is reached where the maximum line pull begins to stall the motor.

The maximum efficiency of the windlass (line pull times hauling speed divided by current draw) occurs somewhere in the middle of the performance curve (point C), and it is here that the windlass should normally be operated. If the windlass continuously operates between points D and E, it is too small and should be replaced.

Operation of the windlass at point E should be avoided at all times. Sometimes, though, the anchor rode will snub up hard when the anchor is near breakout and this could stall the motor. If it does, shut off the windlass power, put a stopper on the chain, and break out the anchor using one of the techniques which will be described later.

Laboratory tests of a number of anchor windlasses were sponsored by *Motor Boating & Sailing* magazine which measured the performance of the

The Ideal, model ACW, vertical electric anchor windlass installed on a Gulfstar 50 sailboat. Note the location of the foot switch close behind the windlass, and the deck pipe forward and to the side of the windlass to accept the chain just ahead of the chain stripper. This windlass is properly mounted on a wood pad; button snaps are visible for attaching a fabric cover when not in use.

windlasses in terms of line pull, hauling speed, and current draw (Table 4-2).

These data point out one distinct feature and that is the high current draw that can occur as the line pull is increased on the windlass. The data from manufacturers often do not show the high current draw which can lead first-time buyers into thinking that they will have no trouble in meeting the electric power requirements of the prospective windlass. Motor burnouts, blown fuses, and burned-up wiring can all result from overloading an inadequate anchor windlass electrical system.

There are a number of ways to prevent overloading an electric windlass. If you are using a rope anchor rode around a warping drum, you can simply slack off on the tension that you are holding on the rope's tail which will allow the rope to slip enough to unload the drum and keep the motor running at an acceptable speed. This simple technique does not work for a chain and wildcat so something else has to be done.

Some windlasses are equipped with shear pins that will shear at a predetermined maximum acceptable line pull. For this concept to be acceptable, the shear pin has to be immediately accessible and easily replaceable.

Table 4.2. Electric Anchor Windlass Performance

Performance curve point →

Type	Manufacturer and model	Application Rope (R), chain (C)	A No load Hauling speed—fpm	A No load Current draw—amp	B 170-lb line pull Hauling speed—fpm	B 170-lb line pull Current draw—amp	C Peak operating efficiency load[a] Line pull—lbs	C Hauling speed—fpm	C Current draw—amp	D Line pull at 20 fpm hauling speed—lbs	E Maximum line pull[b] Line pull—lbs	E Current draw—amp
Vertical	Galley Maid AACW	R/C	58	78	42	108	235	38.9	114	482	850	342
	Ideal A	R	58	48	40	84	370 to 550	30 to 24	108 to 132	737	1,350	360
	Nilsson M800C	R	133	54	68	120	370	51.3	168		850	450
	Nilsson V1000C	R/C	9	48	45	114	350	28	198	745	850	462
	Wilcraft	R	46	36	36	66	370	31	78		550	210
	Benson A 35	R	30	24	31	54	235	27	60	331	550	102
	Denouden Vetus Tiger	R/C	85	48	47	90	370	39	120	1,044	1,350	390
	Good Automatic	R	63	18	24	42	235	20	48	238	370	60
	Powerwinch 412	R	29	18	26	29	370 to 550	23 to 21	36 to 48	582	1,350	114
Horizontal	Powerwinch 612	R	45	12	33	36	370	26	48		370	54
	Powerwinch 2000	R/C	59	72	45	96	550	35	120	1,123	1,350	330
	Simpson-Lawrence Seawolf 520	R/C	36	6	28	24	235	28	24	481	850	102
	Simpson-Lawrence Seawolf 520/20	R/C	41	12	38	24	370	26	36	529	850	84
	Simpson-Lawrence Sealion 526	R/C	33	12	29	18	550	23	42	1,015	1,650[c]	114
	Superwinch	R	40	30	33	54	235 to 370	33 to 29	60 to 84		550	108

Source: *Motor Boating & Sailing*, August 1981. [a]Efficiency is line pull times hauling speed divided by current draw. [b]Deadweight start. [c]Capable of higher load.

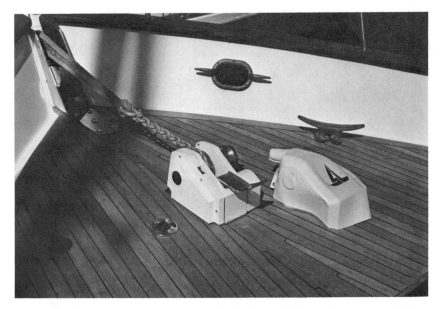

The Simpson-Lawrence Seawolf horizontal electric anchor windlass installed on an Albin 50 trawler. Note the molded plastic cover to protect the windlass from the elements. There is no wood pad between windlass and deck, but one is highly recommended to keep the bedplate from being continually wet due to water flowing across the deck. The foot switch is not in a good location either because it is too easy to accidentally step on it.

Most common of the overload devices is a fuselike arrangement that automatically cuts the power off when the motor stalls. But a simple cartridge fuse is not the way to go. Instead, a slow-blow thermal cutout device is preferred which will allow a second or two of overload without breaking the circuit. That might just be enough of a hard pull to break the anchor loose. If you blow the overload protection device, you will have to wait until it cools down before resetting it, that is, unless you have one of the dual (parallel) overload protection devices that will allow you immediately to set the second and continue weighing your anchor. Avoid blowing the second one, however, because your windlass motor is now heating up and forcing it beyond its limits will be destructive.

Electric motors for windlass drives up to 1,000 pounds of line pull have a ¾ to 1¼ HP rating. They are intended for intermittent service only since cooling is not adequate for continuous duty. While they can be run for "minutes" at low line pulls, they should not be run for long periods when the line pull is high and not for more than one or two seconds if the motor is stalled. All the while you are using your electric windlass, your engine should be running to help maintain the battery charge.

Most recreational boats are equipped with a 12-volt DC electrical system which is not the most desirable voltage for operating a remotely located motor. The distance a motor is from the energy source dictates the size of wiring to be used (Table 4-3). The sizes of wire may amaze you but take a look at the size of wires connected to the electric starter on your engine and you will realize that 12-volt motors do require heavy wiring for proper operation. The goal is to minimize voltage drop along the supply wire, and it takes large wires to do that.

There is a way to use smaller wire sizes and that is to raise the operating voltage of the motor. You may want to consider a higher voltage system in your boat for both engine starting and electric windlass operation (Table 4-4). Larger workboats may already be equipped with 32-volt DC systems which would be very helpful for electric windlass

Table 4-3. Recommended Wire Sizes for Electric Windlasses

Distance from power source to windlass—ft	American Wire Gauge Size Current draw—amps			
	50	100	150	200
0—10	No. 8	No. 4	No. 2	No. 0
10—20	6	2	0	00
20—30	4	0	00	000
30—40	2	00	000	0000

Notes: Assume a 12-volt direct current; a 3 percent line voltage drop at motor; and a fuse rating of 125 percent of current draw.

Table 4-4. Voltage Impact on Wire Size for Plath 3GW Vertical Anchor Windlass

Motor size HP	Supply voltage	Current draw—amps	Recommended fuse—amps	Wire size—AWG
3/4	12 DC	35	60	No. 2
1	24 DC	33	60	4
1	32 DC	23	40	6
1	115 AC	20	30	12

Source: Manufacturer's data.
Notes: Assume distance from power source to windlass = 25 to 35 ft; hauling speed = 37 fpm; and intermittent operation.

operation. Higher voltage motors not only use smaller electric wires but they also operate more efficiently than lower voltage motors.

Availability of other voltage motors for windlasses is quite limited, Plath being a notable exception. If you have a choice, you should consider the following operating voltages for the electric motor drive of your anchor windlass:

> 12-volt DC for line pulls to 1,000 pounds
>
> 32-volt DC or 115-volt AC for line pulls to 2,500 pounds
>
> 220-volt or 440-volt AC for line pulls above 2,500 pounds

Many boats have 115-volt AC electricity available for lights, radar, tools, microwave ovens, and similar uses, and this same power could be used for the anchor windlass. The benefits would be numerous.

Another option for decreasing the power lost in transmission of 12-volt DC current is to locate a separate battery very close to the anchor windlass motor so that the length of heavy cable is kept to a minimum. This battery can then be connected to the engine charging system with much smaller wire, say No. 10 or 12, because the charging amperage would be much less than the draw by the windlass motor. The placing of this separate battery close to the windlass adds more weight forward, but as long as it is not right in the bow and kept low, it can be tolerated on cruising boats, either sail or power.

Wiring of the electric windlass should be done with care and in accordance with the American Boat and Yacht Council's recommendations.*

Control of the electric anchor windlass can be accomplished with a foot switch located near the windlass on the foredeck. This is a momentary switch which must be stepped on with a firm foot to engage, and to hold it engaged. In its simplest form, this switch is a two-position switch that is wired directly into the power supply circuit, and when the foot pressure is released, the switch contacts immediately snap open.

A second version of the foot switch is one that operates through a solenoid in a manner similar to your engine starter solenoid. In this system the foot switch carries only a minimal amperage and the solenoid that it operates is normally located inside the motor housing of the windlass. With a solenoid available, it is now possible to add a remote switch also, placing it in parallel with the foot switch. The latest in high technology electronics provides a cordless remote control switch that can

*American Boat and Yacht Council, Standard E-9 "Direct Current (DC) Electrical Systems for Boats," paper available upon request (P. O. Box 806, Amityville, NY 11701).

operate as far as 40 feet from the receiver unit and gets rid of the trailing cord of the roving switch that is always hanging up on some piece of deck gear.

A reversible motor on an electric anchor windlass allows you both to weigh anchor and to let go the anchor with positive control. This is particularly important if you intend to do your anchoring from the comfort of a wheelhouse on a larger vessel. The reversing switch is a 3-position joystick type that is normally in the center (off) position. Moving the stick to one side or the other energizes the motor in one direction or the other, as chosen.

All electric anchor windlass switches should be of the momentary make or break variety so that the operator cannot energize the circuit and walk off and leave it running. For absolute certainty, any switch on the foredeck that requires the presence of a crew member in the close vicinity of the anchor windlass and rode should be a momentary make or break variety so that if the operator is thrown off balance by a wave, the windlass immediately shuts down.

Electric windlasses which do not have a reversing feature on the motor depend on the operator to manually release the wildcat and operate a clutch much the same as a manual anchor windlass.

There is another switch required in the circuit of an electric windlass and that is a disconnect switch that isolates the entire electric circuit of the anchor windlass from the power supply. When the windlass is not in use, there is no need to keep power in the system, and safety is enhanced if the system is totally deenergized.

Schematic wiring diagrams for electric windlasses are shown in Fig. 4-5. Manufacturers will provide their own recommendations which you must integrate into your boat's circuits, but whatever you do, be certain that the basic safety elements indicated in Fig. 4-5 are also incorporated.

Most electric anchor windlasses include a chain run indicator to tell the operator how much chain has been let out. The indicator is not intended for use with rope since rope slips on the warping drum and a positive indication is not possible. Rope rodes should be marked as will be described in Chapter 5.

Mounting an electric windlass requires the same substantial deck reinforcements as any other windlass. Anchor windlasses that have an electric motor below the deck (all vertical windlasses and some horizontal windlasses) require special reinforcement of the deck where the cutout is made for the vertical drive shaft. One such vertical windlass on the market requires a hole in the deck that is 50 percent of the diameter of the bedplate and that constitutes a serious weakening of the deck. Such an installation definitely requires the use of metal reinforcement under the deck as well as a good-sized wood pad on top.

There usually are four to six mounting holes, a main gear box hole for underdeck motors, an electrical lead hole for above deck motors, a chain pipe for all windlasses, and a deck switch hole. Structural strength of the deck and its ability to keep water out after being penetrated in so many places will be compromised unless you make a first-class design and installation.

All powered windlasses must be backed up with a manual drive option in case of power failure. Although this poses an unwelcome amount of exercise for the crew, it is still better than having to slip the anchor and abandon it and the chain rode.

It is possible to have a windlass, manual or powered, freeze up completely and refuse to turn over no matter what leverage you apply.

*Table 4-5. Troubleshooting an Electric Windlass Failure**

Caution: Stay clear of operating mechanism when making checks!

Identifying the Problem	Probable action required
1. Can you manually turn motor shaft? (*Turn electric power off first!*)	If not, motor, gears, and/or wildcat are frozen. Disassemble, clean, and lubricate.
2. Is there voltage at the foot switch input terminal?	If not, check status of: a. master battery switch b. control circuit disconnect switch c. overload protection device d. foot switch fuse
3. Is there voltage at solenoid input terminal when foot switch is depressed?	If not, foot switch may be defective—replace.
4. Is there voltage at solenoid output terminal (+) when foot switch is depressed? (Can you hear solenoid engage?)	If not, check solenoid coil ground connection (−). Also check continuity of solenoid coil.
5. Is there voltage at motor input terminals with foot switch depressed? (*Stay clear of all mechanisms!*)	If yes and it still doesn't operate, remove motor, check input wiring, and condition of brushes.

Caution: Stay clear of operating mechanism when making checks!

*Refer to Fig. 4-5. Electric anchor windlass wiring schematics.

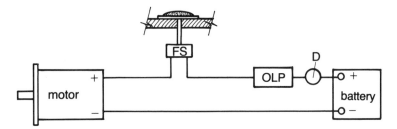

(A) Direct operating deck switch

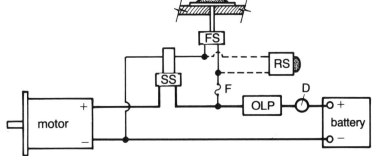

(B) Deck switch to solenoid with optional roving switch

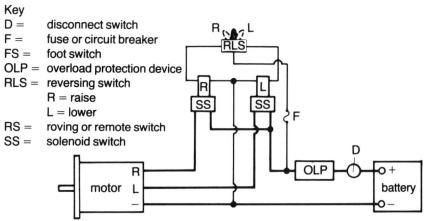

Key
D = disconnect switch
F = fuse or circuit breaker
FS = foot switch
OLP = overload protection device
RLS = reversing switch
  R = raise
  L = lower
RS = roving or remote switch
SS = solenoid switch

(C) Reversing switch with solenoids

Fig. 4-5. Electric anchor windlass wiring schematics.

This is usually due to salt water getting inside which corrodes gears, jackshafts, and bearings. The only solution is to abandon the windlass and get your chain rode and anchor up by other means. One way of doing this on a sailboat is to use a chain grabber on a long pendant which will reach from bow roller to mast winch. With this rig shown in Fig. 4-6, the anchor can be raised one long bite at a time. It will be necessary to use your regular deck chain stopper to hold the anchor rode while you take another bite on it. On a power boat without a winch, it becomes more laborious since a member of the crew will physically have to haul on the chain grabber pendant and belay it while setting the deck chain stopper. Do not attempt to break out the anchor with this rig. Use one of the techniques discussed later.

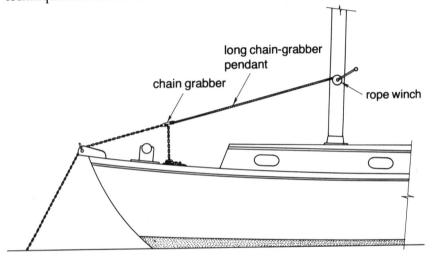

Fig. 4-6. What can be done if your windlass freezes up completely.

HYDRAULIC ANCHOR WINDLASSES

Hydraulically powered windlasses and line-handling gear have been commonplace on workboats for years and are now finding their way onto the larger recreational boats. The hydraulic windlass offers more power than an electric windlass, and it is safer and easier to transmit hydraulic power than high amperage electric power. Hydraulic components are a well-developed state of the art being used on heavy construction equipment and machine tools. They cost somewhat more than an electric drive because of the need for precision machining of pumps, valves, and motors which operate at high pressures. But workboats look to increased reliability and durability as justification for the increased cost. Large recreational boats can take advantage of the same benefits.

Hydraulic anchor windlasses start at rather large sizes because there is a minimum practical size for hydraulic hardware. The Plath model 4H with a line pull of 800 pounds is about the smallest made. Most hydraulic anchor windlasses are above 2,000 pounds of line pull which few moderate size recreational boats need. The hydraulic windlass weighs about

25 percent less than an electric windlass of comparable capability. It can also have a constant hauling speed in contrast to the electric drive where increasing line pull causes the hauling speed to decrease. Stalling of the hydraulic drive does no damage to the system.

The basic elements of a hydraulically powered anchor windlass are shown schematically in Fig. 4-7. The pump is usually driven by belts off the engine and furnishes high pressure oil to the control valve. The control valve modulates the flow governing the speed of the motor in the windlass. A crossover valve can also be used that switches the direction of oil flow to the motor causing it to reverse itself. The pump drive can be disengaged when hydraulic power is not needed to operate the windlass.

Hydraulic power is not stored like electricity; therefore, a prime mover or auxiliary engine must be running when hydraulic power is desired. Typically, a hydraulic windlass developing a line pull of 2,200 pounds at a hauling speed of 40 fpm will require an input power to the pump of about 8 HP. This is not a great requirement even for a sailboat auxiliary engine much less a prime propulsion engine.

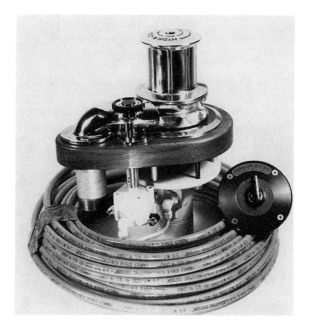

The Hydra-Cap, model 1500M1, vertical hydraulic anchor windlass provides 1,500 pounds of line pull at a hauling speed of 20 to 30 fpm continuous duty. Total weight of the system including an integrated pump and reservoir (not shown) is only 83 pounds. All above-deck parts are stainless steel. Courtesy: Hydra-Cap Systems, Inc.

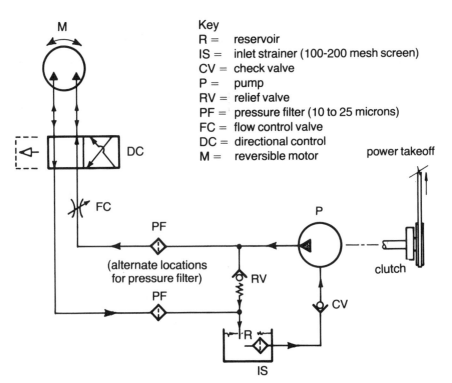

Fig. 4-7. Hydraulic anchor windlass plumbing schematic.

A comparison of hydraulic windlasses will serve to show some of the performance features (Table 4-6). One, the Plath model 8H, is a design for fishing boat use and features a cable drum instead of a wildcat so that a boat can anchor in very deep water using a cable rode.

Like a diesel engine, the secret to successful operation of any hydraulic device is very clean oil and tight plumbing. The high operating pressure of the hydraulic system requires steel tubing or steel-reinforced hose and machined steel connectors. The design and installation of a hydraulic windlass system are best left to a qualified hydraulics shop.

CARE OF THE WINDLASS

As rugged as an anchor windlass is, it still needs some protection from the elements. Because of cost and weight, most anchor windlasses are made with aluminum alloy cases although shafts, gears, etc., are still made of steel or bronze. Manufacturers use the best marine grade aluminum alloy and coat it with durable epoxy paint, but sitting on the foredeck in the wash of green water and occasionally bashed by anchor and chain, the case can have corrosion problems. Likewise, any steel used

Table 4-6. *Hydraulic Anchor Windlass Performance*

Manufacturer and model	Rode size in	Capability		Performance			For boat sizes[b]
		Hauling speed fpm	Line pull lbs	Operating pressure—psi	Flow rate gpm	Power input HP[a]	
Hydra-Cap model 1500	⅜-in BBB chain or rope	20-30	1,500	NA	NA	NA	35 to 50 ft LOA
Plath model 8H	2242 ft of ½-in steel cable	20 (nom) 83 (max)	2,000	900	9	7	anchors to 500 lb
Simpson-Lawrence model 523	to ⅝-in BBB chain or rope	40 (max)	2,240	1,750	4½	8	to 75 ft LOA
Nilsson model H3000	to ⅝-in chain or rope	65 (max)	3,000	2,000	6	10	to 72 ft LOA
Lighthouse model 3002	to ⅝-in chain or 1-in rope	21 (nom)	3,500	2,400[c]	6	7½	to 45 tons

[a] *Specifications for Pumps, Valves, and Power Units* (Savage, MN 55378: Continental Hydraulics, a company brochure).
[b] Manufacturer's recommendations.
[c] Axial piston pump.

in the exposed components of the windlass, even though initially galvanized, will eventually rust.

An anchor windlass should be fitted with a cover that encompasses warping drums, pawls, levers, handwheels, etc., to give some protection from rain and seawater. The cover can be made of sail cover fabric or it can be a soft molded plastic cover which adds a nice cosmetic touch. The latter will also help save bare toes and ankles. The cover should not be airtight but allowed to breathe and to drain water which may be forced up under it. If the cover is form fitted around the drum and wildcat, it will probably not be blown off in heavy winds or torn off by a large wave, but a drawstring tie-down may still be a good idea.

After a windlass has been used for weighing anchor, it should be dried, and the bare metal parts sprayed with a corrosion inhibitor such as WD-40. Tender loving care will make the windlass last the lifetime of the boat.

In general, windlasses need to have the gear case oil checked every one or two years and gear oil added if it is low. (Look for oil leaks around shaft ends if oil has to be added.) A heavy gear oil is usually recommended—SAE 50 to SAE 150. Most gear cases will get along well with an SAE 90 gear oil which sticks to the teeth and can take high gear tooth loads. Do not use engine lubricating oil.

The Lighthouse model 1501 anchor windlass is designed to resist the damaging environment of the foredeck of a vessel. All above-deck components are made of type 304 stainless steel, including the warping drum and wildcat. The case is mounted on a cast urethane deck seal. The below-deck electric motor draws only 80 amperes at its rated line pull of 1,000 pounds at 37 fpm. An optional 2,000 psi hydraulic drive is available with identical, above-deck components. Courtesy: Lighthouse Manufacturing Co.

The cone clutch of a wildcat gets its gripping power from the wedging action of a cone in a mating socket. It can easily become frozen in place if any corrosion develops. To counter this, a very light film of grease should be applied to the conical surface to keep it from jamming but not enough to cause it to slip. Do not put any grease on a band type brake for this is a different gripping action.

Because clutch cones also have to slide back and forth a small distance on the shaft while engaging and disengaging, a grease fitting is usually provided on the end of the shaft for lubrication. Use only saltwater-compatible grease in this fitting. Such grease is available from boat trailer supply stores where it is sold for trailer wheel bearing lubrication.

If you have an electric windlass, you have some vital additional maintenance to do. Electrical faults are the source of many boat fires and the high current draw over an extended period of time by an electric windlass makes it a prime candidate as an arson bug if it is not kept in good condition. Power supply cables should be initially run high and dry through the vessel so that they have a minimum chance of becoming wet and corroding. Terminals should be soldered and any exposed wire between the terminal and the insulation should be sealed with shrink-on tubing or a plastic coating. Corroded wires and terminals increase the electrical resistance of the circuit and undue heating occurs which can cause a fire. Your routine inspection of the boat should include a check on the power supply cables between battery and windlass motor.

Major maintenance of hydraulic windlasses should be left to the hydraulic specialists. Careful torquing of a leaking joint or replacing an O-ring in a connector or changing filters and adding fluid is about the extent of general maintenance that a boat crew should think of doing. There are, however, a number of early clues to potential problems which will tell you whether or not you need a specialist's help. The senses of sight, hearing, touch, and smell can be of great help here:*

> *Sight:* Look for wet hoses or lines, oil stains or low reservoir level.
>
> *Hearing:* Listen for water hammer in the lines or gurgling sounds in the pump.
>
> *Touch:* Feel for vibrating or hot lines.
>
> *Smell:* Any odor of hot oil indicates a problem.

---

*J. F. Briggs. *Trouble Shooting Hydraulic Systems*, Bulletin 5215 (Van Wert, OH 45891: Aeroquip Industrial Division, 1983).

CHAPTER FIVE

Anchor Rodes

You would not expect to use an anchor without a means of connecting it to your boat. The means of connecting the anchor to a boat is called the anchor rode, and it consists of rope and/or chain and a variety of connectors. Sometimes the fiber rope portion of the rode is called a "warp" or a "hawser."

Whatever the name, the rode must be made of materials that will withstand the physical environment in which it will operate. It has to have the strength to hold the boat against wind and wave up to the full holding power of the anchor. It has to be elastic to absorb the shock loads imposed on it by the surging of the boat. It has to be resistant to the marine environment including chemical corrosion and biological action. It has to have good resistance to abrasion as it drags across the sea bottom or chafes against corners of the deck gear. It has to be easily handled by the crew, preferably without special equipment or gloves.

The demands on the anchor rode are many and the candidates for it are few. Steel chain and fiber rope are the prime candidates and these come in an endless array of construction and materials. Oldest and still the most popular rode material is fiber rope. At one time only vegetable fibers were available and ropes made of them when made up as anchor rodes lasted only a year or two. Now with synthetic fiber rope lifetimes are measured in tens of years.

The second most popular anchor rode is chain which solves the abrasion problem and provides a modest elasticity effect as its weight forms a catenary sag in the rode.

THE NEED FOR PROPER SCOPE

The holding power of an anchor is the horizontal resisting force it develops as it digs into the seabed. If there is a significant vertical load on the anchor, the horizontal force will be compromised, and the

resulting efficiency of the anchor reduced. The relationship of the holding power to the rode lead angle, θ, is illustrated in Fig. 5-1. When the
anchor is set in mud, the lead angle is not as critical as when set in a sand
bed, but by the time a lead angle of 12° is reached, anchor holding power
has been reduced a significant amount.*

In general, anchors for small boats are designed for a lead angle of
not more than 8°, and the user should see to it that the lead angle is much
less so that the anchor flukes can dig in with a will.

To get a proper lead angle for the anchor, you must have the proper
combination of "scope" and rode material. Simply put, scope is the ratio of
anchor rode length, L, to the distance of the bow roller above the sea
bottom (D + d) (Fig. 5-2).

Scope is the ultimate secret to successful anchoring, and it is highly
dependent on the materials with which the rode is made. An all-rope rode
at short scope seriously impairs an anchor's holding power (Fig. 5-3). Not

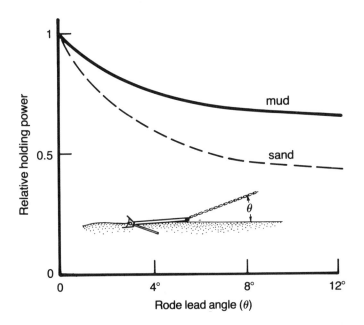

Fig. 5-1. Anchor lead angle effects.

*R. J. Taylor, *Interaction of Anchors with Soil and Anchor Design* (Washington, D. C.: U. S. Navy
Technical Note CEL N-1627, April 1982).

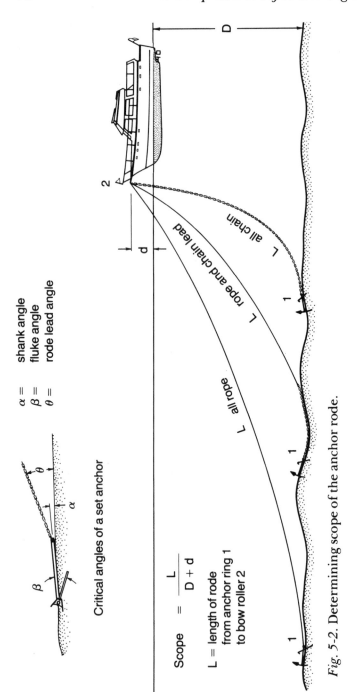

Fig. 5-2. Determining scope of the anchor rode.

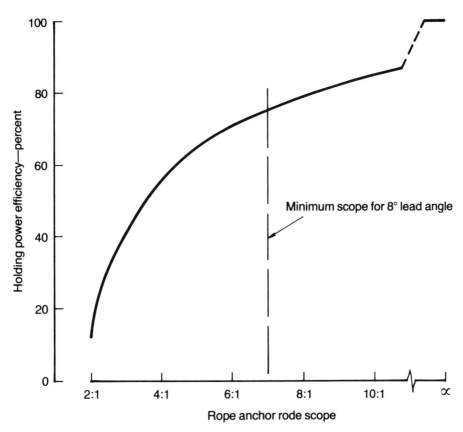

Fig. 5-3. Effect of scope on anchor holding power for the all-rope rode.

until the scope reaches 10 to 1 is the all-rope rode anchor able to realize a significant part of its holding power.

To correct this problem, rope rodes are fitted with short lengths of chain between rope and anchor to hold the anchor lead angle closer to the horizontal than is possible with bare rope alone. The amount of chain needed to make an effective lead on a working anchor rode is quite short, still leaving the rode principally rope. The chain lead, however, is sufficiently long also to keep the rope off the sea bottom, thereby minimizing abrasion problems.

Anchoring with all chain is surely the best way to get maximum efficiency out of your anchor, but it has its drawbacks. Not only is chain heavy, but it weighs down the bow of your boat and tests your resolve in weighing anchor. In addition, chain that is lying on the bottom adds nothing to the shock absorbing capability of the catenary. Furthermore, once that chain is stretched taut, as it may be in a storm, it has no further shock absorbing capabilities and is easily broken. The simple message is that more chain is not necessarily better than less chain.

Experience has given us some rule of thumb methods for the proper scope to lay out based on the type of anchor rode used. For the working anchor with winds no greater than 30 knots and some protection from the seas, the following values have proven adequate in a good holding ground:

Type of Rode	*Minimum Scope*
All rope	10 to 1
Rope plus chain lead (combination rode)	7 to 1
All chain	4 to 1

No single length of rode is suitable for all anchoring situations, but there are some minimums that make sense. Typically, a boat should be able to anchor in water depths equal to its length overall (LOA) as a minimum and should be able to deploy rode scopes of at least 7 to 1 for a combination rode and 4 to 1 for an all-chain rode (Table 5-1).

Boats that operate generally in shallow waters, as on the East Coast of the United States or on inland lakes, may get by with shorter rode lengths. Boats that operate in the deeper waters along the Pacific coast of North America and all those that are oceangoing should consider even longer rode lengths.

As Van Dorn (see Bibliography) points out, in very deep water you can reduce the scope of an all-chain rode, and it has been proven many

Table 5-1. Anchor Rode Lengths (in feet)

LOA	Compatible anchoring depth—D	Minimum rode length[a]	
		Nylon with chain lead[b]	All chain
less than 20	20	160	90
20 to 30	30	240	135
30 to 40	40	310	180
40 to 50	50	390	225
50 to 60	60	480	275
60 to 80	70	560	320

[a]Minimum to yield 7 to 1 scope for nylon rode with chain lead and 4 to 1 for an all chain rode. Includes nominal bow height—d.
[b]Includes length of chain lead.

times. One of the reasons for this is that the wave height becomes a smaller proportion of the total scope allowing the boat to ride easier over the waves.

ANCHOR CHAIN

There is a plethora of chain constructions available, and you should be advised to be certain of the type of chain you buy for your anchor rode. Only two types of chain are in common use for boat anchor rodes and they are Proof Coil and BBB. For many years BBB was the standard in the marine industry with the result that many wildcats were designed to fit that particular link configuration. In recent years BBB has been losing out to Proof Coil which has a broader industrial usage and is superior to BBB with a greater flexibility and less tendency to bind. The fewer number of links per foot also makes it less costly to manufacture.

Proof Coil chain is designated by the National Association of Chain Manufacturers (NACM)[*] as Grade 30 chain. It is frequently called "common chain" and is of utility grade for such uses as log chain, tow chain, guard rail chain, anchor chain, stump pulling chain, etc. Proof Coil chain is not recommended for overhead lifting.

BBB chain was popular because of its greater unit weight which improved the catenary effect and the slightly greater strength offered by the more compact links which distort less under load. BBB chain is still being manufactured because there are a lot of windlass wildcats around that require it. If you are thinking of making an initial purchase of anchor chain, BBB with all of its fringe benefits may give you a problem in regard to its future availability.

Both Proof Coil and BBB chain are made from basic open-hearth low carbon steel with a tensile strength of 55,000 psi. They come in a variety of surface finishes but only the hot-dip galvanized finish should be considered for an anchor rode.

Ship anchor chains are usually made with the stud link design which has as much as a 20 percent higher proof load strength than open link chain. The additional strength is gained from a crosspiece (stud) that prevents the deformation of the link under load. Stud link design chain starts at the ⅝-inch size and goes up to 4 inches in diameter with a breaking strength in excess of 400 tons.

Because chain is so heavy, it comes in discrete lengths for convenience of handling. You will find it in "shots" of 90 feet (15 fathoms) in the larger (⅝ inch and over) sizes. The smaller chain, more commonly used

---

[*] National Association of Chain Manufacturers, P.O. Box 3143, York, PA 17402-0143.

on recreational boats, comes in buckets of about 600 pounds for the small buyer or in large barrels from which you can buy any length. True anchor chain comes with oversize links at both ends which permit the insertion of a single chain shackle for joining two lengths together.

The strength of a chain is determined from extensive test samples of a given construction loaded to the breaking point on a standard test machine. The minimum breaking load so determined is defined as the breaking load for that chain construction.

The proof load is a tensile loading applied to the chain during or subsequent to the manufacturing process for the sole purpose of detecting defects in the material or manufacture. For Proof Coil and BBB chain the proof load is 50 percent of the breaking load of the chain.

The working load is 50 percent of the proof load. Hence, the working load is one-fourth of the breaking strength of the chain (Table 5-2). Chain from reputable manufacturers is proof load tested before shipment. Other chain constructions may have different proof load and working load ratios.

Chains are not considered to be elastic in the same sense that rope is elastic. Proof Coil chain is, however, required to have a 15-percent elongation at the breaking load in order to withstand shock or impact loading without suffering a brittle failure. This much elongation, however, is not elastic and the chain will have suffered permanent deformation. It must be replaced and not put back into use.

The strength of a chain can be seriously compromised if it is subjected to twisting, to bending over a sharp corner, or to any other form of longitudinal disfigurement. Strong men in circuses and carnivals amaze the spectators with their feats of breaking chain using only their bare hands. They do it not by a steady pull on the chain but by twisting the

True anchor chain comes with an oversize link at each end to accept a chain or anchor shackle. If using a bulk length of chain, a chain shackle must first be added to replace the missing oversize link. Courtesy: Campbell Chain Co.

Table 5-2. Physical Characteristics of Anchor Chain

Proof Coil chain (grade 30)

Trade size—in	Number of links per ft	Weight per 100 feet lbs[a]	Feet per bucket	Working load lbs [b]	Proof load lbs [c]	Breaking load lbs
3/16	12-1/2	42	1,000	750	1,500	3,000
1/4	12	76	800	1,250	2,500	5,000
5/16	10-3/4	115	550	1,900	3,800	7,600
3/8	9-3/4	166	400	2,650	5,300	10,600
7/16	8-3/4	225	300	3,500	7,000	14,000
1/2	8	289	200	4,500	9,000	18,000
5/8	6-3/8	425	150	6,900	13,800	27,600

Stud link chain (grade 1)

5/8	3-1/4	406	d	8,310	16,620	23,745

BBB chain

3/16	15-1/2	45	1,000	775	1,550	3,100
1/4	14	81	800	1,325	2,650	5,300
5/16	12	120	550	1,950	3,900	7,800
3/8	11	173	400	2,750	5,500	11,000
7/16	9-3/4	231	300	3,625	7,250	14,500
1/2	9	296	200	4,750	9,500	19,000

[a]Weight before hot-dip galvanizing.
[b]One half of proof load.
[c]One half of breaking load (except for stud link chain).
[d]Supplied in 15-fathom shots.

chain until adjacent links are levered against one another and failure occurs in bending and not in tension. A fine trick for the showplace but not one to be followed in anchoring.

HIGH STRENGTH CHAIN

Chain can be made out of most metals giving a wide range of strength and weight factors. Steel has been the most popular because it is cheap, very workable, and can be alloyed to make it very strong. Common chain (Proof Coil) is a low carbon, unheat-treated steel made in vast quantities. Higher strength chain is made using higher carbon content steel, alloying it with other metals, and then heat-treating it (Table 5-3).

Stud link chain used with an old-fashioned anchor having the early Admiralty pattern flukes. Note the becket on the back of one arm which is used in catting the anchor. Stud link chain sizes start at ⅝-inch diameter— too large for boat anchor rodes but suitable for large moorings.

High Test chain (grade 43) is fabricated from high carbon steel and heat-treated to develop good ductility and a high tensile strength of 85,000 psi. Transport chain (grade 70) is also made from high carbon steel heat-treated to a tensile strength of approximately 120,000 psi. Alloy Steel chain (grade 80) is fabricated from special alloy steel which is heat-treated and tempered or drawn for optimum strength and ductility. This chain has a tensile strength of 180,000 psi, does not work-harden, and does not require periodic annealing to relieve brittleness.

High strength chains get their strength through higher hardness which also makes it difficult to cut the chain except with a torch or grinding wheel. Self-colored or bright finish is normally supplied, neither of which is useful in a saltwater environment. High strength chain can be hot-dip galvanized but at a loss in strength of the following approximate amounts:

Grade 43   10 percent
Grade 70   20 percent
Grade 80   30 percent

Table 5-3. Physical Characteristics of High Strength Chain

Grade 43—High Test chain

Trade size—in	Working load[a]—lbs	Weight per 100 ft—lbs
1/4	2,600	84
5/16	3,900	120
3/8	5,400	176
7/16	7,200	230
1/2	9,200	300

Grade 70—Transport chain

Trade size—in	Working load[b]—lbs	Weight per 100 ft—lbs
1/4	3,150	84
5/16	4,700	120
3/8	6,600	176
7/16	8,750	230
1/2	11,300	300

Grade 80—Alloy chain

Trade size—in	Working load[c]—lbs	Weight per 100 ft—lbs
7/32	2,100	50
9/32	3,500	84
5/16	4,900	120
3/8	7,100	176
1/2	12,000	300

[a]Proof load = 1.7 times working load, breaking load = 3 times working load.
[b]Proof load = 2 times working load, breaking load = 4 times working load.
[c]Proof load = 2 times working load, breaking load = 3.5 times working load.

There is little to be gained through the use of high strength chain in an anchor rode. Chain weight is needed to hold the lead angle of the anchor below 8° and to provide a modest amount of shock-absorbing catenary sag. Using smaller size but higher strength chain only means that you will need a longer length to produce the same weight of chain lead. For the all-chain rode the loss of catenary is serious, and you will certainly need a longer riding stopper to provide needed shock-absorbing capability.

ANCHOR CHAIN CONNECTING ELEMENTS

There are sundry elements to the anchor rode which fall into the category of connecting elements—connecting anchor to rode, connecting chain lead to rope rode, connecting shots of chain, as well as the all-important matter of securing the bitter end of the rode to the boat. These are called splicing links and shackles. Three popular splicing links are illustrated in Fig. 5-4. The riveted joining link forms an integral part of the chain and, when carefully installed, looks and works like any other link. The quick connect link, purely temporary, is about 60 percent longer than a standard link of chain of the same nominal size. The double jaw midlink is the most utilitarian because it may be used for temporary or permanent installation, and it is about the same size as a standard link of chain.

Shackles come in a variety of styles shown in Fig. 5-5. Chain shackles are used to connect the ends of chain to anchor shackles or the ring on the anchor shank. Anchor shackles usually connect rope eye splices to chain or the anchor ring. The bow in the anchor shackle is intended to give more freedom of movement than the chain shackle which behaves more like a chain link.

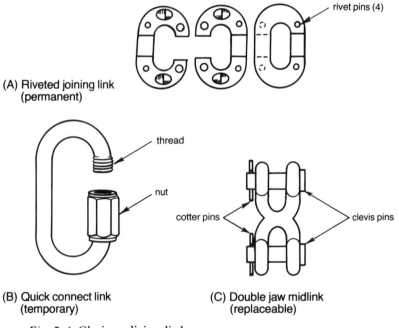

rivet pins (4)

(A) Riveted joining link
(permanent)

thread

nut

cotter pins

clevis pins

(B) Quick connect link
(temporary)

(C) Double jaw midlink
(replaceable)

Fig. 5-4. Chain-splicing links.

The oval pin chain shackle is an excellent connection between shots of chain or for use with chain stoppers because it can be released so quickly and under load. This is done with a mallet, first driving the taper pin out and then the oval pin itself. Unfortunately, it is available only in larger sizes from ship chandleries.

Both anchor and chain shackles come with a choice of screw pin, round pin, or bolt and nut closures. Although the screw pin is somewhat more convenient to use, faulty safety wiring of it has been the cause of many lost anchors. The round pin, on the other hand, is more easily safetied with a cotter pin, and it is a little neater in use avoiding the meat hook characteristic of safety wire.

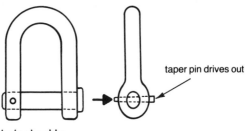

taper pin drives out

(A) Oval pin, quick-release *chain* shackle

screw pin   round pin   bolt, nut, and cotter pin

(B) *Anchor* shackles

How to mouse a screw pin shackle
• double turns of seizing wire in a figure 8 pattern

• frapping turns with both ends of seizing wire (bury ends)

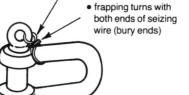

(C) Screw pin *chain* shackle (can also be had in round pin or bolt, nut, and cotter pin)

Fig. 5-5. Ground tackle shackles.

If you anchor only for short periods of time and do not expect the boat to swing in circles, you can use a chain shackle to connect the last link of the chain with the anchor ring (Fig. 5-6 A). If you are leaving your boat on the hook for a long period of time and there is a chance it will swing in circles, then you must insert a swivel between anchor ring and the last link of the chain to prevent twisting the chain (Fig. 5-6 B). Do not connect the jaw fitting of a swivel directly to the anchor shank because the swivel will then be put into a bending position if the boat veers (Fig. 5-7).

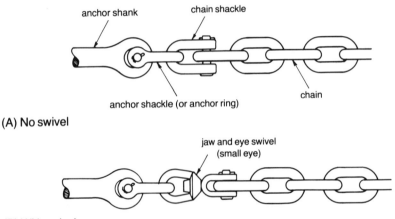

anchor shank   chain shackle

anchor shackle (or anchor ring)   chain

(A) No swivel

jaw and eye swivel
(small eye)

(B) With swivel

Fig. 5-6. Bending the chain rode to the anchor.

Lest you think there is little danger from installing a swivel backwards, as shown in Fig. 5-7, let me cite an example in which I was involved as an expert witness in a lawsuit. In December 1987 an 83-foot Broward luxury motor yacht was anchored at Atwood Harbour, Acklins Island, Bahamas. During the night the wind, blowing in the 20-knot range, veered and the owner found the vessel no longer attached to the bottom. He attempted to motor out of danger, but it was too late and the waves cast the almost-new boat up on the beach (Fig. 5-7(a)).

Because of the value of the vessel, in excess of $1.7 million, an extensive investigation was conducted. Preliminary indications showed that the swivel between the chain rode and anchor had failed. The swivel eye was still attached to the chain, but the rest of the swivel was missing as was the anchor. Divers later found the anchor and, not unexpectedly, the swivel fork was still attached to it in the manner illustrated in Fig. 5-7. The swivel shank, however, was cleanly broken off. Apparently, when the pull on the anchor suddenly changed direction with the veering wind and before the anchor could reset itself to the new direction, the swivel shank underwent an extreme bending load for which it wasn't designed. It broke, separating anchor from boat.

The cost of salvaging this luxury cruiser was $119,000 and the cost of restoring it to its original condition was another $164,000—all because of an anchor swivel installed backwards.

Swivels in an anchor chain can be a source of concern because like all moving parts under stress, they can fail if not properly designed and manufactured. A proper swivel is one that is drop forged—not screwed, riveted, or welded together. In a drop forging the grain of the material is carefully oriented to give not only maximum strength but to relieve the stresses at the corners. Other fabrication processes concentrate stresses or weaken the swivel through welding.

In selecting a swivel, I would use the largest size that fits the chain link without binding.

Many sailors are wary of the strength of chain connecting elements but manufacturers have designed them to be similar in strength to Proof Coil chain to which they are attached (Table 5-4). This is accomplished by forging them out of higher grade steel and, in some instances, making the

Fig. 5-7. If you elect to use a swivel at the anchor end of a chain rode, do not put it on this way. The jaw end of the swivel, as installed here, will most likely break, or, at least, bend the swivel pin when the boat sheers at anchor. The swivel should be installed end for end with an anchor shackle between the swivel eye and the anchor shank.

sections a little larger than standard chain link wire diameter. As an example, anchor and chain shackle pins are 1/16-inch larger in diameter than the chain wire. That is, a 3/8-inch shackle has a 7/16-inch diameter pin that will fit into a 3/8-inch chain link. Using connectors of the proper size will prevent overkill and unnecessary weight.

When you secure the bitter end of an all-chain rode to the boat, do so with multiple turns of tarred nylon lashing which will be easier to sever than a heavier rope (Fig. 5-8). There should be ready accesss to the lashing so that it can be cut free to slip the anchor or to add more chain or rope as the situation may demand.

THE ALL-CHAIN ANCHOR RODE

The principal argument raised for the all-chain anchor rode is that chain can give a shock-absorbing effect to the anchor rode. This comes about through the chain catenary which is, simply, the sag in the chain due to its own weight. It is at a maximum when the chain is horizontal and a minimum when it is vertical. A high end loading on the

Fig. 5-7(a). An 83-foot luxury cruiser hard aground in the Bahamas following the failure of an improperly installed swivel in the anchor rode. Courtesy: Nelson & Associates.

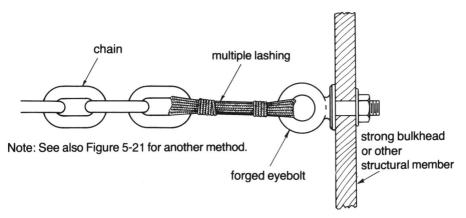

Fig. 5-8. Securing the bitter end of the chain rode to the boat.

chain tends to remove the catenary, and a light loading allows greater sag. Heavy chain produces more of a catenary than light chain.

A boat when anchored with chain in light winds has much of its deployed chain lying on the bottom (Fig. 5-9A). As the boat moves about, the chain is alternately lifted off the bottom and lowered giving a shock-absorbing feature to the rode. This is not a catenary effect, but it acts like one.

As the wind load on the boat further increases, the chain is lifted completely off the bottom providing a true catenary with its shock-absorb-

Table 5-4. Strength of Connecting Elements

Nominal size—in	Safe working load limit[a]—lbs				
	Proof Coil chain	Midlink	Riveted joining link	Anchor or chain shackles[b]	Swivels[c]
1/4	1,250	(use 5/16)	1,325	1,000	900
5/16	1,900	3,250	1,950	1,500	1,300
3/8	2,650	4,500	2,750	2,000	2,450
7/16	3,500	(use 1/2)	3,625	3,000	(use 1/2)
1/2	4,500	7,000	4,750	4,000	3,950
5/8	6,900	9,750	7,250	6,500	5,850

[a]One-fourth of breaking strength.
[b]Applies to screw pin or round pin closures.
[c]Use at least one size larger to give chain-matching strength.
Note that the tabulations in last two columns are from John H. Myers, ed., *Handbook of Ocean and Underwater Engineering* (New York: McGraw-Hill, 1969).

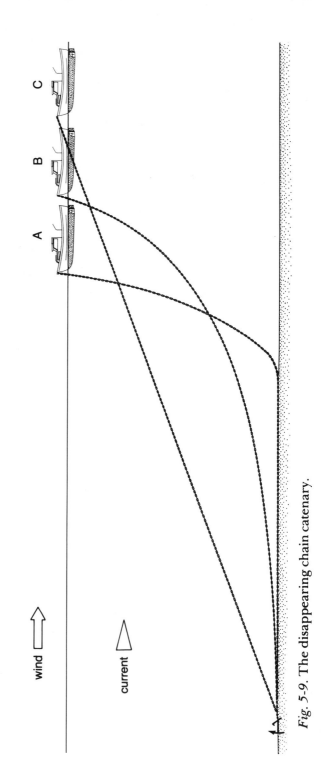

wind

current

Fig. 5-9. The disappearing chain catenary.

ing capability as shown at position B on the same figure. As the wind load increases even further, the catenary tends to disappear as in position C, virtually eliminating the shock-absorbing feature claimed for chain and also increasing the lead angle of the anchor shank. At this point, a sudden gust of wind or a large wave would cause the boat to jerk hard against the taut anchor chain resulting either in upsetting the anchor or breaking part of the ground tackle.

At what point does the catenary disappear? Table 5-5 gives an answer in the form of ground tackle loads as experienced by a hypothetical

Table 5-5. Example of the Disappearing Catenary

(1) Simplified catenary geometry[a]:

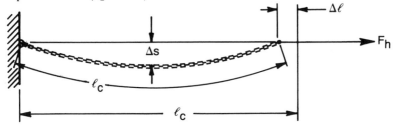

(2) Example boat: ABYC hypothetical powerboat[b]:

LOA = 45 ft, beam = 15 ft

anchor rode = 200 ft of ⅜-in Proof Coil chain

(3) Catenary characteristics of hypothetical boat at anchor:

Wind speed—knots	10	15	20	30	40
Horizontal ground tackle load F_h(lb)	155	350	620	1,400	2,490
F_h as percent of chain breaking strength	1.5	3.3	5.8	13.2	23.5
Catenary sag (Δs) per 100 ft of chain ft	15	6	3	1	0
Extension ($\Delta \ell$) left per 100 ft of chain ft	2.8	1.0	0.4	0.1	0

[a]T. Baumeister, *Mark's Standard Handbook for Mechanical Engineers,* 8th ed. (New York: McGraw-Hill Co., 1978).
[b]From Table 2-1.

powerboat. The calculation has been somewhat simplified by assuming that the chain is stretched horizontally rather than on a slope and that the weight of the chain in water is the same as in air. Both of these assumptions make the catenary look better than it actually will be. The calculation was also made for a 100-foot length of chain for simplicity. Since the powerboat is equipped with a 200-foot chain rode, it conceivably could all be deployed, and the sag and extension would then be double the values given in the table.

The significant factors to look at in Table 5-5 are the sag of the chain, Δs, and the potential extension, $\Delta \ell$. The sag represents the "cushion" in the chain while the extension represents the distance the boat can surge aft before the chain assumes a straight line from anchor ring to bow roller.

At 10 knots of wind the anchored boat is in good shape with the all-chain rode having a 15-foot sag for shock absorption and a possible surge distance of almost 3 feet. But as the wind increases, the catenary is seen to flatten very quickly and by the time 20 knots of wind are reached, there is virtually no extension left in the chain and at 30 knots the sag for all practical purposes has also disappeared. At 40 knots of wind the chain is ramrod straight, and all transient surging forces caused by wind gusts or waves are transmitted directly to the anchor and deck gear as shown in position C of Fig. 5-9.

The surprising aspect of this analysis is how quickly the catenary disappears at loads which are only a fraction of the chain's breaking strength, less than the working load. What becomes obvious, then, is that the catenary which we talk so glibly about as being such a good shock absorber in an anchor rode, just isn't there when the wind pipes up and it is needed most.

Hank Halstead in his Boat Handling column (*Motor Boating & Sailing*, February 1985) had this to say about the role of chain in the November 1984 hurricane Klaus disaster in the U. S. Virgin Islands:

> Interestingly enough, chain proved to be far less effective as a means of securing anchorages than did the nylon anchor rode. Chain does not stretch and therefore when a boat would surge back sharply on a large wave, there was no cushion between the vessel and the anchor. Consequently, the anchor would pull free.
>
> In an extreme case, I saw a Solaris catamaran on which the anchor must have held fast, but when the chain came taut, it generated enough force to rip the windlass right out of the deck.

So if the chain catenary cannot provide "elasticity" when the winds howl, why is it used? Mostly because of its durability under moderate conditions. Chain is an all-around good material for the anchor rode if you can afford the weight in the bow of your boat and have a means of wrestling it to the surface after use. But to use an all-chain anchor rode in a heavy blow, you *must* include an elastic riding stopper in the rode assembly to cushion the blows of wind gusts and wave impacts when the chain is stretched taut.

CHAIN RIDING STOPPERS

The chain anchor rode has great merit from the standpoint of connecting anchor to boat, but it also has some serious demerits that need to be corrected. The greatest of these is the lack of elasticity when the chain is drawn taut as in a heavy wind. Chain also produces ominous rumbling sounds as it shifts position on the bow roller with each swing or

The Coast Guard cutter *General Greene* set out on a rescue mission in the winter of 1960 in what has been described as the worst snowstorm in New England history. During the rescue, *General Greene's* towline became entangled in her propellers, and she was obliged to save herself by anchoring. Two anchors were set, but at the time of the photograph, the starboard chain anchor rode had already parted and the port anchor was being dragged by a rode taut as a fiddle string and totally unyielding to the seas. The *General Greene* went aground but was later refloated.

Under storm conditions such as this, there is no catenary left in a chain rode to absorb surge loads. To survive, a chain anchor rode must have give to it, which is easily done in small vessels with a nylon rope riding stopper. Courtesy: U. S. Coast Guard.

dip of the bow disturbing persons trying to get a sound sleep in the forecastle.

The above problems can be easily corrected by the addition of an elastic riding stopper. This is a length of suitably strong 3-strand nylon rope that is attached between the Samson post or other strong fitting and

A chain grab hook on a rope lanyard is a convenient way to make a stopper for a chain, but it is not recommended as a permanent riding stopper. As the picture shows, the grab hook adds an eccentric loading to the chain.

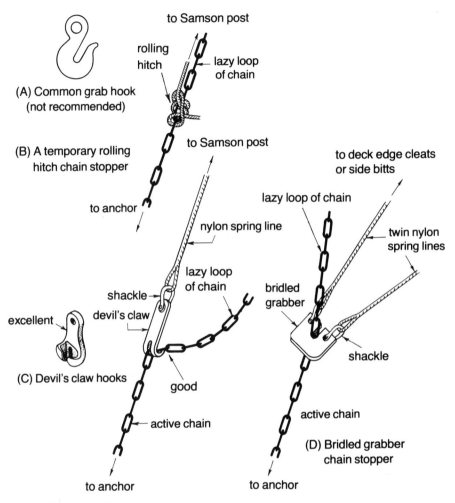

(A) Common grab hook (not recommended)

(B) A temporary rolling hitch chain stopper

to Samson post

rolling hitch

lazy loop of chain

to Samson post

to anchor

nylon spring line

lazy loop of chain

shackle

devil's claw

excellent

(C) Devil's claw hooks

good

active chain

to anchor

to deck edge cleats or side bitts

lazy loop of chain

twin nylon spring lines

bridled grabber

shackle

active chain

(D) Bridled grabber chain stopper

to anchor

Fig. 5-10. Chain-riding stoppers.

the chain forward of the bow, essentially bypassing the section of chain that runs over the bow roller. The attachment to the anchor chain is made by a hook-on device such as the devil's claw, grab hook, bridled grabber, or, in an emergency, a rolling hitch directly on the anchor chain (Fig. 5-10). It should be noted that the common grab hook weakens the chain to

Facing page, below, a preferred riding chain stopper is the slotted steel plate which evenly loads the chain links. Twin bridles tend to dampen the sheering of the boat at anchor.

about 80 percent of its normal strength because of the eccentric grasp it takes on the chain. Therefore, it is not recommended.

The use of nylon rope as a spring brings back the old problem of chafe. Before belaying the spring line(s) to the Samson post or cleats, slip a length of corded rubber hose over the end to take the wear where the rope contacts the deck or deck fittings. One consolation in using an anchor rode spring line is that if the line parts you will still have the lazy loop of chain to take the load directly.

Boats with bowsprits have a particular problem when using a chain anchor rode. If the rode leads from a bow roller at the deck not only will the noise be present but the chain will rub on the bobstay. On the other hand, if the chain is led through a roller near the end of the sprit, there is a very real chance of breaking the sprit when the boat pitches violently in high waves especially if the sprit is long.

The solution to this problem is to provide a riding stopper between hull and anchor chain as shown in Fig. 5-11. The riding stopper not only takes the load off the bowsprit and the rumble out of the roller, but it provides a lower point of attachment. All boats could use this technique by providing a sturdy stem eyebolt at the boot topping.

CHAIN MARKERS

Marking the all-chain rode in order to determine the amount deployed is a problem that has not been satisfactorily solved to my knowledge. Paint gives the most flexibility in marking and can easily be refurbished every year. I use the following sequence of marks which is easily remembered:

Length in fathoms	Color of link and number painted
5	1 red
10	1 white
15	1 blue
20	2 red
25	2 white
30	2 blue
40	3 red
50	3 white
60	3 blue

One difficulty with the painted-link technique is the ease with which a colored link obscured with mud can pass your eye and not be seen. To remedy this, add a nylon electric wire tie to each painted link. These are

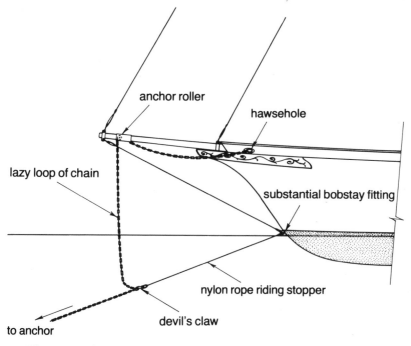

anchor roller

hawsehole

lazy loop of chain

substantial bobstay fitting

nylon rope riding stopper

to anchor

devil's claw

Fig. 5-11. Riding stopper for a bowsprit boat.

durable, easily seen, and easy to attach. Do not cut them off; the long whipping end is part of the eye-catcher (Fig. 5-12).

Regardless of the scheme that you select to mark your chain, you will want to mark the bitter end even though you are absolutely certain that it is securely fastened in the forepeak. About four fathoms from the bitter end paint a dozen or so links a bright yellow color as a warning that you are coming to the end of the chain in the locker.

CARE OF THE CHAIN RODE

One tends to think of chain as being indestructible, but it does have a certain vulnerability to misuse. Here are some suggestions on taking care of your chain anchor rode to prolong its life:

Keep the chain dry and clean.

Do not drag the chain over abrasive surfaces such as concrete.

Eliminate twists before using.

Fig. 5-12. A combination of painted links and nylon ties become chain length markers. Here, two pairs of links are painted red indicating that 20 fathoms of chain have been deployed. Nylon electric wire ties are fastened to the chain at the painted links as eye-catchers when the chain is deployed.

Never knot a chain or insert bolts or spikes to shorten it.

Avoid bending chain links around any sharp corner.

Turn the chain end for end at least annually to distribute the wear on the galvanizing.

Regalvanize the chain before flakes of rust develop. (Regalvanize only twice.)

Avoid the use of dissimilar metals in contact with the chain.

Be certain that end fittings can move freely within the attaching links.

Inspect chain links periodically and after severe strains have been placed upon it (Fig. 5-13).

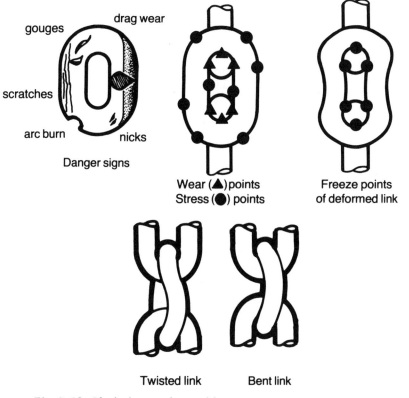

gouges

drag wear

scratches

arc burn

nicks

Danger signs

Wear (▲) points
Stress (●) points

Freeze points
of deformed link

Twisted link   Bent link

Fig. 5-13. Chain inspection guide.

Clean up each shackle or swivel. Be certain to seize the screw pins with wires before putting back into service.

Examine the bitter end attachment to assure its integrity.

Examine rode length markings for legibility. If any are obscured or missing, put new ones on.

ROPE FOR THE ANCHOR RODE

Rope is a general term applied to both fiber and wire products but as used here will apply only to fiber products. One also hears the term cordage, which applies not only to fiber ropes but also to small stuff like yarns, string, marline, and seizing. There is actually very little rope aboard a boat for once it has been fashioned into a specific form, namely, halyard, dock line, anchor rode, etc., it becomes a line.

Manufacturers of cordage have developed rope fibers and rope construction so extensively that you no longer simply buy a piece of rope. Now it is important to match the rope characteristics to the job. Strength, elongation, aging, weight, and cost all enter into your consideration when selecting a rope for a specific use.

Fiber types are conveniently divided into the natural fibers derived from vegetable sources and synthetic fibers which are the products of test tubes. The history of natural fibers is an ancient one, and there is evidence that hemp was used as a rope fiber as early as 500 B. C. Without rope, civilization would have stayed land bound and the age of discovery would not have occurred.

Synthetic fibers, however, have almost totally displaced natural fibers in nautical uses. The reasons are obvious—strength, durability, softness, and the controllability of their mechanical properties. Synthetic rope fibers are continuous filaments of very long molecular-chain polymers. These filaments may be either extruded or spun, and are termed mono-filament (large single filaments) or multifilament (smaller multiple filaments). The chemical characteristics of the polymer material are many and varied giving rise to a vast array of synthetic fibers having interesting possibilities for marine rope. For anchor rode use, only a few are of interest and are listed in Table 5-6.

Nylon

The most interesting property of nylon rope is its elasticity. Nylon is the most elastic and the strongest of the common synthetic fibers. It is highly resistant to mildew, can be stored wet, and even sea grass can grow on it without weakening the fibers. It does not float and its wet strength is 10 to 15 percent less than its dry strength. While it has excellent resistance to aging in general, exposure to sunlight for long periods of time will damage it.

Polyester

These fibers are known under an assortment of trade names such as Dacron, Fortrel, Kodel, and Terylene. The use of polyester in marine rope is of great interest because of low stretch and good resistance to abrasion. Polyester has almost the same strength as nylon but without the wet-strength loss. Recent formulations and constructions have made some polyester ropes almost as stretch-resistant as wire cable. Like nylon, polyester is resistant to deterioration by biological organisms and most

Table 5-6. Characteristics of Rope Fibers

	Fiber Type				
	Manila	Nylon	Polyester	Polypropylene	Aramid
Specific gravity	1.38	1.14	1.38	.91	1.44
Water absorption (percent of dry weight)	up to 100%	9%	1%	nil	nil
Abrasion resistance	good	very good	excellent	good	poor
Resistance to rot	poor	excellent	excellent	excellent	excellent
Resistance to sunlight	good	good	excellent	good[b]	poor
Shock load absorption ability	poor	excellent	good	very good	poor
Strength wet compared to strength dry	up to 120%	85-90%	100%	100%	95%
Recommended working load (percent of breaking test)[a]	20%	11%	11%	17%	11%
Elongation at recommended working load[a]	12%	23%	15%	18%	14%
Elongation at 75 percent of breaking test[a]	19%	42%	29%	37%	21%

[a]Twisted 3-strand construction.
[b]In black color.

petroleums and solvents found aboard boats. Its resistance to sunlight and very low stretch have made it attractive for the running rigging of boats.

Polypropylene
This is the lightest of the common synthetic ropes and it floats making it valuable for towlines and nets. It is only about 75 percent as strong as nylon and even less resistant to sunlight unless it is in the black color. Its low cost makes it very attractive for general-purpose use, and it is commonly used in the fishing industry.

Aramid
This is a modern test-tube miracle fiber having extreme strength-to-weight properties and low elongation. It is used in bulletproof vests, automobile tires, and ropes where very low elongation is important. Du Pont markets one brand under the name Kevlar.

ROPE CONSTRUCTION

Equally as important as the fiber in selecting rope for a particular marine purpose is its manner of construction. The cordage manufacturers have given us a variety of constructions for different purposes. Only two of those, however, are important in today's boating world and they are known as twisted or braided constructions. They are also referred to as rotating or nonrotating, respectively, for the obvious reason that a twisted rope tends to rotate (unwind) when a load is applied, whereas a braided rope with symmetrical right and left hand-laid strands does not rotate. But even the inherent rotation of twisted ropes has now been reasonably quelled.

Braided rope is not one but a whole family of constructions. There may be hollow braid, parallel-core braid, solid braid, double braid, or braid that is plaited. Size for size, double-braided rope is about 20 to 30 percent stronger than twisted rope but is less elastic making it less suitable for an anchor rode. Braided rope is not easily spliced by the novice further rendering it unattractive for anchor rode use.

Some marine chandleries are offering a flat strap form of "rope" construction for anchor rodes which is the worst of all worlds. First, the material is a polyester material which has limited elongation properties. Second, a flat strap construction is even less elastic than any of the round braid constructions. Third, strap construction is susceptible to failure at loads well below its ultimate strength when subjected to sharp jerks.

Three common fiber rope constructions are shown. From top to bottom: 3-strand twisted, double braid (braid on braid), and plaited. Only the 3-strand twisted construction provides sufficient elasticity to make a good anchor rode.

Finally, there are, of course, the inevitable stitching failures from abrasion and age that most certainly will occur in later life. There are no attributes of strap construction that make it attractive to anchor rode use.

Twisted 3-strand rope construction using nylon fibers has become the overwhelming favorite for anchor rodes. It is easily spliced by the novice although the soft-laid ropes do not hold their form well when unlaying during the splicing process. Twisted ropes with their high elasticity can develop hockles when subjected to high loadings followed by a quick release. Once a hockle has developed, the rope has been unacceptably weakened in that spot.

Although practically all twisted rope is of 3-strand construction, there are subtle differences in construction that separate quality twisted rope from cheaply made rope. The major difference is in the number of stages used in forming the rope. In three-stage construction, fibers are twisted into thick yarns and the yarns into strands and, finally, the strands into rope. This type of construction is unbalanced, that is, two elements are twisted in one direction, and only one element is twisted in the other direction. Three-stage construction rope is cheaper to make, it is softer, and, in use, tends to stiffen early and develop hockles.

Four-stage rope has two elements twisted in one direction and two elements twisted in the opposite direction giving it a balanced twist. The additional element is an intermediate "mini-strand" of three-plied yarns. Fibers are first twisted into yarns of smaller diameter than those used in the three-stage rope. Three smaller yarns are then plied together to form the mini-strands which in turn are twisted together to form full strands as in three-stage construction. Three strands are then twisted together to form the final rope (Fig. 5-14).

Four-stage construction rope is much easier to splice because of its firmness of shape, the plied mini-strands actually holding their shape much better than the thick yarns of three-stage rope. In selecting rope for the all-critical anchor rode, it only makes good sense to get the better four-stage construction in your nylon rope.

Selection of the size of rope for the anchor rode (Table 5-7) is determined by the holding power of the anchor and the drag load of the boat. There is a minimum size for handling ease which is ⅜-inch diameter and, if the rope will get hard use, it should be replaced often rather than going to a larger size which would reduce the elasticity.

Twisted 3-strand nylon rope can undergo considerable stretch under working loads as is seen by the graph in Fig. 5-15. For normal day in, day out use, it should not be subjected to loads greater than 11 percent of its breaking strength according to the recommendations of the Cordage Institute. Under these conditions the rope will never wear out from loading although careless use may limit its life.

Working anchors, however, should be able to take anchor loads associated with a moderate gale of 30 knots of wind. There should be no

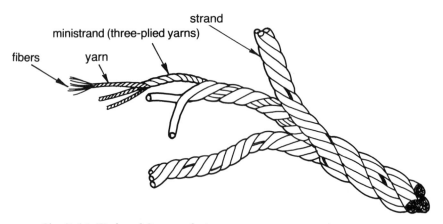

Fig. 5-14. Twisted 3-strand, 4-stage rope construction.

Table 5-7. *Strength of Twisted 3-Strand Nylon Rope*

| Diameter of rope | | Weight | Average breaking | Recommended |
inches	millimeters[a]	lbs/100 ft	test—lbs	working load[b]—lbs
3/8	9	3.5	3,700	410
7/16	10	5.0	5,000	550
1/2	12	6.5	6,400	700
9/16	14	8.3	8,000	880
5/8	16	10.5	10,400	1,140
3/4	18	14.5	14,200	1,560
7/8	22	20.0	20,000	2,200
1	25	26.0	25,000	2,750

[a]Closest metric rope size.
[b]11 percent of breaking strength.

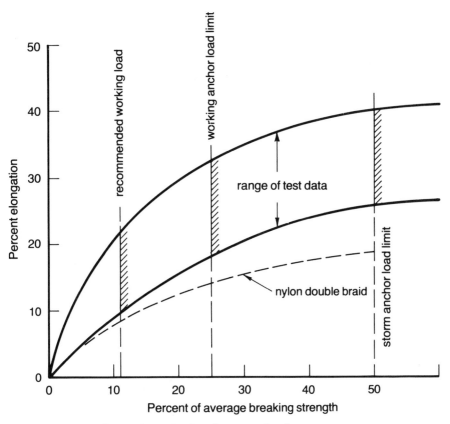

Fig. 5-15. Elongation of twisted 3-strand nylon rope.

need to change anchors or anchor rodes when this occurs since a well-cared-for nylon rope can take an occasional loading to 25 percent of its breaking strength without harm. Chafing becomes the big factor at this point and the line must be carefully protected from wear. Unattended boats lying at anchor during a blow are particularly susceptible to rope failure through wear.

By allowing the nylon anchor line to be stressed to 25 percent of its breaking strength, you get the use of the inherent elasticity of nylon. A nylon rode loaded to 25 percent of its breaking strength will stretch anywhere from 18 to 32 percent of its length giving a shock-relieving feature to your anchor system.

There is a third load limit for the once-in-a-lifetime challenge for your boat to ride out a force 11 storm at anchor. The upper limit of loading on twisted 3-strand nylon rope is 50 percent of the breaking strength of the rope. It is used to gain additional elasticity in the rode and provide further cushioning of surge loads on both anchor and deck gear. This loading reduces the safety factor of the rode to 2, which in a new rope is still enough to account for unknowns of manufacturing variability, aging, moisture content, splicing efficiency, etc.

Although the Cordage Institute does not recommend working nylon beyond 11 percent of the breaking load, it is necessary to do so in order to get the elasticity out of the rope that will prevent shock loads on the anchor system. Putting larger rope on the anchor rode to retain a high safety factor can be self-defeating since the resulting lower elongation will only increase the sharpness of the loads applied to anchor and deck gear. It is better to have the rope stretching than to be pulling deck cleats off or upsetting the anchor.

But this does not mean that your working anchor rode should also be your storm anchor rode even though it is calculated to be the same nominal size. Your storm anchor rode should include new, unused, quality rope kept in reserve for just such an emergency. In use it must be well protected against chafe. After use you should carefully inspect it and if any signs of wear are apparent, convert it to a working anchor rode, and get a new rope for your storm anchor rode.

THE CHAIN LEAD

An essential part of a rope anchor rode is the chain lead between the anchor and rope. It serves three functions—it makes setting the anchor easier, it absorbs the abrasion of the seabed, and it results in a smaller anchor lead angle. The size of the chain lead must match the breaking strength of the rope used. Recommended combinations of chain and rope for combination rodes are shown in Table 5-8.

There is no need to guess at the length of the chain lead if you use a little common sense. You know that anchor weight has something to do with it, so the larger the anchor, the longer the lead. It does not seem to have anything to do with the depth of the water (if the proper scope is deployed) and certainly does not have anything to do with the boat's waterline length except through anchor size.

Simply put, the chain lead should weigh at least as much as the anchor whose weight it is supplementing. For a given chain size from Table 5-8, the minimum length of the chain lead is determined from the formula:

$$\ell_c = \frac{W_a}{w_c} \times f \qquad [Equation\ 5\text{-}1]$$

where ℓ_c = length of chain lead, ft (minimum)
 W_a = weight of anchor, lb
 w_c = unit weight of chain, lb/ft (Table 5–2)
 f = anchor materials factor: 1 for steel anchors
 1.6 for aluminum anchors

As an example, for a 20H Danforth Hi-Tensile anchor with a ½-inch twisted 3-strand nylon rode, you would use at least 17 feet of 5/16-inch Proof Coil chain weighing 1.15 pounds per foot.

In the case of a 7-lb Fortress aluminum anchor with a ½-inch twisted 3-strand nylon rode, you would use at least 11-lbs of 5/16-inch Proof Coil chain

Table 5-8. Matching Combination Rode Components

| Chain lead | | Rope rode | | Rode loading limits | | |
| Galvanized Proof Coil | | twisted 3-strand nylon | | Recommended working | Working anchor | Storm anchor |
size in	breaking load—lbs	diameter in	breaking load—lbs	load lbs[a]	load limit lbs[b]	load limit lbs[c]
1/4[d]	5,000	3/8	3,700	410	925	1,850
1/4	5,000	7/16	5,000	550	1,250	2,500
5/16	7,600	1/2	6,400	700	1,600	3,200
3/8	10,600	5/8	10,400	1,140	2,600	5,200
7/16	14,000	3/4	14,200	1,560	3,500	7,000
1/2	18,000	7/8	20,000	2,250	4,500	9,000
5/8	27,600	1	25,000	2,750	6,250	12,500

[a] 11 percent of breaking load of rope.
[b] 25 percent of breaking load of rope or chain whichever is smaller.
[c] 50 percent of breaking load of rope or proof load of chain whichever is smaller
[d] Minimum recommended chain size.

(10 feet) as a chain lead. Weight is the key to making an anchor penetrate the seabed as well as to preventing planing of stock-stabilized, pivoting fluke anchors. The lead cannot be made shorter simply because of lighter anchor materials.

COMBINATION RODE CONNECTIONS

The rope-chain connection in a combination rode can be made with the familiar eye splice over a thimble in conjunction with a bow shackle (Fig. 5-16). This is a bulky connection but it is simple to make and is easily refurbished.

A proper eye splice for the anchor rode is made with a minimum of six tucks and the last tucks are seized to the standing part of the splice. A simple way to taper this splice is to tuck one strand two more times and one strand one more time beyond the sixth full tuck. The thimble should be tightly seized with the eye under tension to prevent it from popping out when the eye stretches under load.

One technique to tighten a nylon rope eye splice over a thimble is to boil the entire splice in water including the thimble. The nylon rope will shrink onto the thimble making a professional-looking splice. No harm will be done since nylon can withstand water at 250 degrees fahrenheit for 10 hours of immersion without any damaging effect.

It is also possible to splice the rope portion of the combination anchor rode directly to the chain lead (Fig. 5-17). This eliminates the bulky eye splice and anchor shackle allowing the joint to pass smoothly through the navel pipe and around the windlass warping drum. The rope-chain splice efficiency is approximately 85 to 90 percent, the same as a long splice. It does have one point of concern, though, and that is the eventual breakdown of the zinc galvanizing on the chain link and subsequent rusting. Since rust is the enemy of nylon, when you see it starting, cut off the original end link and make a new splice. Although the breakdown in the zinc coating on the end chain link cannot be stopped, the transfer of the deleterious rust to the rope strands can be slowed. To do this, slide pieces of

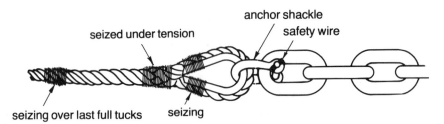

Fig. 5-16. The thimbled eye splice rope to chain connection.

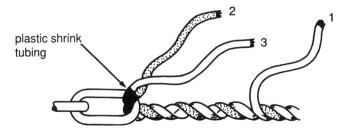

(A) Lay back 1 strand (#1) for 12 turns and the other 2 strands for 6 turns. Insert the paired strands (#2 and #3) in the end link of the chain as far as they have been unlaid.

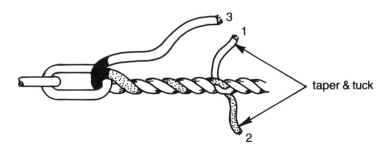

(B) Lay strand #2 in place of strand #1. Strands #1 and #2 are then knotted together with an overhand knot as in the long splice. The ends are then tapered by cutting away one-half the fibers and then tucking each across the lay of the rope 2 or 3 times.

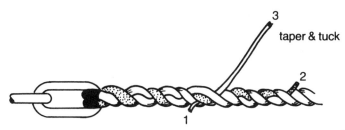

(C) Strand #3, which was left standing at the end link, is now tucked against the lay until it reaches the crossover of strands #1 and #2. It can be either cut there or tapered as the others and further tucked against the lay for neatness.

Fig. 5-17. Steps in making the rope to chain splice.

plastic shrink tubing used in electrical work onto the rope strands where they pass through the end link to serve as rust buffers.

The common, open, teardrop-shaped thimble (Fig. 5-16) is a poor design to consider for your storm anchor rode. Under heavy load the rope eye will stretch and the thimble will tip allowing the sharp ends of it

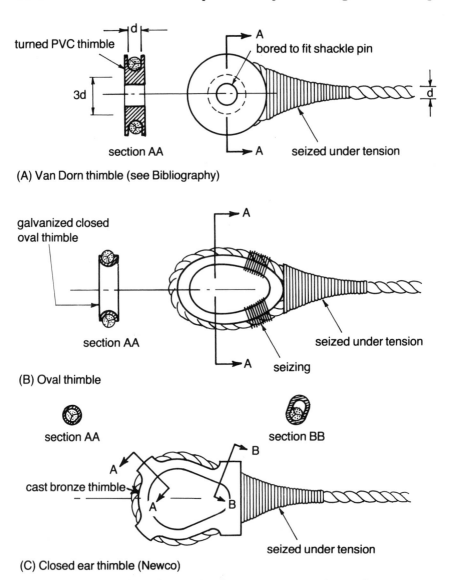

Fig. 5-18. Preferred thimbles for rope storm anchor rodes.

to contact and, possibly, sever the rode. Figure 5-18 shows three thimbles all superior to the common teardrop thimble for use on a storm anchor rode. The Van Dorn thimble can be made, but the others must be purchased.

The obvious shortcomings of metal thimbles are overcome in the Samson Nylite Connector shown in Fig. 5-19. This connector uses a spool

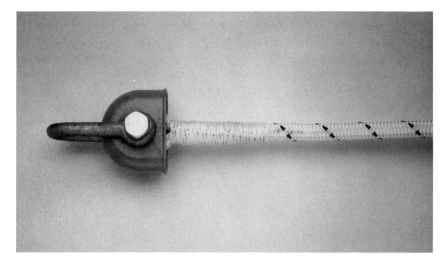

Fig. 5-19. The Samson Nylite Connector is a 3-part assembly—a spool, a shield, and a special shackle. It can be used with either braided or twisted synthetic rope. This is a major advance in the technology of ground tackle. Courtesy: Samson Ocean Systems, Inc.

made of a high strength composite nylon with a flexible shield of tough urethane, and a special high strength shackle to transfer the rope load to the chain lead.

The connector spool is pushed into a small premade eye in the rope. The shield is pressed over the spool by hand and the special shackle is inserted into the bore of the spool and safetied in place. The urethane shield prevents the rope eye from coming out of the spool's groove and also protects the rope from abrasion. The lubricant in the spool allows it to move freely under high loads.

The Samson Nylite Connector has been approved for use by the U. S. Coast Guard and the U. S. Navy for use on towing hawsers.*

Rarely should a rope be bent directly to the anchor without the use of a chain lead. However, there are times when it is expedient to do so as in using a grapnel which does not depend on weight to do its job. Also, there may be times when you put out a kedge anchor from a dinghy and would rather not wrestle with chain for a temporary situation. In such cases it is perfectly proper to bend the rope rode directly to the anchor ring, but it should not be done haphazardly.

---

*G. P. Foster, "No Longer the Weakest Link," *Sea Technology*, September 1985.

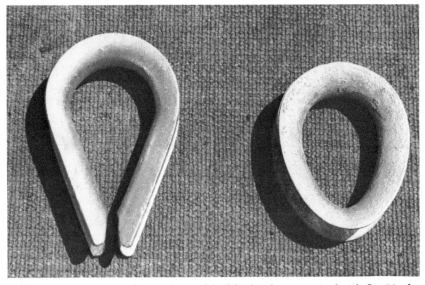

A common teardrop rope thimble is shown on the left. Under extreme load, as in storm anchoring, it tends to tip in the eye splice, and the pointed end digs into the rope and damages the fibers, possibly causing the rope to fail. The oval thimble to the right is a far superior thimble for use in practically all eye splices. Unfortunately, it costs more to make and cost-conscious buyers, ignoring the safety aspect, settle for the cheaper, but less safe, teardrop thimble.

Bending the rope rode directly to the anchor ring can be done with common knots which are quick to tie, do not slip, provide some resistance to chafe, and can be untied when the exercise is over. The anchor bowline and the fisherman's bend (sometimes called the anchor bend) are two of these (Fig. 5-20). Note that they both use an extra turn around the anchor ring which minimizes the motion of the rope against the ring thereby helping to prevent chafe. Note also that the fisherman's bend has the first half-hitch of the bitter end passed inside the round turn to prevent loosening of the knot.

From a strength standpoint an eye splice is always preferred to a knot as can be seen from a comparison of their efficiencies:

Bowline	60 percent of rope strength
Anchor bend over a ⅝-inch diameter ring	75 percent of rope strength
Eye splice with thimble	90-95 percent of rope strength

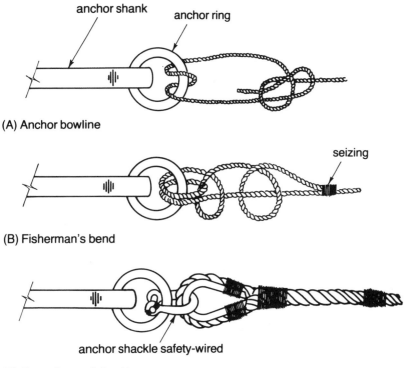

anchor shank

anchor ring

(A) Anchor bowline

seizing

(B) Fisherman's bend

anchor shackle safety-wired

(C) Eye splice and shackle

Fig. 5-20. Bending the all-rope rode to the anchor.

The last connection to be made with a rope rode is to secure the bitter end to the structure of the boat. This can be done down in the chain locker (Fig. 5-21). Make the knot accessible, though, so that in time of need it can be untied rather than having to sever the rope rode above deck. The bitter end attachment should never be depended on to carry the ground tackle loads on the boat. It is there only for the purpose of preventing loss of ground tackle should Murphy's Law prevail.

A rope anchor rode like the chain rode must be marked to tell when an adequate length has been deployed to yield the proper scope. These markings are readily available at chandleries as colorfast yellow vinyl strips marked for 30, 50, 70, 90, 110, 120, and 150 feet. The strips are easily woven between the strands of the rope and their locations must include the length of the chain lead used (Fig. 5-22).

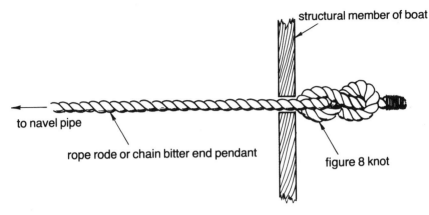

Note:
- This can also be used to secure the end of a long pendant on a chain rode to allow the bitter end of the chain to come above deck for severing.
- Keep a serrated-edge knife handy for severing a bitter end attachment. A serrated blade is far better than even a razor-sharp, smooth blade.

Fig. 5-21. Securing the bitter end of a rope rode.

Fig. 5-22. Excellent depth markers for rope rodes are made of yellow vinyl strips with a waterfast printing. These are inserted between the strands of the rope and will last for years.

CHAFING PROTECTION

A rope anchor rode must be given adequate chafing protection if you are to get real security while at anchor. At the anchor end of the rode, a proper chain lead will absorb the abrasion of the sea bed. But at the other end of the rode you must look for wear on the rode where it passes over the bow roller and also where it may contact the cheeks of the bow roller trough.

If wear over the bow roller (or chock, if used) seems to be a persistent problem, then consider the use of a chain riding stopper as illustrated in Fig. 5-23. This stopper allows a length of chain to take all of the wear of the bow roller (or chock) and is completely adjustable for any length of rode deployed. The rope pendant can be made of either nylon or polyester material. I prefer a polyester twisted 3-strand rope with a soft finish to give the best possible grip on the anchor rode. The pendant should, obviously, be of the same strength as the rode rope. Braided rope should

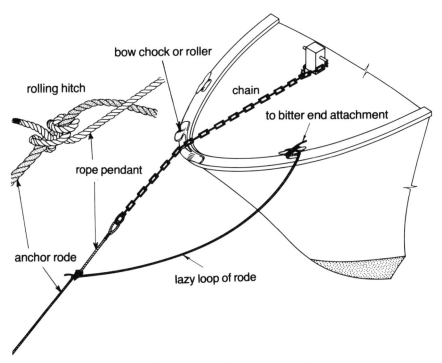

Fig. 5-23. Chain riding stopper for a nylon rode.

be avoided because it does not have the gripping quality of twisted rope. By carefully working the rolling hitch tightly into place on the anchor rode, a secure grip can be assured.

Wear on an anchor rode due to contact with items of deck gear can be minimized by taking a fresh nip on the rope rode every day or two to distribute the wear on the outer whiskerlike fibers of the rope. Once these wear away, the inner rope fibers become exposed to wear, and there is subsequent loss of strength in the rope.

Leather sewn in place on the line itself is the best possible chafing protection. Barring that, canvas or leather sheet can be wrapped around the critical area and tied in place. Possibly the best "portable" chafing protection is a length of corded hose with holes punched in the ends so that it can be securely tied in place. The rope must not slide inside the hose or it will again wear itself, which you want to avoid.

Chafing protection is a must, especially on the anchor rode to which you trust the security of your boat. You must do whatever is necessary to preserve that line. A weakened rode can part at loads much lower than your anchor system was designed for and that would certainly spoil your whole day.

CARE OF THE ROPE RODE

While synthetic fibers have made ropes almost indestructible by chemical and biological action, it is still up to the boatowner to prevent mechanical damage to the rope. At least once a year the rope rode should be stretched out on land and examined foot by foot for damage. Take the following steps to assure the longevity of your rope anchor rode:

> Wash sand, grit, and salt out of your nylon rode with a low pressure water hose or slosh it in fresh water in a loose coil.
>
> Turn a nylon rode end for end every year to equalize wear.
>
> Inspect the nylon rope for chafing or hockles. If they are present, either replace the whole rope or cut out the affected section and short splice the line back together. Do not use it for a storm rode after splicing.
>
> Examine the nylon rope internally for broken or frayed fibers or fibers that appear to be fused together due to excessive heat caused by high loadings.
>
> Check the thimbled eye splices in the rope for looseness or rusting of thimbles.

Replace your nylon rope with new rope and use the old rope for making dock lines if it shows signs of undue wear or aging.

Clean each shackle or swivel in the rode. Safety the shackle screw pin with new wire.

Examine the bitter end attachment to assure its integrity. Be certain to reattach it when you are through with the inspection.

Examine the rode length markers for legibility. Replace if necessary.

Inspect the chain lead as previously described for the all-chain rode.

CHAPTER SIX

Anchor Options

An anchor can be described as a metal forging, casting, or weldment consisting of one or more flukes to grasp the seabed; a stock to properly position the flukes for digging in; and a shank connecting the flukes and stock assembly to the ring which is attached to the anchor rode.

An anchor is not simply a weight, it is a carefully formed metal claw or scoop that grips the bottom. Mooring sinkers, often erroneously called anchors, will drag across the surface of the seabed but a properly set anchor can hold to the breaking strength of the weakest part of the ground tackle system.

Arguments for and against certain anchor designs arise principally from the compatibility of the anchor used with the seabed in which it is placed. You must remember that an anchor is a blind fastening to an undefined seabed. If you are lucky, the anchor sets with ease. Otherwise, you try a different location or a different anchor until you find a combination on which you are willing to stake the safety of your boat.

It is convenient, if not rigorous, to classify anchor designs as being either burying or hooking types. The lack of rigor comes from the nature of the seabed itself. If the seabed is soft mud, all anchors will bury themselves. If the seabed consists of numerous coral heads, all anchors will hook themselves. Nevertheless, each anchor has a primary holding mode which can be described as burying or hooking.

Although the variety of anchors is great, the terminology is essentially the same. The flukes provide the gripping power, the stock provides roll stability, the shank carries the fluke loads, and the ring connects the anchor to the anchor rode. Interestingly, the old-fashioned anchor displays most of the components of both early and modern-day anchors (Fig. 6-1). The only component of some modern anchors that is missing is a pivot or hinge between flukes and shank.

BURYING ANCHORS

Burying anchors have broad flukes angled in such a manner that they are drawn into the seabed as a horizontal load is applied by the

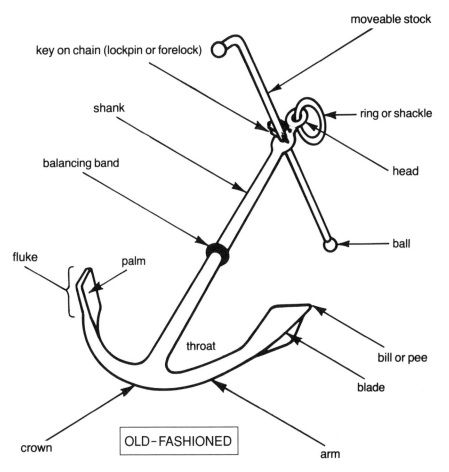

Fig. 6-1. Anchor nomenclature.

anchor rode. If the seabed is not extremely hard, they will bury themselves in a short distance along with some part of the anchor rode. Burying anchors depend mostly on driving their pointed flukes into the seabed to get penetration while it is the area of those flukes that eventually provides the holding power. Weight by itself is less important in modern anchor design, although that is not true of the Navy stockless anchor which is an old design.

Burying anchors are popular because most of the continental shelf seabeds are composed of sediment covering underlying rock and that is where our anchoring is primarily done. (A discourse on seabeds and anchor compatibility is presented in Chapter 7.)

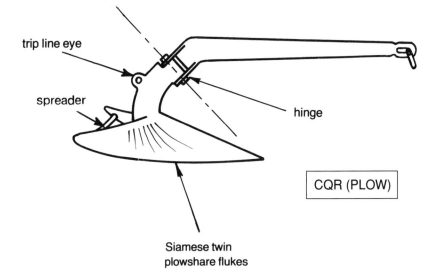

CQR (PLOW)

Siamese twin
plowshare flukes

The CQR (Plow) Anchor

The CQR is a stockless anchor whose Siamese twin flukes are shaped like a pair of plowshares back to back. The anchor lies on its side when lowered to the bottom and tips upright when a horizontal pull is applied to it and the bill digs into the seabed. Although no unique fluke angle can be attributed to this design, it works equally well in sand and stiff mud with some capability in weeds because of a fair-sized throat.

The particular merit of the CQR anchor is that it is virtually nonfouling and will adjust its set as tide or wind shifts the boat's position. The shank of the anchor is hinged allowing 75° of sideways motion (each side). As the shank swings, it also lowers itself because of the angular displacement of the pivot pin tending to keep the flukes dug in during rotation. If the boat swings more than 75°, the sideways leverage of the shank causes the flukes to rotate while still imbedded until the anchor aligns itself with the new direction of pull.

The CQR anchor is made of three steel drop forgings—the shank, the horn including shoe and pivot pin, and the wings forming the flukes. The wings are welded to the horn with a spreader tube welded between the wings. The entire anchor is hot-dip galvanized.

Although the origin of this design dates back to 1933, it is very popular today with cruising and fishing boats because of its efficiency.

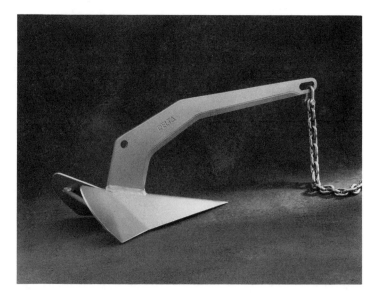

The Delta anchor is a variation of the CQR concept by the same manufacturer. The principle visual difference is that it does not have the hinged shank of the CQR. There are other more subtle differences such as an improved fluke shape, a shank allowing the anchor to deploy automatically from the bow roller, and a very low center of gravity. The shank is made of manganese steel welded to the "delta blades" and the entire anchor is hot-galvanized. It can be expected to gain a significant share of the market represented by the CQR and Bruce anchors. Courtesy: Simpson Lawrence Ltd.

The Bruce Anchor

The Bruce anchor is a one-piece heat-treated steel casting, hot-dip galvanized for corrosion protection. It is U-shaped, and the upper leg is the shank and the lower leg is a single large fluke made in the shape of a three-palmed scoop. When deployed, it lies first on its side with one outer palm in contact with the seabed. As a horizontal pull is exerted on it, that one palm digs into the seabed causing the anchor to swing upright so that the center palm and, finally, the other outer palm digs into the seabed.

The holding power comes from the large size of the fluke and, once set, it is claimed that the scope can be reduced to as little as 2 to 1 while still retaining 50 percent of the holding power. The breakout force of the Bruce anchor is low because the fluke is placed far down the shank which gives the shank good leverage to tilt the anchor up when the pull is in a vertical direction. It is especially efficient in small sizes.

A further claim for this anchor is a full 360° veering capability. With a nonfouling design, its simplicity of construction is a real merit. Furthermore, since it has no moving parts, it is easier to handle (but not stow) on deck.

The Bruce anchor was introduced to the boating scene in the late 1970s, and it caught on rapidly. It is a refinement of the immense Bruce anchors that have moored North Sea oil rigs for many years.

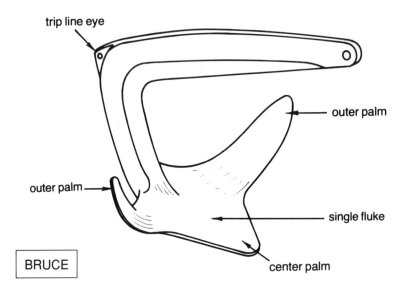

The Stock-Stabilized, Pivoted-Fluke Anchor (SSPF)

This anchor has the same pivoting fluke arrangement and hawsepipe stowability as the Navy stockless anchor, but there the similarity ends. Its unique features are: (a) large-area, pivoted flukes positioned close to the shank; (b) an inward-sloping crown plate (tripping palm) that lifts the rear of the flukes to force the bills into the seabed; (c) a stock that positions the flukes horizontally for symmetrical penetration of the seabed; and (d) lightweight, strong flukes with sharpened edges to aid in penetration.

Originally developed in 1939 by R.S. Danforth, it became known as the Danforth LWT (lightweight) anchor, and saw extensive service on World War II landing barges. The U.S. Navy Mark II LWT anchor is another one of its versions.

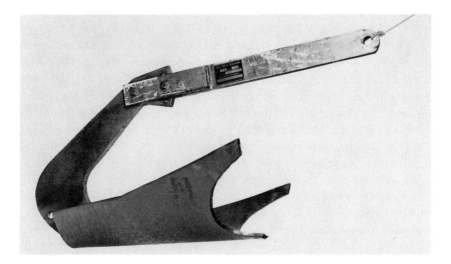

The MAX is a new spade anchor design whose ungainly appearance belies its capability. This anchor has tested well in soft mud seabeds. Although basically a burying anchor, the trio of sharp bills at the leading edge of the spade-shaped fluke assures penetration in hard bottoms and also gripping of coral or rocks. It has an adjustable shank angle to enhance holding power in seabeds ranging from sand to soft mud. Materials of construction are high tensile steel coated with hot-dip galvanizing. Courtesy: Creative Marine.

Danforth anchors are composed of four basic parts—a pair of flukes, a stock, a crown assembly, and a shank. The parts are made of steel and hot-dip galvanized. The Danforth Hi-Tensile model has flukes made of heat-treated, forged steel while the Danforth Standard LWT model has rolled sheet steel flukes. The Standard LWT is neither as efficient nor as strong as the Hi-Tensile model. Both anchors, whose names are registered trademarks, are intended for recreational use and are manufactured by a private company established by Danforth.

The Danforth LWT anchor has its flukes set at an optimum angle for sand (32°) making its holding power excellent in sand and other hard bottoms it can penetrate.

Fouling a Danforth LWT anchor is possible when it is only partially buried in sand. Fouling by other means is also possible should the flukes engage any seaweed or trap a rock (or even a beer can) between them. Then the chances are that the anchor will not set.

The new Danforth Deepset anchor (Fig. 6-2) is said to have 50 percent more holding power than a conventional Danforth anchor. The reason for this is said to be the thin shank which minimizes the vertical drag of the shank as the flukes pull downward in setting the anchor. The very flexible spring steel shank can bend sideways up to 80° if the boat shears to one side. In bending, the shank pulls the anchor around in its set thereby reducing the tendency of the anchor to roll out of its set.

Danforth has also replaced the angled tripping palm of the original design with a drag claw much like the Navy Mk II versions of the anchor. This claw also contributes to the drag of the anchor.

Since expiration of certain of the Danforth patents in the 1970s, other interesting versions of the stock-stabilized, pivoting-fluke anchor have appeared on the market. One of the most interesting is the Fortress aluminum anchor. It is made of a hardened high tensile strength marine grade aluminum-magnesium alloy anodized for corrosion resistance. Because the Fortress is made of aluminum, you would not expect it to be as abrasion or corrosion resistant as a steel anchor. For short-term anchoring, though, the material aspects should pose no problem. The anchor weighs only about 40 percent of a similar size Danforth Steel Anchor.

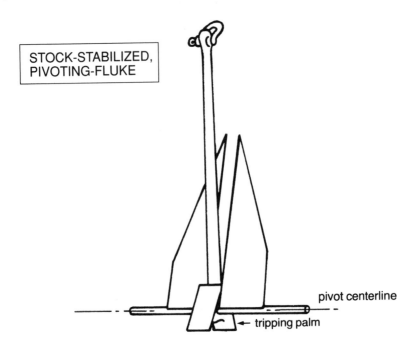

STOCK-STABILIZED,
PIVOTING-FLUKE

pivot centerline

← tripping palm

Many lightweight anchors patterned after the Danforth stock-stabilized, pivoting fluke design were used by the U. S. Navy. This 30-pound forged steel version is a treasured find at a surplus equipment store. Note that there is no tripping palm on the crown as used in today's small boat anchors. Instead there is a scoop which digs into the seabed and pivots the flukes so that they can penetrate the bottom.

The Fortress is manufactured in five basic elements which the owner assembles for use and can disassemble for compact stowage. The disassembly feature makes it of particular interest for light displacement monohull and multihull boats whose owners like to take their anchors apart and stow them near the centers of the vessels. Another of its unique features is the ability to choose different fluke angles for sand and mud bottoms. The anchor was introduced to the market in the late 1980s with considerable fanfare and has

Fig. 6-2. The Danforth Deepset anchor is a revolutionary design using a spring steel shank to improve both the holding power and the capability of the anchor to rotate in its set as the boat swings. Courtesy: Danforth/Hooker Division, Rule Group.

lived up to its performance predictions. It is truly the new kid on the block and only time will tell whether it can develop a reputation as a hook on which you are willing to stake the safety of your boat.

The Wishbone Anchor

The Wishbone anchor is neither a traditional looking anchor nor does it have an extensive history of use to make it well known. Yet, it does have merit for use on small boats of all categories. The single broad fluke is rotated into position by the kicker plate. The fluke angle is set at a compromise of 40°, making it equally useful in sand and mud but not optimum for either. The pointed fluke can also hook onto rock or coral much like an old-fashioned anchor, and it is virtually foolproof. When lowered into the water from a moving vessel, the Wishbone will not plane (kite) in the manner of the lightweight stock-stabilized pivoting-fluke anchors. Today's Wishbone anchor is an advanced version of the old Piper anchor invented in 1822. They are now out of production.

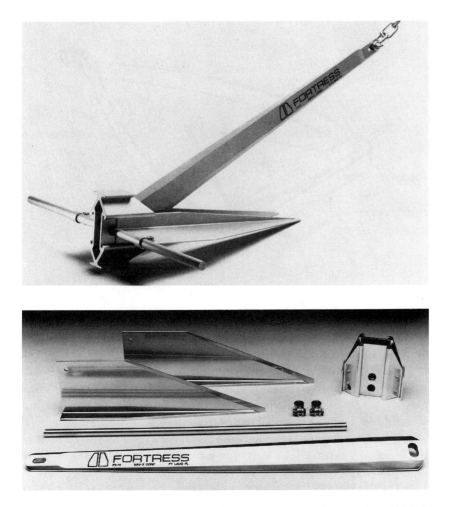

The Fortress aluminum anchor, a derivative of the stock-stabilized, pivoting-fluke design by Danforth, is an excellent candidate for stowage below deck on light-displacement racing sailboats. The lighter weight of this anchor makes it easier to handle although the chain lead must be equally as heavy as that for a steel anchor of the same dimensions to assure penetration and prevent "planing or kiting" of the anchor. Courtesy: NAV-X Corp.

The Navy Stockless Anchor

The popularity of this anchor is due to the absence of a well-defined stock which allows the anchor shank to be readily drawn up into the vessel's

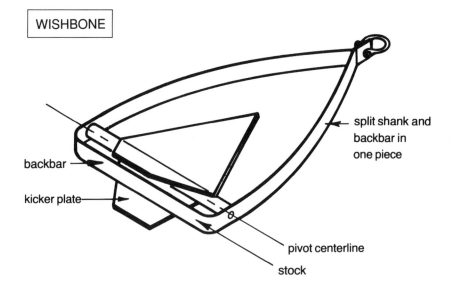

WISHBONE

split shank and backbar in one piece

backbar

kicker plate

pivot centerline

stock

hawsepipe by its own chain rode. When the anchor is stowed, the flukes nestle snugly against the hull plates.

The twin flukes and crown of the Navy stockless anchor are cast in steel as a single unit (head) and are pivoted at the base of the anchor shank. Weight is the key to making this anchor dig in as the flukes are quite blunt. The rolling tendency of the stockless anchor is dampened by widely spaced flukes. These anchors still have a tendency to roll out of a set, especially in mud. The only cure is to weld stock-extending stabilizers to the fluke base.

The Navy stockless anchor has less holding power than an old-fashioned anchor of the same weight and much less than today's lightweight anchors. Generally, though, this higher mass, lower efficiency anchor is less sensitive to seabed conditions. The flukes are set at an angle of 45° favoring mud seabeds. At best its holding power is seven times its weight in penetrable sand and three times its weight in good mud. This is an especially difficult anchor to set in a hard sand seabed because of its blunt flukes.

The Navy stockless anchor design goes back to 1821 and the Hawkins patent anchor which was the first real improvement in anchor design since 600 B.C. The stockless anchor is used today only on large boats, but it is universal on ships where ease of handling and stowing by mechanical means is more important than anchor weight.

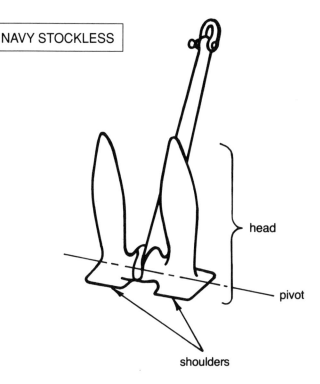

NAVY STOCKLESS

head

pivot

shoulders

The Mushroom Anchor

The mushroom anchor is excellent for permanent moorings and is commonly used for mooring lightships, channel buoys, and navigational aids. Weather buoys are anchored in depths of 1,000 fathoms or more using mushroom anchors supplemented by huge concrete sinkers or kellets. The anchor is rarely found on board large boats although it is commonly seen on small fishing skiffs operating in protected waters over muddy seabeds.

Mushroom anchors are made of iron or steel castings with a long shank welded into the crown. The small mushroom anchors used by fishermen are generally a single casting with a short shank. Mushroom anchors are virtually foulproof.

The holding power of a mushroom anchor that is not well set is, at best, approximately twice its weight. As the anchor is allowed to oscillate in place, it buries itself deeper into the seabed gaining increased holding power with time. When well "silted in," its holding power can be as much as ten times its weight. This depends to a large extent on the nature of the

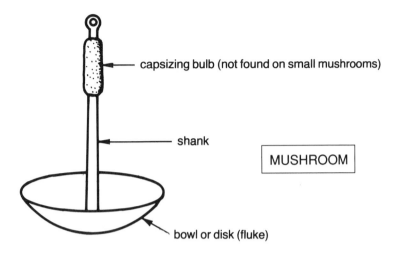

capsizing bulb (not found on small mushrooms)

shank

MUSHROOM

bowl or disk (fluke)

seabed. A mushroom's best performance is usually found in seabeds with a soil soft enough for the anchor to bury itself and yet cohesive enough to have good shear strength.

Mushroom anchors for moorings should be set early in the season to assure that they will be well silted in by the time the hurricane season arrives.

The Dor Mor pyramid anchor is a recent development of the familiar mushroom anchor for mooring use. Its pyramid shape assists the anchor in setting itself rapidly by presenting a cutting edge to penetrate the bottom when a force is exerted in a circle about it. The short shank allows mooring in shallow water without chain wrap-up and potential hull damage.

HOOKING ANCHORS

Hooking anchors are designed primarily to hook into the seabed; consequently, they have smaller flukes than burying anchors, and they are often heavier to assure penetration and larger in order to have some fluke area for softer seabeds. A hooking anchor is intended for use in rocky bottoms or seabeds covered with weeds where long arms can penetrate through the weeds.

The Old-Fashioned Anchor (also known as the Fisherman, Yachtsman,
Admiralty Pattern, Kedge (erroneously), and Herreshoff)

Probably nothing symbolizes seafaring more than the old-fashioned anchor which has been around for over two thousand years looking in general much like it looks today. But the old-fashioned anchor has two basic faults—its lazy arm pointing upward easily fouls a slack anchor rode and the small flukes have little holding power in soft seabeds.

These anchors are usually made of steel forgings and are hot-dip galvanized for corrosion protection. It is also possible to get one made of bronze at a premium price. To improve stowability, the anchor can have a movable stock. Another scheme is to make the anchor in three parts— stock, shank, and arm/fluke assembly—allowing all three parts to be laid side by side for stowage in the bilge.

The old-fashioned anchor with a fluke angle of about 45° works best in difficult bottoms like rock, shingle, shelf coral, and heavy weed. With a

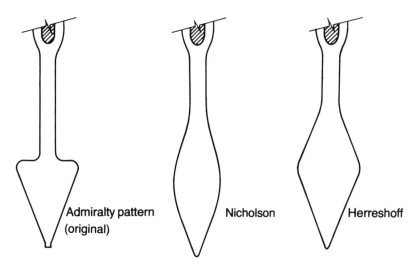

Fig. 6-3. Fluke-shape modifications minimize fouling and provide a better bite in the seabed.

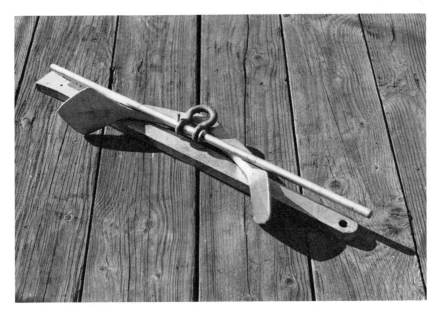

The old-fashioned anchor has been damned by the boat owner because it is so difficult to stow, but its versatility has never been challenged. To counter the anchor's clumsy stowage problem, Paul Luke has designed a take-apart version that can be stowed under a cabin sole. It uses the larger Herreshoff flukes to give better holding in muds and clay.

sharp bill and enough weight, it can penetrate sand and will give a good account of itself even though it is not fully buried. In soft sand or mud it is helpless.

The Northill Anchor

The true Northill anchor is probably the most sophisticated of all anchors. Its late 1930s design was aimed at lightness, stowability, and corrosion resistance for use on seaplanes. The arms of the Northill are set at right angles to both shank and stock, and the flukes are set at an angle carefully determined to give a quick and positive bite in the seabed. The sharp bill enables the anchor to dig quickly into the bottom. The broad fluke provides good gripping power once it is set. Fabrication of the true Northill uses stainless steel sheet rolled to various shapes and then welded together. Both the arm and stock halves are hinged on stainless steel bolts.

A new version of the Northill anchor which appeared in the late 1980s is being built under the name Pekny. The light weight, good holding power,

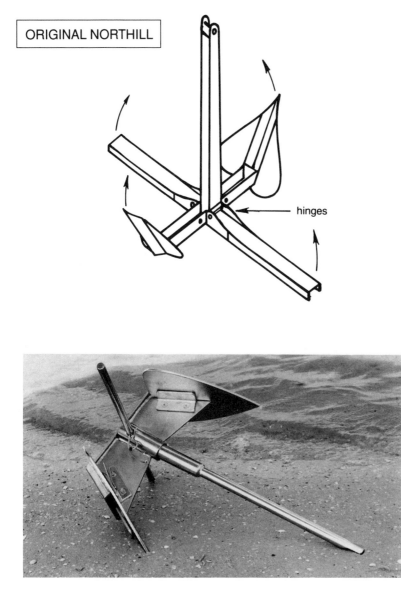

ORIGINAL NORTHILL

hinges

    The Pekny anchor retains the basic design of the original Northill
anchor which made it so effective, namely, the stock in crown, broad flukes,
and stainless steel construction. It replaced the folding feature with a
take-apart capability requiring no tools to improve stowability. Optional fluke
designs include rock picks and muck flaps for very soft seabeds. Courtesy:
Pekny Industries.

and disassembly characteristics of the Pekny anchor make it a prime candidate for use as a working anchor on multihull and ultralight displacement boats.

The Danforth Utility anchor made of hot-dip galvanized cast steel is a variation on the basic Northill design and is considerably more rugged and heavier. Only the stock folds, not the arms. Northill invented his anchor while in the employ of Northrop Corporation. I suspect that the original stainless steel Northill anchors were made by many manufacturers during World War II. They went out of production in the late 1940s and the patents expired. Danforth's Utility version appeared in the 1960s. The Northill anchor suffers from the potential problem of having the slack rode foul the lazy arm sticking up from the seabed. These anchors are, therefore, not good swinging anchors and your boat should not be left unattended on them.

The Hans C-Anchor is a revolutionary concept in ground anchors combining many of the features of the plow, SSPF, and Northill anchor designs. The arrow-shaped flukes and crown make up a diamond-shaped body attached to the stock. The fluke angle is adjustable according to seabed composition. It is manufactured of hot-galvanized steel. Courtesy: Hans C-Anchor, Inc.

The Coral Pick Anchor

This anchor has proven itself valuable in deep-water anchoring over seabeds of coral and rock. The long shank with hooked end is simply a steel rod, sometimes a length of rebar. A hook is bent into the bar forming

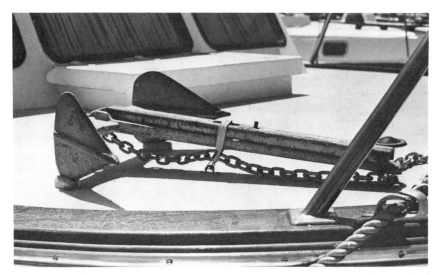

One model of the Danforth Utility (Northill) anchor used a sliding stock to simplify stowage. This is a very versatile anchor but difficult to handle aboard the vessel. Like the old-fashioned anchor, it also has the potential of fouling the anchor rode should the boat swing in circles about the anchor.

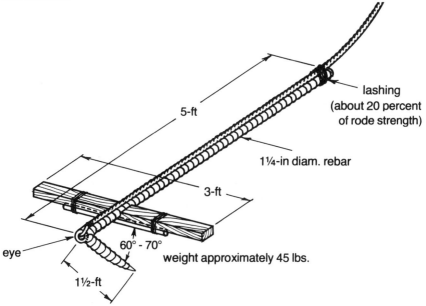

Fig. 6-4. Coral pick design. (Note: the dimensions shown make an anchor suitable for about a 40-foot boat.)

an arm and it, in turn, is flattened to form a fluke. A short length of steel rod is welded across the shank as a partial stock. The rest of the stock is a buoyant piece of wood lashed tightly to the steel crossbar.

Because this is a hooking anchor and likely to get its fluke wedged into a coral or rock crevice, it is essential to scow the rode as shown. The crown attachment of the chain rode suggests that this is not an anchor to use where the boat will do a lot of swinging, nor is it an anchor on which to leave your boat unattended. (See Chapter 9 for retrieval method.)

The Grapnel

The grapnel is really not an anchor but a multiple hook device to be used for recovering lost articles on the sea bottom. It is made with four, five, or six clawlike arms secured to a common shank having an eye at the head. When used for grappling, it is dragged along the bottom until it snags the missing objects and is hoisted aboard.

As an anchor the grapnel has limited use. It is worthless in sand or mud but great in rock or coral. It is also sometimes useful in weedy bottoms if the weeds are not deeper than the length of the arms. Whenever used for anchoring, the grapnel should be fitted with a trip line.

If you are gunkholing the shallow waters of the Intracoastal Waterway or navigating bayou and tule areas, you will find the grapnel very useful for anchoring along the shoreline where mangroves and brush abound. Simply throw the grapnel into the brush and snub up tight for the evening.

GRAPNEL

ANCHOR ROLL STABILITY

In order for an anchor to have good holding power, it must also have good roll stability—the two are inseparable. An anchor in setting must first orient one or more flukes downward to penetrate the seabed.

The Babbit stockless anchor depends on widely spaced flukes for stability and saves on weight by having a narrow crown.

Then it must have sufficient roll stability so that the fluke(s) continues to dig in even though the seabed is a heterogeneous mix of soil and rock.

Anchors get their roll stability by different means. The CQR and Bruce anchors are unique in that their fluke design gives them an inherent stability. These anchors are probably the most roll stable of all, and they will engage the seabed even when they are deployed on their sides—which is most of the time.

Stock-stabilized anchors get their roll stability from a stock which is placed at 90° to the shank. The old-fashioned, Northill, Danforth, and Wishbone anchors are typical of this concept. In action, the stock leans against the seabed positioning the fluke(s) so that it will penetrate into the seabed. The longer the stock, the better the roll stability. Very long stocks, however, can become an anchor-handling and fouling problem.

Roll stability of stocked anchors is enhanced if the center of the fluke(s) is close to the shank. The old-fashioned, Northill, and Wishbone anchors are ideal in this respect because their single penetrating fluke is right on the shank centerline. The Danforth design, on the other hand, requires a gap between flukes to clear the central shank, and therefore has less stability.

Stockless anchors, in general, have poor roll stability as well as poor holding power. When setting, if the flukes experience any dissymmetry in penetration of the seabed, the anchor will tend to roll out of its set because there is no stock to react against the roll. When this happens in a mud or clay seabed, the elevated fluke usually comes out with a "clod" affixed to it. If that happens, the fluke may not be able to reimbed itself, and the anchor must be weighed for cleaning before trying a reset.

There have been many attempts made to improve the roll stability of stockless anchors through fluke design and wider spacing. The Forfjord, Babbit, FOB, and Sea Claw patent anchors are typical of these attempts to improve on the Navy stockless design. Although some improvement may be noted, even the best of these patent designs must still be said to have poor roll stability, and any anchor with poor roll stability is going to give erratic holding performance.

TESTING FOR HOLDING POWER

The anchor has but one function in life and that is to get a grip on the seabed and hold on in spite of wind and wave forces on the boat. While the function is simple to identify, it is a complex job for the anchor to accomplish. The anchor must first be able to penetrate the seabed as well as any weed covering that might be there. It must be able to progressively bury itself deeper and provide increased holding power as wind and wave increase the load on the boat. It must be able to take up new positions as the boat swings and pulls on it in different directions. It must be strong enough to resist the breakout forces applied by the rode without structural failure. And, finally, it must easily break out from its set when it is time to weigh anchor.

Supplementing the anchor's primary function of holding onto the seabed, there are a number of other subjective requirements needed to make it acceptable as a practical piece of boat gear. The crew's ability to handle the anchor is all-important and that involves both its weight and shape. In the past, anchors have been notoriously heavy and ill-shaped for stowage. Recent developments in anchor design, construction materials, and manufacturing methods have yielded concepts which are both light and more easily stowed. The ugly duckling of boat gear is beginning to assume a position of respectability in the boating scene.

Testing anchors for holding power is difficult to implement with any degree of consistency. Seabeds, having the desired characteristics of soil composition, compacting, evenness, weed growth, and small stone or rock distributions (collectively, these are known as the "competency" of the seabed) are not in great abundance nor can two seabeds ever be found that are alike in all features. Consequently, there are wide variations in test results. The most consistent results come from anchor comparison testing wherein a series of anchor designs are tested at one location using the same testing procedures. But, since anchor performance is so dependent on seabed features, the same set of anchors may yield different results when tested at a different time in a different location.

The testing summarized here is believed to be consistent and unbiased for the selection of seabeds used. The results are useful for choosing which anchor(s) will perform best for the conditions where the reader does his or her boating.

Holding Power in Sand

As part of its development program of the aluminum Fortress anchor, the NAV-X Corporation sponsored and/or participated in a number of anchor holding power tests. Most notable were the tests in sand bottoms conducted at Biscayne Bay, Florida, and those in mud bottoms conducted at San Francisco Bay, California. Although NAV-X had a vested interest in the outcome of the tests, they were objectively performed in the presence of representatives of other manufacturers and representatives of a number of American and European boating magazines. Anchors used were purchased "off-the-shelf" at local marine stores and all were subjected to the same test procedure and conditions.

The seabed for the sandy bottom tests was described as "firmly compacted fine-grained coral sand."* The test vessel was the 70-foot twin screw (2 × 450 HP) diesel tug *Hercules*. The anchor rode consisted of 95 feet of 1¼-inch three-strand nylon rope coupled to a 6-foot length of ½-inch High Test (Grade 40) chain. A water depth of 15 feet plus a 5 foot stern freeboard on the tug yielded a 5:1 scope for all of the tests. Loads were measured by Dillon analog dynometers having calibration certificates from the U.S. Bureau of Standards.

Anchors were selected in a revolving order. Each in turn was attached to the combination rode and put over the transom. Set was established with the tug coasting forward as the full rode became deployed. After set was assured, the tug moved forward under power and increased the pull until the anchor reached (1) a predetermined test limit based on a factor of 2.5 times the manufacturer's listed holding power or, (2) until it failed or, (3) until shore bearings indicated the anchor was dragging or upset. The tests measured only straight-line pull.

In this series, ten anchors were tested in 56 separate tests. From four to seven pulls were made for each of the ten anchors. The results are shown in

---

* "Comparative Performance Tests of Popular Recreational Marine Anchors. Part I" (Miami, FL: NAV-X Corporation report, February 1990).

Fig. 6-5(a). The confidence of the Fortress anchor manufacturer in its aluminum anchors was justified as the results show them to have the highest holding power in sand of the group tested.

It should be noted, though, that the 11-pound chain lead used helped all the anchors to set themselves. This was of particular importance to the very lightweight Fortress anchors. Subsequent tests conducted by Underwater Capabilities, Inc.[*] found that the aluminum anchor would not always set depending on the position of the flukes. When the flukes were pointed upward, it would literally "fly" instead of digging into the seabed. This phenomenon has been previously noted with other lightweight anchors if boat speed is excessive when deploying the anchor (see Chapter 9—Technique of Anchoring).

The diesel tug *Hercules* under strain on a test anchor in a sand seabed during Fortress-sponsored holding power tests. The seawall in the background served as a reference to determine anchor movement in the seabed. Note the crew and observers standing clear of the towing bitt and nylon rode for obvious safety reasons. Courtesy: NAV-X Corporation.

---

[*]Letter report, Underwater Capabilities, Inc., to Creative Marine, Inc., dated August 1991.

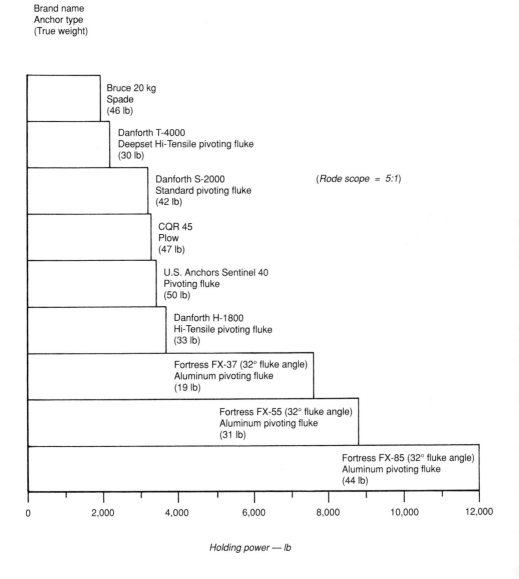

Fig. 6-5(a). Anchor holding power test results in sand seabed

Holding Power in Mud

A second series of anchor holding power tests were conducted in San Francisco Bay, California, by the NAV-X Corporation with additional sponsorship by West Marine Products of Watsonville, California. The tests were conducted off the Hunter's Point area where the bottom was described as "soft gray-brown mud without an apparent binder content, such as clay."* The test vessel was the 60-foot twin screw (1400 SHP) commercial push tug *Pacific Rose*. The anchor rode was 120 feet long, made up of a six-foot length of ⅜-inch High Test chain, 100 feet of ⅞-inch 3-strand nylon, and 14 feet of 1½-inch 3-strand nylon at the tug end. At a total rode length of 120 feet, the scope varied from 4.2:1 to 6.3:1 depending on local water depth and the state of the tide which varied from seven to eight feet. Loads were measured by Dillon analog dynometers having calibration certificates from the U.S. Bureau of Standards.

Anchors were selected in a revolving order. Each in turn was attached to the combination rode and deployed slowly over the bow. Set was established with the tug slowly backing down. After set was assured, the tug backed down under increasing power until the anchor either dragged or pulled out of its set as determined by side bearings taken against eight buoys alongside the test course. The tests measured only straight-line pull.

In this series of holding power tests a primary group of eight anchors were tested in 48 separate tests. Six "pulls" were made for each of the eight anchors. The results are shown in Fig. 6-5(b). The standard nonadjustable sand anchors all had reduced holding on the order of 13 percent of that which they were able to produce in the sand seabed tests.

For comparative interest a secondary group of nine anchors was given partial tests. Among them the 40-pound spade-type "Max" anchor, which in two pulls exhibited an 800-pound holding power—higher than any of the universal anchors tested in the mud bottom.

The U.S. Navy has always had an objective interest in anchors and has conducted many tests on ship-size anchors. Although their holding power tests are not directly applicable to boat-size anchors, some of the ancillary results are rather enlightening.

One variable found in testing the holding power of anchors in a mud bottom in the early 1960s was the criticality of fluke angle—β. Holding power tests were run on a U.S. Navy Mark II anchor (a heavyweight version of the Danforth stock-stabilized, pivoting fluke lightweight anchor), but having a

---

* "Comparative Performance Tests of Popular Recreational Marine Anchors. Part II" (Miami, Florida: NAV-X Corporation report, April 1990).

variable fluke angle capability (Fig. 6-6(a)).[*] Two things are apparent from the test results: (1) the efficiency of the anchor changes rapidly with small changes in fluke angle, and (2) the optimum fluke angle varies greatly depending on the nature of the seabed.

---

[*] R.C. Towne and J.V. Stalcup. "New and Modified Anchors for Moorings" (Washington, D.C.: U.S. Navy Technical Report CEL M-044, March 1960.)

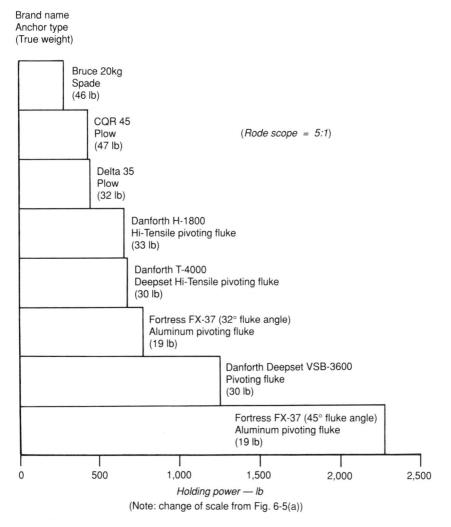

Brand name
Anchor type
(True weight)

Bruce 20kg
Spade
(46 lb)

CQR 45
Plow
(47 lb)

(Rode scope = 5:1)

Delta 35
Plow
(32 lb)

Danforth H-1800
Hi-Tensile pivoting fluke
(33 lb)

Danforth T-4000
Deepset Hi-Tensile pivoting fluke
(30 lb)

Fortress FX-37 (32° fluke angle)
Aluminum pivoting fluke
(19 lb)

Danforth Deepset VSB-3600
Pivoting fluke
(30 lb)

Fortress FX-37 (45° fluke angle)
Aluminum pivoting fluke
(19 lb)

0   500   1,000   1,500   2,000   2,500

Holding power — lb
(Note: change of scale from Fig. 6-5(a))

Fig. 6-5(b). Anchor holding power test results in mud seabed.

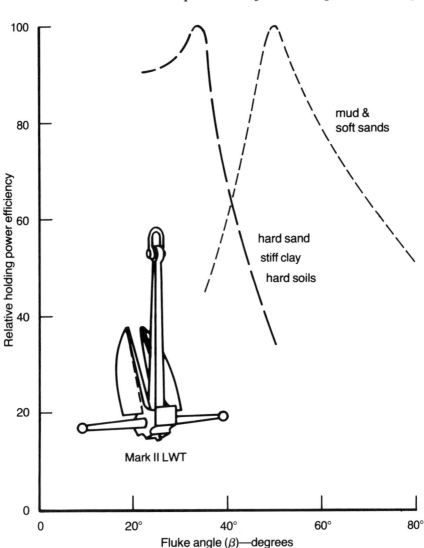

Fig. 6-6(a). Effect of fluke angle on holding power. Navy MK II anchor.

You can see that 34° appears to be near optimum fluke angle for this anchor in hard sand and 50° is near the optimum range for mud. Some ship anchors have been built with a variable (preset) fluke angle capability, but, until recently, nothing had been done with that concept for small boat anchors. Some anchors, like the Wishbone, use a compromise angle nearer 40°, while the Navy stockless anchor uses an angle of 45° based on their observations that the majority of seabeds are mud or soft sand.

NAV-X Corporation, recognizing the importance of a variable fluke angle, redesigned their Fortress series (originally having only a 32° fluke angle setting) to allow presetting of fluke angles to either 32° for sand or 45° for mud. Limited tests[*] were made in the San Francisco Bay series on Fortress anchor models FX-37, FX-85, and FX-125 with 32° and 45° fluke angle settings. These showed the higher fluke angle to give approximately three times the holding power in mud than the optimum sand setting (Fig. 6-6(b)). The 32° fluke angle which worked very well in sand did not work well at all in the mud seabed. On the other hand, the 45° fluke angle worked very well in the soft mud seabed. The adjustable fluke has given the Fortress anchor a dual capability provided that the user knows his or her seabed characteristics beforehand.

The criticality of proper fluke angle on an anchor's performance is quite amazing—just a few degrees' change in the angle can have a major effect on its holding efficiency. It is easy to see why an anchor with bent flukes is an unreliable anchor and why look-alike anchors may perform differently than their progenitors.

Another interesting result from Navy tests was the strong influence of the amount of anchor chain that was buried along with the anchor in the seabed. In an extreme case the Navy test results showed that the chain rode

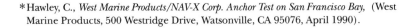

[*] Hawley, C., *West Marine Products/NAV-X Corp. Anchor Test on San Francisco Bay,* (West Marine Products, 500 Westridge Drive, Watsonville, CA 95076, April 1990).

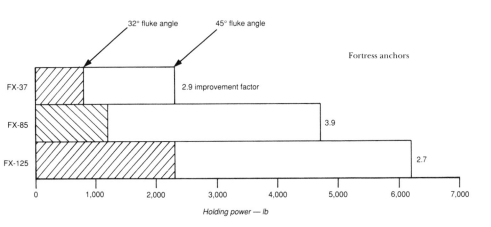

Fig. 6-6(b). Effect of fluke angle on holding power in mud.

could produce up to two-thirds of the total holding power of the anchor system in mud. One would not expect this same degree of contribution in a hard sand bottom but it does explain one source of discrepancy in anchor holding power test results (Fig. 6-7).

This Danforth standard anchor with its bent fluke is of little value to its owner. It would be very difficult to straighten the fluke to make it a reliable anchor once again. The proper action would be to give it the "deep six" and replace it with the stronger Danforth Hi-Tensile model.

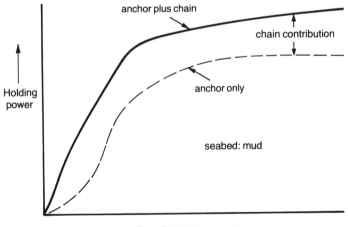

Fig. 6-7. Typical holding power test results for an anchor with a chain rode in mud. Source: Taylor, R. J., and Walker, G. R., *Model and Small-Scale Tests to Evaluate the Performance of Drag Anchors in Combination,* U. S. Navy Technical Note CEL N-1707, October 1984.

Holding Power Tests on the MAX Anchor

Creative Marine, inventor and builder of the MAX anchor, sponsored a series of tests by two organizations to compare their unusual spade anchor design with other select anchors. The tests were carried out by the American Bureau of Shipping (ABS)* and Underwriter Capabilities, Inc. (UCI).** Results are shown in Fig. 6-8.

The ABS test program included two MAX anchors—67-pound and 150-pound and a standard 200-pound Navy stockless anchor. The tests were conducted at Gulfport, Mississippi, using the 1,000 HP tugboat *Admiral* as a platform. The anchor rode in all cases consisted of 42 feet of 2½-inch chain and 150 feet of 3-inch nylon line in approximately 20 feet of water. The sand seabed test of the two MAX anchors culminated at the plotted values when the shanks bent. The shanks have since been redesigned, but no additional test data have become available.

The very low holding power of the standard Navy stockless anchor is clearly evident. At 200 pounds its holding power is equivalent to a 47-pound MAX anchor. The only thing in favor of the Navy stockless anchor is its almost indestructible design, certainly not its holding-power-to-weight efficiency.

The UCI test program included three MAX anchors, a CQR, and a Bruce. The tests were conducted at Escambia Bay, Pensacola, and the adjoining waters of the Gulf of Mexico. The test platforms were capable of bollard pulls of 1800 and 3300 pounds. The rode was a ½-inch diameter double braid nylon line bent directly to the anchor with no chain lead. A scope of 5:1 was maintained in waters of 20 to 25 foot depth. Three tests were made on each anchor in the two seabeds.

The Fortress FX-37 aluminum anchor was included in the tests but difficulties were experienced in making it set, no doubt due to the lack of a chain lead to prevent "flying." It did set in the soft sand with a holding power of 600 pounds, but it would not set in the soft mud.

Qualitative comparisons can be made between these results and those in Figs. 6-5 (a) and (b), recognizing that test conditions were not the same. The MAX anchor does, indeed, show that it has comparable capability to many of the old standby anchor designs and even the new aluminum pivoting fluke, stock-stabilized anchor. Both the MAX and the Fortress anchors have to be viewed as the "new kids on the block" and win approval of the boat owner who may at some time gamble the life of his boat on the capability of his anchor. Such a challenge is not taken lightly by most boat owners.

---

* *Report on Test of Two (2) Anchors,* Report No. 92N0348, dated 26 March 1992, by American Bureau of Shipping.

** Letter report, Underwater Capabilities, Inc. to Creative Marine, Inc., dated August 1, 1991.

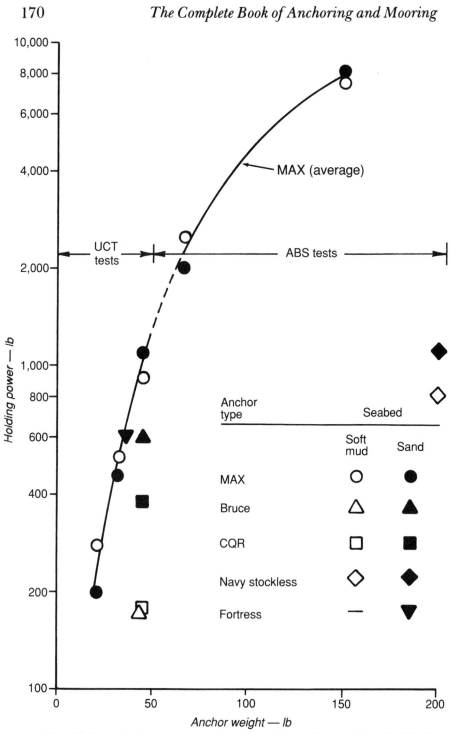

Fig. 6-8. Drag load tests on a variety of anchors. Source: Creative Marine.

French Tests of Anchor Holding Power in Sand

The French marine products company, Wichard, sponsored a series of tests to demonstrate that modern lightweight anchors have equal, if not superior, holding power when compared to heavy anchors. The tests[*] were intended to provide sufficient data by which French Government regulations could be modified to recognize the capability of lightweight anchors aboard French vessels.

The tests were conducted in the sand seabed between Ile St. Marguerite and Ile St. Honorat off Cannes, France. The test platforms were two 44-foot Island Gypsy trawlers, each with twin 275 HP diesel engines developing an approximate bollard pull of 11,000 pounds maximum each.

The rodes consisted of 180 feet of ⅝-inch nylon 3-strand rope and seven feet of ⅜-inch chain. Each anchor was pulled six times starting at the same point marked by a buoy. The boat pulled until the anchor yielded. Strain measurements were made on a Dillon analog spring dynometer and a Tractel electronic load cell dynometer. When each anchor was recovered, the drag distance was measured for that test.

The results of these tests are summarized in Table 6-1. The superiority of the Fortress anchor is again evident. However, in these tests, the Bruce

Table 6-1. French Tests of Anchor Holding Power in Sand.
Source: Wichard Co.

Brand Name	Anchor Type	True weight (pounds)	Holding power (pounds)	Drag distance to fully set (feet)
FOB HP 16kg	pivoting fluke	35	840	130
Britany 20kg	pivoting fluke	44	1,080	165
FOB Light E220	pivoting fluke	15	1,180	200
Bruce 20kg	spade	44	2,865	33
CQR 45	plow	45	3,835	50
Fortress FX-23	pivoting fluke	14	4,740	16

[*] *Procès-Verbal D'Essais D'Ancres à Cannes.* April 28, 1992. Mediterranée Expertises Maritimes.

and CQR anchors performed much better than in other tests quoted here. The most interesting new data to come out of these tests, however, is the distance each anchor had to drag to fully embed itself in the seabed to develop its full holding power. The Bruce, CQR, and Fortress anchors yielding the greatest holding power all had significantly shorter drag distances.

The Fortress anchor, which was the primary subject of the test program, dragged a short 16 feet in distance. A diver recovering the Fortress after a 5500-pound pull had broken the rope portion of the rode, noted that the anchor was completely buried with only about three feet of the chain lead exposed above the seabed. Although quantitative evidence is meager, one suspects that the Fortress digs more steeply into the seabed than any other anchor tested.

Veering Tests

These are the most difficult tests to perform and seemingly impossible to repeat. The latest tests were sponsored by the Simpson-Lawrence Company in Ardminish Bay on the Island of Gigha on the West Coast of Scotland.[*] They tested three anchors in a fine sand seabed—a Danforth 20H, a 10-kilogram Bruce, and a 25-pound CQR. The series of tests applied to each anchor consisted of three different drag loadings to a 300-kilogram load (660 pounds). This was considered representative of an anchor load on an average size boat in nominal wind conditions. (Refer to Table 2-1 for equivalent wind speeds and boat sizes.) The rode consisted of 25 meters of $5/8$-inch diameter 3-strand nylon rope followed by ten meters of $5/16$-inch short link chain. Water depth was $4\sqrt[3]{4}$ meters and the scope was held at 5:1. Drag loads applied by the fishing trawler *Vestra* were measured onboard with a recording strain gauge. In addition, a diving team followed the events with an image-intensifying video camera to record the anchor behavior on videotape.

Tests were made on the three anchors as follows:

1. A straight line pull to 300 kilograms, at which point the load was released.

2. A pull at 90° to the anchor as left set in (1) until the drag load again reached 300 kilograms and the load was again released. This simulated a 90° veering of the wind.

3. A pull at 180° to the anchor as left set in (2) until the drag load again reached 300 kilograms and the load was again released. This simulated a full turn of the tide.

[*] *Underwater Study on the Behavior of Anchors.* Gigha Island, 23-26 June 1987. Simpson-Lawrence Limited.

A total of 18 tests were made. Typical results from three selected consecutive pulls on each anchor are illustrated in Fig. 6-9. The test team made the following observations on the behavior of each anchor based on the quantitative data and their impressions from the video recordings:

Danforth 20H: The Danforth anchor consistently landed flat on the seabed and upon initial setting buried its flukes to about 30 percent of their area before rearing up to stand with the two flukes fully open and pointing into the seabed at 50-60°. Under further loading the flukes dug into the seabed until completely buried with both stock and shank lying flat on the seabed. This is the textbook version of how a pivoting fluke anchor works. Unfortunately, in several tests, the anchor was seen to tip over until it rested at an angle on one fluke, one stock end, and the shank head, readily dragging itself and not wanting to set.

Properly buried, the Danforth gave high holding power because of its large fluke area. When the applied load exceeded the anchor's ability to resist, it "flipped out" of its set and assumed the angled three-point attitude until resetting. In both the 90° and 180° veering tests, the anchor "flipped out" of its set immediately and dragged before resetting.

10-kilogram Bruce: The Bruce anchor lands on the seabed in a variety of positions but shows the ability to set rapidly from any of them. The setting motion is not what one would expect as the palm tips seem to rake the seabed surface rhythmically "hopping and dragging," alternately loading up and releasing its resistance. In all three categories of tests, the Bruce proved itself the quickest setting of the three anchor types.

In both of the veering tests, the Bruce remained embedded while veering but continued to exhibit the characteristic "hop and drag" action.

25-pound CQR: While the CQR could also land in any number of positions, it righted itself on loading with one wing carving its way into the seabed until the anchor rolled upright and eventually buried itself symmetrically.

In the veering test, the CQR would remain in its original position until the full swing of the pivoted shank was reached, at which time it would roll out on its side and again carve an arc into the seabed to realign itself with the direction of pull before resetting as mentioned above.

While the above analysis and the accompanying excerpts from the strain gauge recorder traces are representative, there are caveats to all the results. Although the tests were all run in the same seabed, a total of only 18 tests were made, some of them repeat tests to try and understand what the anchor was actually doing. This was particularly true in the case of the Danforth, which in the first three tests would not set. The tendency of the Bruce to "hop and drag" may have been due to an accumulation of seabed material on one or more flukes preventing it from digging in. Although the seabed

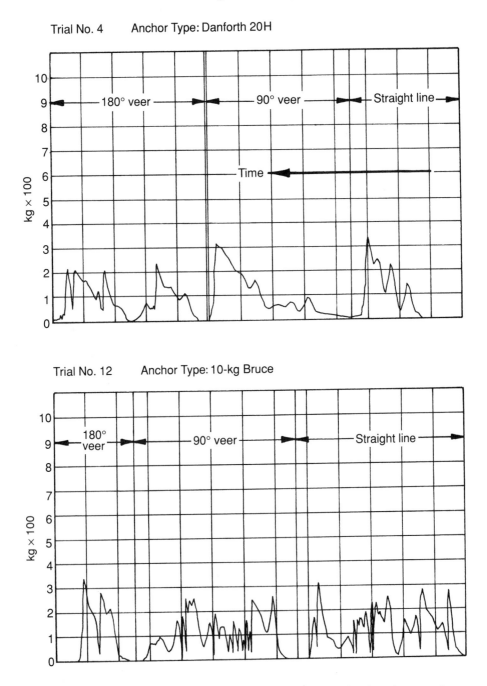

Fig. 6-9. Strain gauge readings from veering tests. *Continued on next page*

Trial No. 8   Anchor Type: 25-lb CQR

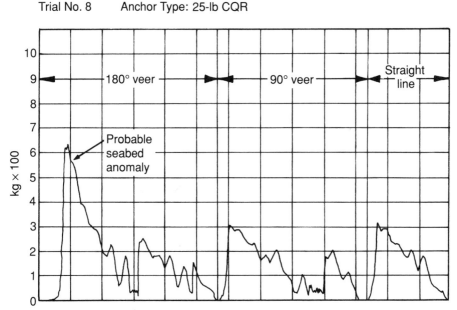

Fig. 6-9—Continued

was described as fine sand, there is no mention of the homogeneity of the seabed horizontally or vertically. Since seabeds are notoriously heterogeneous, some of the anchor antics experienced in these tests may have been due to pockets of mud, clay, rock, weeds, and other irregularities. Nevertheless, any seabed will probably be no better than this one, and the boater can expect greatly varied performance and stability from his or her favorite anchor.

Putting Holding Power in Perspective

After reviewing results from hundreds of anchor holding power tests, I am left with the feeling that the only truly stable anchor is the old-fashioned hooking anchor. It is safe to assume that all burying anchors can at some time break their set under unusual conditions of seabed, loading, and veering. Repeatability is, at best, a will-o'-the-wisp in the world of anchoring. No one anchor yet appears best for all purposes and no one anchor can overcome the inconsistencies of the person setting it.

When an anchor is caught in a rock by its fluke tip(s), what is the possibility that it will structurally fail due to wind loads, surge, or an extra-strong windlass pull? This is the ultimate load on an anchor and a measure of its physical strength.

The Boating Safety Division of BOAT/US together with _Cruising World_ magazine sponsored a series of tests on the physical strength of anchors, simulating the case of an anchor fluke tip caught in a rock crevice. The tests were conducted by the Com-Tex Development Corporation using laboratory facilities of the University of Lowell at Lowell, Massachusetts.[*]

The Danforth H-1500 stock-stabilized, pivoting fluke anchor in the Tinius Olson testing machine at the University of Lowell. Courtesy: _Cruising World_.

---

[*] B. Holman and M. Clarke, "The Power to Hold," _Cruising World,_ May 1989) and B. Holman, "A Show of Strength,"_Cruising World_, October 1990).

The test procedure was as follows: each anchor was secured head end up in a hydraulic tensile testing machine and the load was applied through a steel cap slipped over the fluke tip (both fluke tips in the case of a pivoting fluke anchor design). A tensile load was gradually applied between anchor ring and fluke tip and the ensuing separation distance (distortion) was measured at 1,000-pound loading intervals. Loading was increased until failure occurred or the fluke-shank angle opened to 90°. Results of these tests to destruction are summarized in Table 6-2.

In general, the anchor destruction tests showed that anchor physical strength was adequate for the maximum holding power possible in sand or mud for each anchor. Some of the better built anchors actually resisted loads that would unnecessarily challenge the proof loading of the rode and the strength of deck gear. Anchoring in rocky seabeds simulated by these tests is not recommended as a general practice. Should it be necessary, always buoy the anchor with a trip line and avoid the necessity of testing the anchor's strength on retrieval.

Table 6-2. Results of Destruction Tests*

Brand Name Anchor Type Weight	Construction	Type of Failure	Max. load in Pounds
Sentinel 15 Economy Pivoting Fluke 15 pounds	Galvanized steel, slip ring design, one-piece crown	Crown bent as soon as load was applied to flukes. Weld failed between shank and crown.	300
Sea Hook, Fluke Type Pivoting Fluke 20 pounds	Stainless steel, welded joints	Shank bent sideways 40° just above crown plate.	1,150
Sentinel 22 Pivoting Fluke 22 pounds	Galvanized steel, welded joints, two separate crown plates	Shank drove through crown causing a rolling shear failure of crown plate. Shank bent sideways 30°.	1,250
Danforth S-1600 Pivoting Standard Fluke 24 pounds	Mild steel, welded joints, galvanized finish	Shank drove through crown, both flukes bent and one fluke weld tore away from crown.	1,500

Continued on next page

* Source: *Cruising World*, October 1990

Table 6-2—Continued

Brand Name Anchor Type Weight	Construction	Type of Failure	Max. load in Pounds
Fortress FX-11 Pivoting Fluke 6 pounds	Hi-tensile aluminum magnesium alloy, weld-free components, anodized finish	Shank bent sideways 35°, stock bent slightly.	2,000
Danforth T-400 Deepset Hi-tensile Pivoting Fluke 30 pounds	Heat-treated chrome-molybdenum alloy, spring steel shank and flukes, welded joints, galvanized finish	Shank deflected, twisting with increasing load, springing back when unloaded. Weld failure at 2,600 pounds caused crown plate to shear off. *Crown plate has since been redesigned.	2600*
Fortress FX-23 Pivoting Fluke 14 pounds	Hi-tensile aluminum magnesium alloy, weld-free components, anodized finish	Anchor held its shape well until stock broke into three clean pieces at 4,650 pounds.	4,650
Danforth H-1500 Hi-tensile Pivoting Fluke 20 pounds	Hi-carbon alloy steel flukes, drop forged steel shank, welded joints, galvanized finish	Shank strap failed at 5,250 pounds, then crown broke.	5,250
Seaspike 35 Plow 35 pounds	Hi-tensile, two-piece cast steel, galvanized finish	Swivel pin sheared at 3,400 pounds.	3,400
Danforth P-1500 Deepset Plow 27 pounds	Mild steel plow chrome-molybdenum steel shank, welded joints, galvanized finish	Tensile failure occurred when swivel bushing parted at the plow neck.	5,700
Harborfast 35 from Simpson-Lawrence Plow 35 pounds	Two-piece cast steel, galvanized finish	Swivel pin caused tensile failure of swivel bushing.	8,150
Luke Storm Anchor Old-fashioned 25 pounds	Steel stock, steel shank, one-piece cast-iron flukes	Shank began bending at 3,000 pounds and continued to bend until test stopped at 9,000 pounds. Fluke arm remained undistorted.	9,000
CQR 35 Plow 35 pounds	Drop-forged hi-tensile steel, galvanized finish	After loaded to 4,000 pounds, shank bent gradually and twisted until test stopped at 13,250 pounds.	13,250
Bruce 33 Spade 33 pounds	One-piece, heat-treated cast, galvanized finish	No distortion whatsoever, then shank gradually bent and twisted until test stopped.	18,500

CARE OF THE ANCHOR

Next to the ballast on a vessel, the anchor is probably the most neglected component of a boat. If it is able to take care of itself in a rocky seabed, certainly it can take care of itself anyplace! Not so. Anchors have their points of vulnerability just as any other man-made article has. Fortunately, it is easy to inspect an anchor and the proper time to do so is after weighing, when it is clean and being stowed in its saddle.

> Look for any signs of bending of fluke(s), shank, or stock that would impair its performance in the next set. Also look for proper sharpness of the bill(s) to assure penetration on the next set.
>
> Inspect ring (or shackle) for deformation, wear, and freedom of movement.

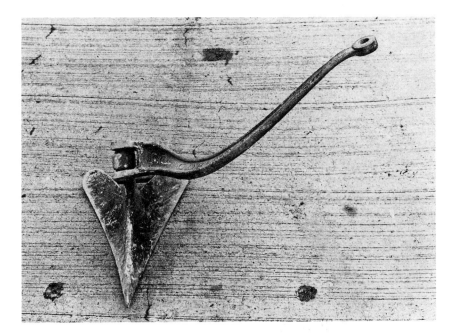

While the owner of this CQR anchor was enjoying an afternoon of spinnaker flying, his anchor wedged solidly in coral and was tested to the utmost. The anchor held, but the shank was corkscrewed by the sheering of the boat during the fun.

Examine pivot and hinge points, if they exist, to assure yourself that they are not excessively worn.

Regalvanize when the anchor shows signs of rusting. If you do so at the first sign of rust stains, you will avoid the need for sandblasting.

Paint your anchor a white color to improve its visibility in the water. This will help you in setting the anchor by making its orientation and location more apparent.

Take good care of your anchor and it will take care of you in that blow that you would just as soon not think about.

Would you trust your valuable boat to any of these look-alike or homemade anchors? *Above,* lightweight, stock-stabilized, . . . (see following page)

. . . *above*, welded old-fashioned, and *below*, lightweight stockless with sliding ring

CHAPTER SEVEN

Anchor and Rode Selection

The right anchor for your boat is the one that is matched in type to the seabed and in size to the applied loads. As you have already seen how to determine the applied loads (Chapter 2), you will now take a look at the nature of the seabed from which the anchor will get its resisting force.

NATURE OF THE SEABED

It is not simple to describe the seabed because its qualities are as diverse as those of the land, and they are mostly hidden from view. Therefore, you have to depend on the results of oceanographic surveys or on some spot-checking by the lead as was done in the days of sailing ships. Knowing the nature of the bottom will materially assist you in determining which anchor is the best to use and how to set it.

Geologists have spent a great deal of time examining the seabed that surrounds continents, islands, and sea mounts. By a variety of sampling techniques they have determined that the continental shelves are made up of rock covered with a sediment that has accumulated over millions of years. Marine sedimentation is a slow process and one involving a great diversity of materials and material sizes. For convenience of interpretation geologists have classified sediment as gravel, sand, or mud depending on particle size and composition. By size these groups are defined as follows:

Gravels: Boulder—particles larger than 256 mm (10 inches)
               in diameter.
            Cobble —particles between 64 and 256 mm (2½ to 10
               inches) in diameter.
            Pebble —particles between 4 and 64 mm (1/6 to
               2½ inches) in diameter.
           Granule—particles between 2 and 4 mm (1/12 to
               1/6 inches) in diameter.

Sands: Particles between 1/16 mm and 2 mm in
                    diameter. These are further subdivided into very
                    fine, fine, medium, coarse, and very coarse sands.

Muds: Particles less than 1/16 mm in diameter. These
                    are further subdivided into silts if larger than
                    1/256 mm in diameter and clays if less than
                    1/256 mm in diameter.

Sand is the most common of the sedimentary materials found on the
ocean floor and is believed to have gotten there from three sources. One
source is the weathering of rocks on land and the subsequent washing of
this rock debris into the ocean waters. This terrigenous sand is predomi-
nately quartz but may contain other minerals such as feldspar, mica,
hornblende, and augite. The second source of sand includes seashell
fragments, coral fragments, and the calcareous skeletons of other marine
organisms. A third and the smallest source of sand is from the direct
precipitation of chemical solids out of the ocean water. More often than
not, the three types of sand are found mixed together. Sand is a loose
material with no cohesive attributes.

The second most common sedimentary material found on the ocean
bottom is mud which is a fine earthy sediment characterized by a stickiness
which gives it body. Mud can be distinguished from very fine sand in that
it will hold together when dried, whereas sand will fall apart.

Clay, as a particular form of mud, is characterized by three properties: plasticity, fineness, and the presence of large amounts of hydrous
aluminum silicate in its makeup. Clay, when mixed with water, forms a
pasty, moldable mass that will preserve its shape when dried and can even
be baked into a stony substance.

Silt is another mudlike substance which tends to be plastic when wet
but crumbles when dry. Extremely wet silt loses its cohesiveness and,
having little mass, will remain in suspension in water as particles.

The third most common sedimentary material is gravel which is
nothing more than coarse fragments of rock in large quantities covering
the bedrock of the ocean floor.

Underlying all of the sediments and sometimes exposed over large
areas of the seabed surrounding the continents is the rock bottom which is
made up of the same rock materials as found on land. This rock is
sometimes covered with coral or coral-like growth that obscures the true
rock bottom but produces the same impenetrable type of surface.

Oceanographic studies have sought to classify the seabed in a scientific manner, carefully defining its constituents. Unfortunately, time

and ocean currents have so mixed up the sediment of the seabeds that it is rare to find deposits which can be singularly described in concise geological terms. Furthermore, from the mariner's standpoint, anchor use preceded the scientific development of undersea geology so that the mariner has come to know the ocean bottom by somewhat different terms.

Navigation chart makers use a list of 85 descriptors to define the nature of the seabed to normal anchoring depths (Table 7-1). These descriptors were to a large extent based on seabed samples brought up in the process of sounding with a lead.

The sounding, or hand lead, at one time called the "blue pigeon," is a cone of lead weighing from 5 to 14 pounds (deep sea leads may weigh as much as 100 pounds). The base of the lead has a cavity which holds tallow, soap, or grease to pick up a sample of the seabed where it touches. From an examination of these seabed samples, a skipper would know its nature and could estimate its potential for anchor holding.

Over the years this technique, as well as more scientific types of surveys, have revealed the nature of shallow seabeds so that now you need only look at the descriptors printed on the charts to know whether you have a good holding ground or not. Not all of the descriptors affect your ability to set an anchor firmly; some, such as color, only help you to identify your location, provided that you have obtained a sample of the local seabed for analysis.

Although it is conceivable that boaters could at some time or other find themselves trying to anchor in any or all of the seabeds described by the chart makers, you really need to be concerned only about a few categories. These are defined as follows, consistent with chart symbols which differ somewhat from the geologist's orderly definitions given earlier:

Sand. A loose siliceous material made up of small particles ground from rock by the action of waves on or near a coastline. Coral sand results from the erosion of coral (coral is made up of the calcareous skeletons of minute polyps).

Clay. An earthy material which is plastic when moist and very tenacious. Clay can be very compact so that an extremely sharp anchor bill is required to get a bite. This is probably the best holding bottom.

Mud. A very fine, earthy sediment in water characterized by a stickiness that gives it body. It is not as heavy nor as sticky as clay. Relatively dry mud makes a good holding bottom, but soft mud has little gripping power.

Table 7-1. Seabed Quality Descriptors

1	Grd	Ground	38b	Ma	Mattes
2	S	Sand	39	f; fne	Fine
3	M	Mud; Muddy	40	c; crs	Coarse
4	Oz	Ooze	41	so; sft	Soft
5	Ml	Marl	42	h; hrd	Hard
6	Cy; Cl	Clay	43	stf	Stiff
7	G	Gravel	44	sml	Small
8	Sn	Shingle	45	lrg	Large
9	P	Pebbles	46	sy; stk	Sticky
10	St	Stones	47	bk; brk	Broken
11	Rk; rky	Rock; Rocky	47a	grd	Ground (Shells)
11a	Blds	Boulders	48	rt	Rotten
12	Ck	Chalk	49	str	Streaky
12a	Ca	Calcareous	50	spk	Speckled
13	Qz	Quartz	51	gty	Gritty
13a	Sch	Schist	52	dec	Decayed
14	Co	Coral	53	fly	Flinty
(Sa)	Co Hd	Coral head	54	glac	Glacial
15	Mds	Madrepores	55	ten	Tenacious
16	Vol	Volcanic	56	wh	White
(Sb)	Vol Ash	Volcanic ash	57	bl; bk	Black
17	La	Lava	58	vi	Violet
18	Pm	Pumice	59	bu	Blue
19	T	Tufa	60	gn	Green
20	Sc	Scoriae	61	yl	Yellow
21	Cn	Cinders	62	or	Orange
21a		Ash	63	rd	Red
22	Mn	Manganese	64	br	Brown
23	Sh	Shells	65	ch	Chocolate
24	Oys	Oysters	66	gy	Gray
25	Ms	Mussels	67	lt	Light
26	Spg	Sponge	68	dk	Dark
27	K	Kelp	70	vard	Varied
28	Wd	Seaweed	71	unev	Uneven
	Grs	Grass	(Sc)	S/M	Surface layer and
29	Stg	Sea-tangle			Under layer
31	Spi	Spicules	76		Freshwater
32	Fr	Foraminifera			springs in seabed
33	Gl	Globigerina	(Sd)		Mobile bottom
34	Di	Diatoms			(sand waves)
35	Rd	Radiolaria	(Se)	Si	Silt
36	Pt	Pteropods	(Sf)	Cb	Cobbles
37	Po	Polyzoa	(Sg)	m	Medium (used
38	Cir	Cirripedia			only before S
38a	Fu	Fucus			(sand)

Source: "Table S. Quality of the Bottom," *Chart No. 1: United States of America Nautical Chart Symbols and Abbreviations,* 8th ed. (Washington, D. C.: Department of Commerce, 1984).

Gravel. Small loose fragments of rocks, pebbles, small pieces of stone, or rock that present no gripping power in themselves and, because they cover the bottom, can prevent an anchor from properly digging in.

Shelf rock and coral. A continuous, or nearly so, surface of rock or coral which has only small crevices or pits roughening the surface. Sharp hooking anchors are needed to get a bite on it.

Weed. Any of a large variety of seaweeds that are found in shallow waters, which can range from low-growing grass to giant kelp; has no holding power of its own. An anchor must pass through it to grip the underlying seabed.

Marl. A loose or crumbly earthy deposit composed of varying mixtures of sand, silt, or clay with little cohesion of the particles that make it up; not a suitable holding material.

Silt. A very fine earthy sediment resulting from the deposit of fine sand, earth, and clay at a river mouth; not considered to have any holding power whatsoever—ooze.

The relative holding power of these seabeds (competency) has been estimated by the U.S. Navy* to be:

Firm Sand	1.00
Stiff-dense clay (plastic)	1.50
Sticky clay of medium density	0.66
Soft mud	0.33
Loose coarse sand	0.33
Gravel	0.33
Hard bottom (rock-shale-boulders)	0.00 (unless anchor is hooked under a massive rock)

CHOOSING THE ANCHOR TYPE

The burying type of anchor certainly deserves its popularity because most of the seabeds in shallow waters are composed of alluvium, and that is where most anchoring is done. Anchors with sharp bills like the CQR, Danforth, and Wishbone designs are able to penetrate the hard-packed surface of sand and clay and get a grip in these materials. Duller

* R. S. Crenshaw, Jr., *Naval Shiphandling* (Annapolis, MD: Naval Institute Press, 1975).

bill anchors such as the Bruce and Navy stockless will dig into softer sands, clays, and muds with ease. Anchoring in marl requires an anchor with considerable throat as well as a pointed bill to penetrate the bottom. Danforth and Navy anchors are susceptible to fouling the space between the flukes in marl. They have also been known to pick up beer cans and rocks between flukes.

Hooking anchors are basically rock anchors with the old-fashioned and Northill anchors having enough palm area on the flukes to be modestly effective in heavy sand and clay. As kedges, they probably have no peer. The Wishbone with its single, sharp fluke is also a good hooking anchor along with its capability to work well in sand and clay. (It is not good in mud because of a relatively small fluke area as compared with the CQR, Danforth, and Bruce.) A weed hook requires a long, narrow fluke that can penetrate layers of weeds to actually reach the bottom. Oftentimes burying anchors will hook onto weeds and give you the feeling of a proper anchor set, but they have not reached the bottom and their holding power is only what the roots of the weeds provide.

Table 7-2 summarizes where common small boat anchors seem to do their best work. You can see from this table that there is no single anchor suitable for all seabeds, and so you will have to make a compromise selecting an anchor that handles the majority of seabeds in your area of operations. It is only good sense to carry more than one anchor (Table 7-3), and it is also good sense to carry different styles of anchors.

Table 7-2. Where Common Anchors Seem to Work Best

Anchor style	Type of Seabed				
	Sand or clay	Mud	Gravel	Rock	Weed
Burying anchors:					
CQR/Delta	X	X			X
Danforth/Fortress	X	X			
Bruce/MAX	X	X	X		
	(soft)				
Navy stockless	X	X			
	(soft)				
Mushroom	X	X			
	(soft)	(soft)			
Hooking anchors:					
Old-fashioned	X		X	X	X
Northill	X		X	X	X
Hans C–Anchor	X	X		X	X
Grapnel				X	

Table 7-3. Recommended Minimum Anchor Complements

Type of Boat	Class of Anchor			
	Working	Stern	Storm	Other
Day sailer or powerboat less than 7 meters (23 ft) in length[a]	1			
Day sailer or powerboat 7 meters (23 ft) in length or greater[a]	1	1		
Ocean racing sailboat[b] (LOA less than 28 ft)	1			
Ocean racing sailboat[b] (LOA 28 ft or more)	1	1		
Coastal cruising—sail or power driven[a]	1	1		
Blue water cruising—sail or power driven[a]	1	1	1	Old-fashioned
Blue water working or fishing—power driven[a]	1		1	Grapnel

[a]In addition to carrying appropriate ground anchors, it is recommended that power-driven vessels also carry a sea anchor.
[b]Recommendaton of the Offshore Racing Council, London, England.

Probably the hottest debate in anchor selection occurs between the CQR plow and the Bruce anchor. Both are good cruising anchors, but both are difficult to stow unless you have a bow roller. I do not think that there is an answer as to which is best, and I will tell you why.

In 1984 we were cruising the Line Islands south of Hawaii and made a stop at Palmyra Atoll. The holding ground in the lagoon is a coarse coral gravel which you might call small cobblestones. The Offshore 40 yawl, *Valera Linda*, was already there, and she was anchored with a 44-pound Bruce on an all-chain rode. She was still there in her original position when we left two weeks later. We anchored our Morgan Out Island 41 ketch, *Horizon*, nearby using a 60-pound CQR and an all-chain rode. Within 24 hours we had dragged a perceptible distance. We then reanchored with greater care on the other side of *Valera Linda*, but the anchor did not hold there either. So we rowed a line ashore and put it around a palm tree. Score one for the Bruce.

Our next port of call was Fanning Atoll where the anchorage consisted of coral sand with random coral heads. The strong tradewinds had a fetch of five miles across the lagoon so good holding was a necessity to keep you off the leeshore. We again set our 60-pound CQR on chain and did not touch it until we left 17 days later. In the meantime *Valera Linda* arrived and set her 44-pound Bruce on chain in the same bottom and it failed to hold. Not finding a suitable bottom for the Bruce to hold against the tradewinds, *Valera Linda* departed after a few days. Score one for the CQR.

At Christmas Island both boats shared the same reef anchorage which consisted of coral sand with long streaks of solid coral running seaward. Both boats hung on their same bow anchors and both boats remained securely anchored for their stays. Score that one a tie.

Cruising Boat Anchor Preferences:

In 1991 the members of the Ocean Cruising Club[*], all experienced blue-water sailors, were asked what attributes they would look for in their ideal long-distance cruising boat and how they would equip it. In the category of ground tackle for an "ideal boat" of 39 to 47 feet length of medium displacement they made the following ground tackle selection

> The nature of long-term cruising—in waters where marinas are rare, where lying alongside may be inadvisable or expensive, and where common mooring methods, bow- or stern-to a dock, involve judicious anchor work—means that anchoring is the norm rather than the exception. Most long-term cruisers view their anchors as their best insurance and take particular care in their choice. What is detailed here represents thousands of days of bitter experience and many miles of anchor dragging.
>
> *Number of anchors.* Nearly two-thirds of respondents decided on four, usually of different sizes and weights. The typical choice was: primary, CQR; secondary, Danforth; storm, CQR or Yachtsman; spare, Yachtsman.
>
> *Main anchor.* With 87 percent voting for the CQR as the main anchor, this preference would seem to be based on more than mere reputation. Weights suggested ranged from a minimum of 45 pounds to over 70 pounds, with 60 pounds the most popular. Almost without exception all-chain rode was specified, $\frac{3}{8}$ inch in size, and in lengths between 200 feet and 330 feet, the shorter lengths being backed by rope.
>
> *Secondary.* The burying characteristics, frontal area, and resulting straight-line holding power of the Danforth type are

---

[*] Ocean Cruising Club, P.O. Box 996, Tiptree, Colchester, Essex CO5 8XZ, England.

[**] Source: *Sail,* June 1992. Reprinted by permission of *Sail* Magazine, copyright 1992, Cahners Publishing Company.

well known and make it particularly useful as a kedge. Sixty-two percent chose the Danforth, 15 percent the CQR, and 11 percent the Bruce.

The most frequently specified weight of the Danforth type came out at a manageable 35 pounds, with between 16 feet and 33 feet of ⁵⁄₁₆-inch chain and the rest rope.

Storm anchor. The storm anchor is the one that, with its few feet of superheavy chain, lives in the bilge acting as ballast until needed in earnest. It is normally seen as the third anchor.

With a CQR as main anchor and Danforth as secondary, this would suggest the Yachtsman, with its superior holding power in kelp or on rocks. The Yachtsman did fare well in this category, but so did the CQR. The suggested weight of 65 pounds hints that even with good handling gear, anything much heavier could be difficult to deploy and, more important, to recover.

Spare anchor. Such is the importance attached to ground tackle that 65 percent said they would carry a fourth anchor as backup. After the Yachtsman and the CQR, a wide variety of anchors were specified, some for specialized use, like the grapnel for coral.

Stowage. Half our sample chose to carry an anchor in the bow roller; 28 percent opted for on-deck stowage; 22 percent for bow anchor lockers.

Handling. That every member of our sample requested an anchor windlass is no surprise; 76 percent specified electric windlasses. We attribute this to the size of the boat and the weight of the anchor and its rode. Electric windlasses, especially vertical-axis types, offer greater line speed than manual ones, making shorter work of anchor recovery.

Racing Boat Anchor Preferences:

Anchor requirements for racing boats are set by race sponsors who seek to provide an adequate level of anchoring capability for specific races without burdening the boat with excessive weight.[*] Numbers of anchors may be specified, but the type, size, and stowage are left to the contestants.

Since weight is the number-one criterion in race boats, lightweight anchors of the stock-stabilized, pivoting fluke design are preferred. These, when made in aluminum, provide a reasonable capability for mud and sand

[*]"Recommendations for Offshore Sailing Including ORC Special Regulations." United States Sailing Association, Newport, R.I., 1992.

bottoms at a minimum weight. For uncertain bottoms, a Northill design would provide great versatility at a modest weight. Again, if the boat carries more than one anchor, they should be of different designs to better match the variety of seabeds over its race course. Boats that race extended distances through large groups of islands, such as in the western Pacific, which may be subject to adverse weather conditions, should also include a heavy storm anchor as a survival piece.

Although a nylon rode is preferred for its lightness, adequate chain lead as described on pages 128-130 should be included to assure that the anchor will perform to its specifications. It would not be expected that the racing boat would carry a windlass on the foredeck because of its added weight. Instead, the racing boat with its large crew can easily manhandle the ground tackle.

Anchor stowage location is the second most important criterion for racing boats. Conventional stowage at the bow is not desirable except when approaching land. Anchor and rode are best stowed amidships as low in the hull as is possible, but still readily accessible for quick use. The location should be dry and well-ventilated to preserve the materials of both ground tackle and boat construction. Weight and weight distribution are all important in the dedicated racing boat. but safety in an emergency must also be assured.

SELECTING WORKING ANCHOR AND RODE SIZE

There are two decisions that have to be made when selecting anchors for your boat—what type and what size. To an extent, these are independent choices. There is no universal, unbiased source of truth on anchor performance. Therefore, your selection must place in balance (1) the likely wind and seas that your boat will face; (2) the size of anchor that is compatible with the size of your boat; and (3) the nature of the seabed in which you will anchor.

The working anchor is the one that you will use most. Preferably, it will be a lightweight, efficient anchor suited to the type of holding ground found in the normal operating area of your boat. Whether fishing, cruising, or gunkholing, anchoring should not be a physical tussle. Too often one thinks that if a 20-pound anchor is good, then a 35-pound anchor must be better. That only leads to an unnecessary escalation of ground tackle weight and cost together with greater frustration when it comes time to weigh anchor. The net result is that you will anchor less with heavy gear than with light gear.

I was brought up on the heavier-is-better philosophy until I took pencil and paper and compared the holding power of anchors with the strengths of chain and rope and predicted maximum wind and surge loads on my boat. That quickly convinced me that there was both strength and efficiency in lighter weight ground tackle and that it would be to my muscular and financial benefit to take advantage of a more scientific and balanced approach to ground tackle.

The anchor choice is yours. In Chapter 6 you have the characteristics of commonly available anchors for small boats from which you can choose a type of working anchor. Choose either a burying or hooking type depending on the type of seabed common to your boating area. You may even want to get one of each (the second as a stern anchor) before you are through because you are going to need two anchors to give you a mooring capability in constrained anchorages, or where wind and current may play tricks on you.

Conservatism must be followed to a point in making an anchor selection because the anchor has to work in a hidden environment, but ultraconservatism must be avoided. Lightweight anchors of great holding power have become the norm for everyday use, but the old-fashioned

The oldest anchor designs still in use—the old-fashioned and a version of the stockless patent anchor.

anchor still has not been surpassed as a general all-around anchor if you can afford the weight and have handling space.

To simplify the task of selecting a working anchor size, I have constructed Table 7-4 which presents suggested anchor and rode sizes for a variety of working anchors. It is based on (1) the horizontal design loads promulgated by the ABYC; (2) the capabilities of chain and rope rodes stressed to appropriate working anchor load limits; (3) the identification of each anchor by its primary seabed capability; and (4) data offered by the manufacturers on the holding power of their anchors together with such other experimental data as was available in the literature.

The first part of the table presents burying anchors—CQR, Delta, Danforth Hi-Tensile, Bruce, Navy stockless, and the Fortress. The middle part of the table presents hooking anchors—old-fashioned, Pekny, and the Danforth Utility. The third part of this table presents compatible rode sizes for all chain or a a combination of chain and rope. The independent variable by which anchor size and rode size can be determined is the overall length

A well-made and well-matched bow anchor system. The 50-kilogram (110-pound) Bruce anchor is an appropriate size for this 80-foot cruising sailboat. The bow roller appears substantial although it could use more flare in the cheeks. It is fitted with keeper-pin holes, and there is a swivel between chain and anchor.

Table 7-4. Suggested Anchor and Rode Sizes for a Working Anchor System[a]

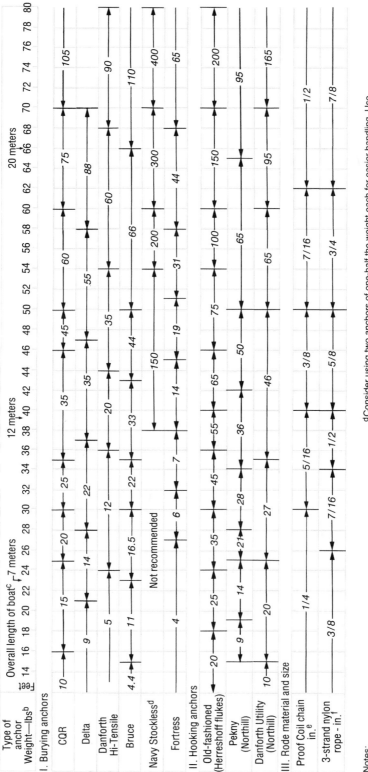

Notes:
[a] For medium displacement boats and 30 knots of wind.
[b] Anchor weights correspond to manufacturer's production weights and not to a product numbering system.
[c] For the ABYC "nominal" boat of Table 2-1 or an equivalent (see text).
[d] Consider using two anchors of one-half the weight each for easier handling. Use only an all-chain rode of compatible size.
[e] Based on working loads of new Proof Coil hot galvanized steel chain.
[f] Based on using new twisted 3-strand nylon rope at a working load up to 25 percent of the breaking strength.

of the nominal ABYC boat or an equivalent based on similar horizontal ground tackle loads.

Because of the great overlap in anchor capabilities and the discrete sizes available, there is no single answer as to which is the proper size anchor to use under all conditions. You are faced with selecting from a variety of anchor types in the context of the most likely seabed that that anchor will see.

The procedure for making an anchor and rode selection is diagrammed in Fig. 7-1. The illustration identifies the various steps that must be taken in selecting the working anchor and the rode for your boat from the information given in Table 7-4.

CHOOSING A STERN ANCHOR

A stern anchor is a necessity for most boats longer than, say, 23 feet. It gives the skipper greater flexibility in anchoring and mooring situations and serves as a backup in case the working anchor is lost. The stern anchor rode, itself, can be equally useful as a spare working anchor rode, tow line, or a spring line for docking in unusual circumstances.

The stern anchor can be smaller than the working anchor—about 70 percent of the working anchor's size, or, roughly, one size smaller for a given style. Because the stern anchor is to be a utility anchor, it should be light and as easy to handle as an anchor can be. It is often used for kedging or carrying ashore but it need not be an old-fashioned anchor, although on large boats this might make a practical choice.

The best all-around stern anchor style is the stainless steel Pekny, but both the Danforth (Hi-Tensile) and the Fortress are very acceptable. It is wise to choose a style of anchor different from the working anchor to give added flexibility in matching seabeds and solving difficult anchoring problems.

The stern anchor rode should be a combination chain and rope matched to the stern anchor size with an overall length equal to the working anchor rode. It should carry depth markings. Do not use an all-chain rode for the stern anchor since that will decrease its utility value.

Deck gear for the stern anchor system should follow the same design guidelines as given for the bow anchor system. A roller guide based on the criteria of Figure 3-1 (Chapter 3) can be useful in minimizing chafe and transferring loads to the hull. Many boats simply use fairleads but a careful eye should be kept on chafing of the rode where it passes through the fairlead.

On boats under 40 feet in length, there probably is no need for a separate anchor windlass to take in the stern anchor rode. Any winch

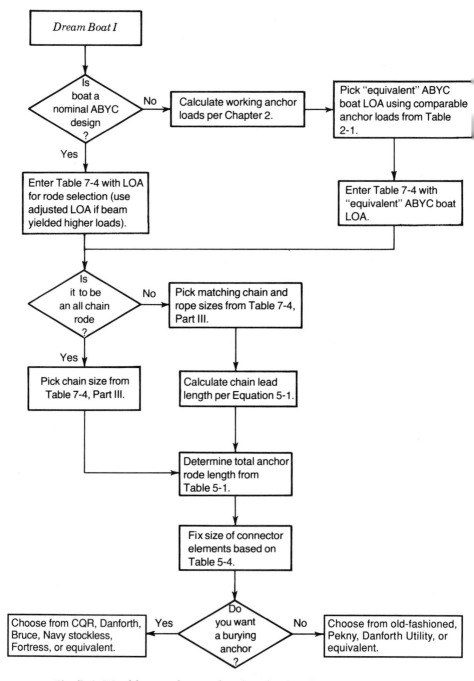

Fig. 7-1. Working anchor and rode selection flow diagram.

already installed for some other purpose can be used provided that the anchor rode has a fairlead from stern roller guide to the winch. Generally, the weight of the stern anchor and rode is not so great that it can't be handled by hand.

On boats longer than 40 feet with no winches available, a light duty anchor windlass properly located can be helpful. It should be aligned with the anchor roller guide and have a separate means for belaying the anchor rode such as a bitt or an oversize horn cleat.

Except on very large boats, the stern anchor rode is usually stowed separately below deck and brought up through a hatch when needed.

CHOOSING THE STORM ANCHOR

Most boats are never faced with the need to anchor out in a storm. With good weather forecasting, a prudent skipper will never leave a secure harbor when a storm is brewing. But there still is a need for storm anchors on boats whose operation might just find them away from well-protected waters when a storm strikes and they will have to put up with less than good protection from the elements.

A storm anchor by definition must be able to handle wind and surge loads up to four times what the working anchor has to handle. There are, of course, even more severe storms than that represented by the 60-knot storm wind definition used in anchor terminology. There are, indeed, winds that exceed 100 knots in speed whose forces are 11 times those expected to be encountered by a working anchor. Anchoring in the ultimate storm is discussed in Chapter 12 along with some examples of boats that have survived.

Storm anchoring cannot depend on brute force to be successful, there has to be a strategy involved also. A big anchor with an unyielding chain connecting it to the boat will cause either the anchor to be upset or the chain or deck gear to fail when the boat experiences a large surge. Big, by itself, is not enough. The system also has to have some give to it.

Provided that you have elasticity in your storm anchor rode, you can get by with a storm anchor that is only one size larger than your conservatively selected working anchor. Going two sizes larger only adds handling weight and is not necessary for reasonable holding grounds. Of course, if you regularly operate in areas of poor holding ground, you may want a larger storm anchor, or you can use tandem anchors as discussed in Chapter 10.

Boats that regularly operate away from well-protected waters such as fishing boats and blue water cruising boats should be very conservative in the selection of ground tackle. A variety of anchors, a collection of chain and combination rodes in good condition, plus plenty of chafing gear will see them through severe storms. Neither the severity of a storm nor the physical conditions surrounding the anchored boat are predictable beforehand. The crew with good ground tackle and a knowledge of how to use it will weather the storm.

PART II

THE ART OF ANCHORING

The how-to of anchoring and mooring a boat in diverse situations with considerations of crew capability, legality, and heavy weather encounters.

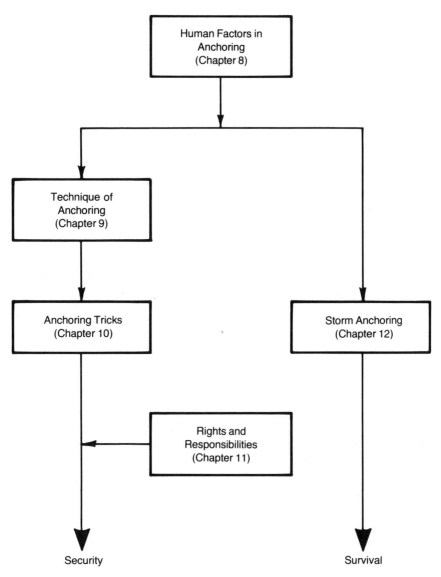

CHAPTER EIGHT

Human Factors in Anchoring

Recreational boating is supposed to be fun, and it usually is between periods of setting and weighing anchor. Fun is a human emotion, and when it comes into conflict with the hook, the fun often ends. This happens all too frequently on the foredeck where the crew is expected to do some back-wrenching work with gear unsuited to the job. Maybe you first need to give some thought to crew capabilities, and then think about the gear that will be needed to assist them.

Rarely is the number of crew needed to anchor a boat considered in the crew makeup, but it is an important factor. I would seriously question trying to operate a boat 50 feet long with a crew of only 2 persons. I would even question it on any boat over 40 feet long. There is a minimum number of crew who can safely handle the heavy and obstreperous pieces of ground tackle, especially in storm conditions. Experienced husband and wife cruising teams can usually handle the routine anchoring chores on 40-foot boats, but boats larger than this need a third person with a certain amount of muscle. Even then, under storm conditions, this may not be enough.

Physical capabilities of your crew must be considered when you have to confront an anchoring situation. While all people are created equal, some people have greater physical capabilities than others, and that important fact must be taken into account.

Powered windlasses take much of the backstrain out of weighing anchor, but who or what finally lifts the anchor into its stowed position? If it takes plain muscle, don't ask one of the weaker crew members to do such a task. And, except for very large boats that have a powered windlass to bring a stockless anchor home into its hawsepipe, every anchor will require some muscle power.

A good example of this problem showed up at the Cabo San Lucas disaster of 1981. The Pardeys, writing in *Sail* magazine (June 1983), observed that sailboats over 37 feet in length with crews of 2 or 3 persons got into trouble handling their ground tackle whereas crews of 4 or more were able to handle theirs adequately. One skipper of a 35-foot boat said that a couple just can't handle the ground tackle in a real emergency—the gear is too heavy and the forces too large. This disaster is discussed in more detail in Chapter 12 and emphasizes with real life experiences how important the crew really is as a functional element of the total anchor system.

With the crew at hand, you should attempt to develop, if only for the weekend, a procedure of handling the ground tackle. Put beef and experience on the foredeck and use the others for gofers—to go for shackles, safety wire, additional chafing gear, and the like. You will never know ahead of time when a blown sail, a stopped engine, or some other undesirable incident will force you to anchor quickly, and under adverse conditions. It is nice to know that your crew has some capability to handle the ground tackle without hazard to themselves.

CREW INFLUENCE ON GEAR SELECTION

Deck gear is the connection between the tug of the anchor and the mass of the boat. Mechanically, the deck gear must be capable of handling the loads applied to it by the anchor rode. It must also be of a functional design so that it is within the capability of the crew to use it without undue effort, knowledge, or hazard. Your deck gear should make any crew member the equivalent of a deck ape strong enough to bring home the anchor. It should not leave a crew member a sobbing basket case because the anchor won't budge, and the skipper is yelling such endearing terms as "you bloody landlubber," and the like. Failure of the foredeck crew to handle the anchor properly and expeditiously is more likely due to inadequate or improper deck gear than any lack of physical or mental will.

I have said it before, and I will say it again—handling anchors and chain can be tiring to your muscles, hazardous to your limbs, and can jeopardize your peace of mind when not done correctly. To save yourself undue problems, your ground tackle should be set up so that you do not have to manhandle it every time you want to set or retrieve your hook.

Every boat should have at least a working anchor stowed in the "at ready" position at all times. The reason is obvious: to prevent the boat from going on the rocks when propulsion or steering fails or the wind quits, or other unforeseen events occur. Racing boat sailors will certainly object to carrying an anchor near the bow, and they have to accept the risk attendant with making up an anchor after the crisis has started. Weekend sailors, fishermen, and blue water cruisers can all sacrifice a small bit of performance in order to have the ground tackle ready for use at all times.

In the ideal case your anchor should be stowed in the ready-to-use location, and the rode should be attached and ready to run out. In other words, the foredeck crew should have nothing more to do than to release a brake to let go the anchor. Similarly, when weighing anchor, the foredeck crew should only have to haul in on the rode by mechanical means (or by hand on a small boat) and the anchor will bring itself aboard. The rode should be self-stowing as should the anchor.

If you are going to use an all-chain rode, you most likely will also have a windlass to bring it aboard. If it is a powered windlass, you will need to consider a backup system should the power fail. Most powered windlasses are fitted with some kind of mechanical backup but few give you the needed mechanical advantage to haul in the anchor by simple manpower.

Studies of human capabilities for operating machines* have revealed much about our strength in doing different types of jobs. These studies have shown, for instance, in a backlift motion such as heaving in on an anchor, that a deck ape can exert a maximum pull of 520 pounds while a well-conditioned man and woman can exert 360 and 200 pounds, respectively. But how many of us can lay claim to such good physical condition?

These studies also show that people are strongest in their late 20s, by age 50 their strength is reduced to 85 percent and by age 65 to 75 percent of their peak strength. In general, females are about two-thirds as strong as males.

Of course, the strength of an individual varies with the type of task. Fore and aft lever motions at shoulder level are better handled than the same motions when bent over as in windlass pumping. The poorest motion of all from the strength standpoint is a circular motion. The strength available for a horizontal circular motion at a crouched level, as in grinding a sheet home on a sailboat, is poorest of all. If the circular motion is in a vertical plane near chest height as with "coffee grinders" on "maxi" racing sailboats, then the strength input is at its best.

Today's ground tackle has not been designed with consideration for the best strength and motion of the human body. One vertical powered anchor windlass I have seen had a one-and-one-half-foot-long bar inserted across the top of the capstan for the emergency manual drive lever. That gave only a 5- or 6-to-1 mechanical advantage and in the worst

---

*Wesley E. Woodson, *Human Factors Design Handbook* (New York: McGraw-Hill Book Company, 1981) and A. Damon, H. W. Stoudt, and R. A. McFarland, *The Human Body in Equipment Design* (Cambridge, Mass.: Harvard University Press, 1966).

possible plane of motion for applying a person's strength. It is hoped that in the future boat and equipment builders will give more consideration to the capabilities of the human body in doing heavy physical work on a boat than they have in the past.

To decide what is an adequate mechanical advantage for backup manual operation of a powered windlass, examine some of the manual windlasses and see what has proven satisfactory to an average person when faced with hauling in a chain rode and anchor. The Simpson-Lawrence 555, which I have used for many years, has a mechanical advantage of 14 to 1 for high-speed operation and 40 to 1 for low-speed operation. When taking in on the chain rode, I generally use the 14 to 1 ratio for speed, but when anchor rode comes up and down, I shift to the 40 to 1 ratio, trading the lower speed for less muscle requirement.

I would rather have a slow speed, high mechanical advantage for the manual backup on a powered windlass than the other way around. Inasmuch as the backup operation will, most likely, have only one speed, a mechanical advantage of about 25 to 1 is a sensible compromise.

Don't put your head in the sand when buying a powered windlass. Murphy's Law says that something will eventually fail, and you may be left with an inadequate manual mode which cannot handle your anchor and chain without the help of a deck ape.

ON CHOOSING AN ANCHORAGE

At some time or other every boat is going to anchor and it will be up to the skipper to have properly prepared the boat ahead of time and be able to follow through with alacrity. You must bear in mind that when you anchor your boat you will be in shallow water and near land—both of which constitute the maximum hazards to which you can expose your boat. To ensure the safety and comfort of the boat and crew while at anchor, the skipper (with help from the crew) should investigate a number of characteristics of the anchorage (Fig. 8-1).

Location

Choose your anchorage carefully and with the safety of your boat in mind. Start with a thorough examination of the physical features of the intended anchorage which can be done using charts, Sailing Directions, and local guidebooks. But remember that Sailing Directions were written for ships and may overlook many small harbors which make ideal havens for small boats. Look first for an area specifically set aside for anchoring small boats. Stay out of ship or quarantine anchorages unless that is why you are there. Special anchorages for small boats will be noted on charts and they

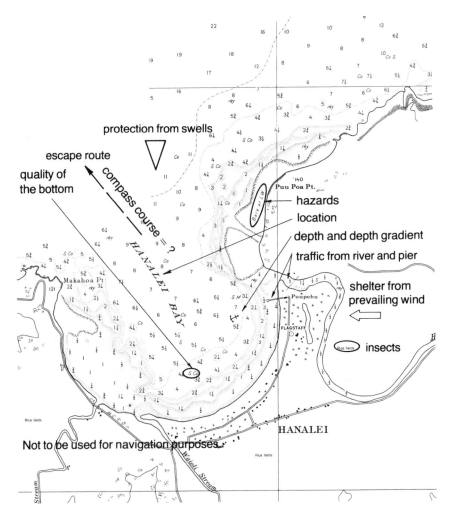

Fig. 8-1. Factors in choosing an anchorage.

are located to give shelter, provide convenience to shore facilities, and be out of the way of commercial traffic.

If there are no designated anchorages, look where other boats anchor, especially fishing boats. Fishermen will usually pick a well-sheltered and secure anchorage for overnighting or ducking a storm period. If other pleasure boats are anchored in a bight, try to determine if they really have found a secure anchorage or if the blind have been leading the blind. If the anchored boat is a local boat, in all probability the owner knows the area and there is some merit in the location he has chosen to drop his hook.

Shelter

Lacking local knowledge or printed advice, you must decide for yourself what constitutes a safe anchorage for your purpose. Start with an assessment of the shelter offered from both the wind and seas. It is usual practice to anchor in the lee of land to gain some protection from the prevailing wind but will that spot also offer protection from waves and breaking surf? I have anchored within many reef-fringed lagoons where the highest windbreak was a 75-foot-tall coconut tree and been perfectly happy for the holding ground was good and the reefs broke the swells.

On the other hand, I have anchored in the lee of mountainous terrain where the wind would howl down the canyons and cause violent sheering of the boat at anchor. My fears were not that the boat would drag across the bay onto a lee shore for there was none. Instead, a dragging anchor would blow the boat into the broad Pacific with no backstop for thousands of miles.

When you look at the protection offered, give some thought to the "What if's?" What if the wind shifts? Does it leave you close to a lee shore? Will it swing your boat into rocks or kelp? Or will it swing it into shallow water where you will ground, or deeper water where your anchor may slide off the bottom shelf if it drags? Your boat should never touch ground except in careening.

What if there is a change in current direction? Will your boat gradually swing with the current without upsetting the anchor? Or, will you ride right up over the anchor? Maybe you should consider the use of two anchors if the current change is severe.

Finally, a really good anchoring location is one that will allow you to shift your berth to another part of the anchorage should the wind change its direction.

Depth

If the geography of the area still looks good to you, what about the water depths? Charts will give you the surveyed depths but be certain that you know whether they are recorded in feet, fathoms, or meters. While checking the chart for scale, also check for the reference datum used. It may range from simple low water (LW) to mean lower low water (MLLW). Then check the Tide Tables for the tidal height at the time you are doing your anchoring.

I recall one Fourth of July cruise to Cat Harbor on Catalina Island

Beneath the placid surface of a tropical lagoon lie many coral heads. This was true inside the barrier reef surrounding the island of Pohnpei, but there were places where a boat could swing on one hook with safety.

when we owned a Cal-30 which drew 4½ feet of water. Most of the good anchorage areas had already been implanted with permanent moorings leaving only the very deep or very shallow areas for individual anchoring. The deep area was too near the entrance so we elected to slip inside the inner row of moorings. The lead line told us we had about 6 feet of water at the time and a quick calculation with the Tide Tables said the level would drop to 4½ feet about 0200. It was marginal but seemed safe enough since the bottom was mud. Sure enough, shortly after midnight I felt the keel softly scrape bottom but that was all. I went back to sleep satisfied with my brief calculation.

While you are scanning the chart for a suitable water depth, look also for steeply sloping bottom profiles that may allow you to set your anchor easily in one direction but which make it difficult to set in another direction (see Fig. 8-2). On a steeply sloping bottom, the determination of scope becomes a bit more troublesome. Technically, it should be measured at the depth of the anchor location, but you can see from the illustration that the effective scope can differ drastically from the measured scope.

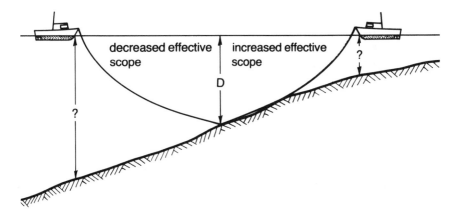

Fig. 8-2. Effective scope depends on the bottom profile.

Even though you have found an area of shallow water allowing you to use the proper scope of rode, there may still be problems. Shallow water found close to the beach can be attractive in saving a long dinghy row ashore. But it can also end up in breakers if the weather deteriorates or large swells arrive from far-off storms.

You do not even have to be close to the beach, itself, for the problem to develop. When the bottom shows a long shoal area to seaward, all of which is good anchoring depth, worry a little about what happens if there is a change in wind direction. Can the whole area become exposed so that wind waves pile up on the shoal and become breakers?

This happened to us on a cruise south from California along the coast of Baja California. We had anchored for the night in San Quintin Bay which is a large area of partially sheltered water from 20 to 30 feet deep. The winds were from the north and the bay calm. By morning the winds had switched to south-southeast, and we now faced a lee shore problem in addition to a large buildup in the waves over the shoal area. There was only one thing to do and that was to abandon the anchorage immediately even though we had not yet been ashore for a visit. We weighed anchor therefore and set off down the coast, thankful that a stronger wind had not developed during the night.

Quality of the Bottom

The quality of the bottom is very important to the success of anchoring, because it directly affects the ability of the anchor to dig in and hold. In most cases charts will tell you what you need to know about the quality of the bottom, whether it is sand, coral, pebbles, boulders, or what have you (see Nature of the Seabed in Chapter 7). What charts do not always tell you is whether the sand is soft and penetrable or whether the mud is loose and slippery with no holding power. That you will have to find out when you test your anchor's set.

In anchoring, you must match your anchor's capability in a particular bottom to the quality of the bottom actually present. If the bottom is weedy, you will want an old-fashioned or Northill anchor. If it is mud and sand, you will want a burying anchor. If it is rocky, you will want a hooking anchor. If it is smooth, unpacked sand, then most any anchor will work and you are home free. Obviously, few boats carry such a variety of anchors, so where you choose your anchorage depends to some extent on what kind of bottoms your anchor inventory can handle.

Hazards

When selecting your anchorage, look also for underwater hazards such as a pinnacle of rock, an unmarked wreck, or old tree stumps if yours is a flooded area. Look for coral heads that may stand out of an otherwise smooth bottom. If the waters are too murky to eyeball the bottom and the chart indicates possible trouble, look for another anchoring area. While you may get your hook down all right, you may never get it back.

A case in point—we had sailed *Horizon* from the Austral Islands south of Tahiti with an engine on the fritz and on-board repairs had proven futile. At the entrance to Papeete Harbor the winds were nil because the harbor is in the lee of high mountains. Without engine or wind we had no way of entering the harbor until a French sportfishing boat offered us a tow. We took the offer and, with our meager supply of French, conveyed to him that we would like to take up a position along the shoreline away from the busy harbor area. All went well and he dropped the tow where we thought was a good place to hang our hook until the engine could be brought back to life. It turned out to be a very good spot for several days of work during which we got the engine running again. But when we started to weigh anchor, it refused to come up. Three hours later with the help of a scuba diver, the anchor and chain were retrieved from an unmarked wreck that we had unknowingly selected as our berth.

Insects

These can make or break a good anchoring experience. If you anchor close to marshlands, expect mosquitos during the night. This is of particular consequence in malarial country where it is better to anchor a half mile offshore or at least upwind from the buzzing critters.

Flies can also be a nuisance around shorelines where animals graze or where there is an abundance of seaweed. Although they will not affect the security of your anchorage, insects can make life at anchor unpleasant enough to make you want to leave.

You may also find that shorebirds and their droppings can become obnoxious.

Traffic

Give some thought to the traffic patterns in the anchorage area, particularly commercial traffic. Equally as bad as the noise from these boats are the waves created by commercial vessels whose missions are not tempered with pity for the lazing boater. Avoid, if possible, anchoring near any fairway where commercial traffic plies, and be sure that if the wind changes, your swinging radius does not bring you into such a fairway. By all means don't anchor in an area where charts or signposts indicate a cable crossing.

Escape Route

If you have to leave your anchorage in a hurry for any reason, can you get out? At night? That is a most important factor to consider in your anchoring plans. It is not only insects that may drive you from an anchorage, but a buildup of adverse weather could force you to leave under the most trying of circumstances. There is a variation of Murphy's Law that states if something is going to happen, it is going to happen at the worst possible time. Be sure you choose an anchorage that you can leave against stiff winds and rising seas.

Prudence

Choose your anchorage with care and foresight. Be pessimistic. Consider all of the "what if's." It is better to shift your anchorge in the daylight than wait until after dark when the storm has risen and your mental capabilities have been dulled by a sound sleep. To be safely anchored, you have to know the area and have done a good job of setting your anchor. Anything short of that is to invite trouble and discomfort.

WHEN NOT TO ANCHOR

There can be times when it is more prudent not to anchor. My favorite example of this circumstance happened as hurricane Iwa was driving down on the Hawaiian Islands in 1982. *Phat Duck,* a Morgan 45, was returning from a three-year South Pacific cruise and intended to make landfall at Nawiliwili Harbor on Kauai's east shore. The skipper of *Phat Duck* had been plotting Iwa's position against his own and knew that he could make Nawiliwili before Iwa arrived but, and this is what separates good from bad seamanship, he reasoned that the protection offered by a harbor against the eye of a hurricane is poor at best. He chose to keep *Phat Duck* at sea and battened down the hatches in preparation for the blow.

Phat Duck survived the eye of the storm which registered 99 knots of wind, that being the top of the scale on its anemometer. All of the boats in Nawiliwili Harbor were either sunk, beached, or impaled on battered docks and pilings.

A more common reason not to anchor is simply that the anchorage is already overcrowded and adding one more boat only increases the congestion and reduces the chances of you and the neighboring boats having a pleasant weekend. In a crowded anchorage boats have been known to anchor on short scope to avoid fouling and thus get more boats into the anchorage. This is a common technique practiced at Ensenada, Mexico, after the finish of the Newport Beach, California, to Ensenada, Mexico, yacht race which annually sees more than 550 boats heading for "Tequila Town." Can you imagine a worse situation if the winds freshen and even one boat starts dragging? Good seamanship tells you never to anchor with less than adequate scope and plenty of swinging room.

I have been in many anchorages where bow and stern anchoring is a necessity because of adjacent rocks or reefs. We had such an anchorage off the village of Haka Maii in the Marquesas Islands. The enticements of the village warranted a stop in the rockbound anchorage, but we kept an eye on the weather and were ready to leave on short notice.

In the end it is the skipper who must make the decision to anchor or not to anchor. If there are any doubts about the security of the anchorage, don't use it.

ARM SIGNALS FOR ANCHORING

Nowhere in boating is the Captain Bligh syndrome more evident than when the skipper takes the foredeck to handle the anchor chores leaving his wife, children, or friends in the cockpit to handle the boat. The distance between foredeck and cockpit as well as engine noise causes the skipper's voice to become an unintelligible string of commands taking on a tone of blue as the boat fails to respond to his directions. The shade of blue deepens in proportion to the number of other boats present in the anchorage.

There is a solution to this all-too-common problem and that is clearer communications. Since sound won't do it, use visual signals. Such signals need not be complicated nor are many required to accomplish the purpose. Unlike communications between ships or ship to shore, there is no need for standardization except on your own boat.

The arm signals used on *Horizon* during her several Pacific voyages are illustrated in Fig. 8-3. The key to these signals is the use of arm motion which assures the helmsman that the foredeck crew members have not lost their powers of concentration because a bikini-clad sailor is on the next boat. The key uses extended arm movements to get away from momentary vision impairment by mast, dodger, or other obstructions. Hand motions by themselves are inadequate.

To be sure that the foredeck crew and helmsman understand each other's need for proper signals, it is good practice to have them exchange duties occasionally. Then they will have the proper appreciation for the other person's communication needs.

THE ANCHOR WATCH

The final step in your anchoring exercise is to determine the need for and the nature of an anchor watch. An anchor watch is a crew person who attends the boat when it is at anchor under particularly dangerous conditions and who sees to the safety of the boat while it is at anchor.

At one time, the anchor watch was posted when the ship was at a wharf with anchors stowed on deck, "lest some miscreants from ye other ships about steal ye anchors while the crewe sleepe."

Before posting the anchor watch, get a fix on the boat's anchored position, which is much like taking any other fix (Fig. 8-4). Take compass bearings on two objects ashore, preferably 90° apart, one in line with the bow and one athwartship or as close as they can be selected. Draw the lines of position on your harbor chart for the crew to see. Lie back for half an hour or so and determine whether these angles are changing. If they do not change, you are assuredly set for the time being. If they do change, determine if the change is due to the boat swinging, tidal height changes, a slackening or a freshening wind. If the boat is really dragging its anchor, then take appropriate action.

The anchor watch should periodically check the lines of position previously determined; inspect the anchor gear for wear and secure hitches; keep a wary eye on other boats in the anchorage; and also keep track of the weather, especially wind direction changes. It is essential to employ an anchor watch when the winds exceed 30 knots or the weather

The Complete Book of Anchoring and Mooring

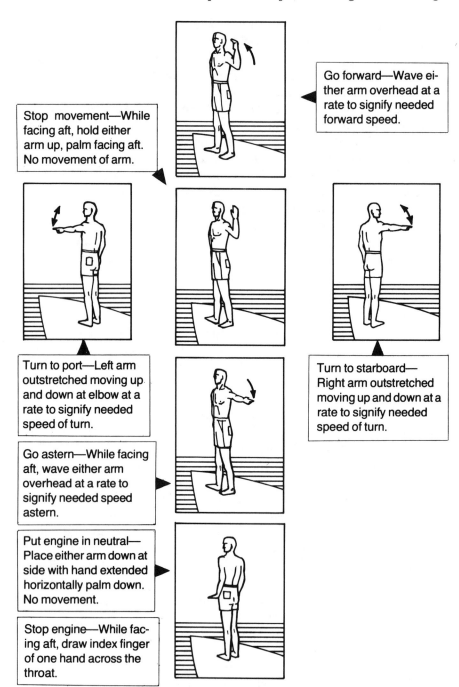

Go forward—Wave either arm overhead at a rate to signify needed forward speed.

Stop movement—While facing aft, hold either arm up, palm facing aft. No movement of arm.

Turn to port—Left arm outstretched moving up and down at elbow at a rate to signify needed speed of turn.

Turn to starboard—Right arm outstretched moving up and down at a rate to signify needed speed of turn.

Go astern—While facing aft, wave either arm overhead at a rate to signify needed speed astern.

Put engine in neutral—Place either arm down at side with hand extended horizontally palm down. No movement.

Stop engine—While facing aft, draw index finger of one hand across the throat.

Fig. 8-3. Foredeck arm signals for anchoring.

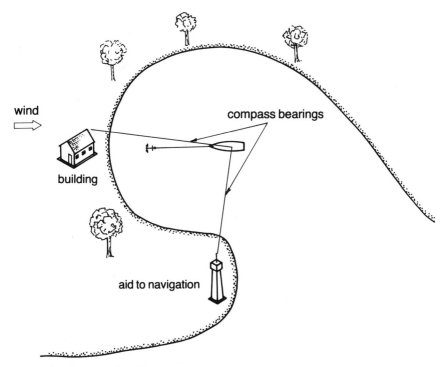

Fig. 8-4. Anchor lines of position.

becomes threatening. We have stood anchor watches on *Horizon* in what are normally secure harbors, atoll lagoons, bights of land that we didn't want to leave, and open roadsteads. It gives real peace of mind to stand by your vessel when the weather deteriorates, knowing that she will stand by you when the chips are down.

There are times when the conditions of anchoring suggest that dragging may be an imminent possibility as, for instance, in a poor bottom with an expected wind buildup. Then it is nice to have a drag-alarm system in place which will supplement your visual bearings. It can take the form of a drift lead, which is a heavy lead lowered to the bottom with a small amount (about one boat-length) of slack in its line. Any significant movement of the vessel will cause the line to tauten. The drift lead should be placed near the bow of the boat to minimize the effect of the boat sheering at anchor.

To avoid having to watch the lead line continuously, tie it to a pan set high on the cabin top which will come tumbling down with much racket should the slack be removed from the lead line. A more sophisticated alarm system connects the lead line to a switch which throws electric power to a bell when the lead is pulled off the bottom. These schemes work well at night when your visual ranges are darkened. One single-hander I read about tied the lead line to his toe, so that it awakened him directly when the boat moved beyond its allotted distance.

Besides a drag alarm, you may want to consider a wind strength alarm which tells you when the wind exceeds a predetermined force (Fig. 8-5). The boat rides to its anchor through the light bypass section of rode until the wind increases in force and breaks the bypass rode. The boat will fall back a distance equal to the slack in the primary rode where it comes up short with a light jolt on the boat. Then you know it is time to tend your anchor.

Anchorages should not be thought of as infallible protectors of the anchored boat. Before you tuck in for the night, make an inspection of the ground tackle, the anchorage layout, and, most important, your escape

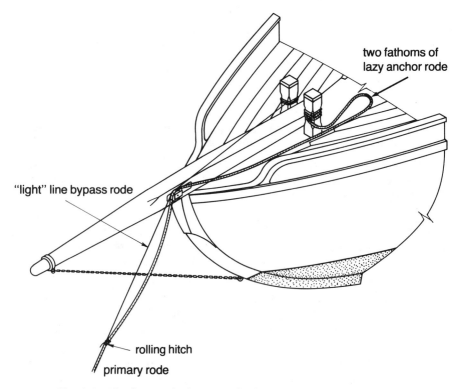

Fig. 8-5. Rigging a wind-strength alarm.

route. If your escape route is a simple direct run to the open ocean, record on a piece of paper at the compass the proper compass course. If the course is involved with a dog leg or two, plot it on your harbor chart with all the dead reckoning information such as compass courses, speeds, and time to run, etc. Then make certain that your foredeck is clear and ready to weigh anchor. As in all boating, a neat boat is a safe boat.

Finally, give some thought to what you will do if the weather deteriorates. Consider the alternatives—(1) stay put where you are and increase the holding power of your anchor system; (2) move to a better berth within the harbor; (3) if you are a sailboat—put out to sea and heave to on an offshore starboard tack while waiting for the weather to improve; or (4) make a run for a nearby harbor or a better known shelter. Whatever your plan of action, prepare the boat for it ahead of time. Have your decks clear and the dinghy ready to take aboard. Tie in the necessary reef in your mainsail. Don't let your crew wander too far away from the vessel. Instruct them on what procedures will be followed should the weather deteriorate. Then sit back, splice the main brace, and hope that the weather remains quiescent.

CREW SAFETY IN ANCHORING

Of all activities that take place in boating short of working in a boatyard, anchoring has to have the greatest potential for human danger. Lifting anchors and chain can be damaging to the back; catching your finger in the windlass wildcat can result in severe damage to the digit; standing with your leg inside the anchor rode coil can sweep you off the deck as the rode pays out rapidly; and grasping a wildly running rode with your hands will certainly cause a severe rope burn.

Anchors are heavy, unwieldy, and awkward, and the simple act of stowing the anchor can result in pinched fingers or worse. I cannot emphasize too strongly the need for caution when handling any portion of your ground tackle. Wear gloves and shoes (not sandals) to protect yourself while working with ground tackle, and your happy hour need not be a first aid class.

One of the biggest mistakes made by boaters in anchoring is to deploy the chain or rope anchor rode manually under the assumption that there is little load on it. That should never be done. If you don't have a windlass to control the rode mechanically, at least take a hitch around the Samson post or a husky cleat. The boat snubbing up hard against the anchor in a solid set could be damaging to your hands.

Even the best sailors occasionally are overtaken by a moment of carelessness and pay the price. Eric Hiscock, the dean of small boat sailors, paid the price off the coast of Baja California when he attempted to free a chain jammed in a too small navel pipe. While in the act of freeing it by hand, the chain jumped a couple of notches in the wildcat carrying the thumb of his hand between chain and wildcat, crushing it badly.*

Alain Colas, one of France's and the world's greatest single-handed sailors, suffered serious leg damage when a loop of anchor rode snatched up tight around his leg. He was hospitalized and out of sailing for nearly a year while it healed. If it can happen to those who are experienced, the weekend sailor has to be extra careful.

Weekend sailors on tight schedules are particularly vulnerable to taking shortcuts in boat handling which may endanger their well-being. I served as an expert witness in a legal case involving a ground tackle system. In this instance, the foredeck crewman was hauling in the combination rode with an electric capstan. After the chain had reached the warping drum, he continued to haul in on the rode with the chain now wrapped around the warping drum. An unexpected movement of the boat brought the rode up taut and, in his attempt to prevent the rode from running back out, he grasped it firmly; as a result, his hands were drawn into the capstan and he lost several fingers.

---

*Eric Hiscock, *Southwest in Wanderer IV* (London: Oxford University Press, 1973).

CHAPTER NINE

Technique of Anchoring

The science of anchoring is the proper selection of ground tackle and the study of available information on the anchorage. The rest of anchoring is an art learned by repeated practice under a variety of conditions. One never becomes an expert in anchoring—only more proficient as the years go by. Each anchoring exercise is a new experience confounded by the unknowns of the seabed, the vagaries of wind and current, and a new set of neighbors who have rearranged the anchorage. Even the most proficient seamen will, on occasion, be thwarted by a weedy bottom, debris, or a rocky outcropping. There is no panacea for anchoring problems, but the following procedures can help assure a satisfactory anchoring exercise.

A perfect anchorage in the summer months—Hanalei Bay on the island of Kauai, Hawaii.

PREPARING TO ANCHOR

Having selected your berth, get the ground tackle ready to go. If your anchor is stowed on a bow roller with the rode attached, lower it over the roller until it is just clear of the water. Your windlass should be clear with the operating handle in place and tied to the bow pulpit with a safety line.

If your anchor is stowed separately, bring it to the foredeck. Lead the unattached rode through the chock or fairlead and under the pulpit and then over the top of the pulpit (Fig. 9-1). Bend the rode to the anchor and safety wire each and every shackle pin. Hang the anchor over the bow, being careful not to bang up the topsides. The rode can then be short snubbed to a cleat or the Samson post while the final boat maneuvering takes place. Single-handers will often lead the rode in a loop back to the cockpit where they can belay it until time to let go.

Rodes that are stowed in chain lockers will usually come out freely, but not always. For example, crossed links in your chain can jam at the navel pipe entrance or a rope can develop a kink at this point. Chain, which normally piles up in a conical heap in the locker, can tip over in a rough sea and pin itself down by its own weight. This happened to us on a return passage from New Zealand.

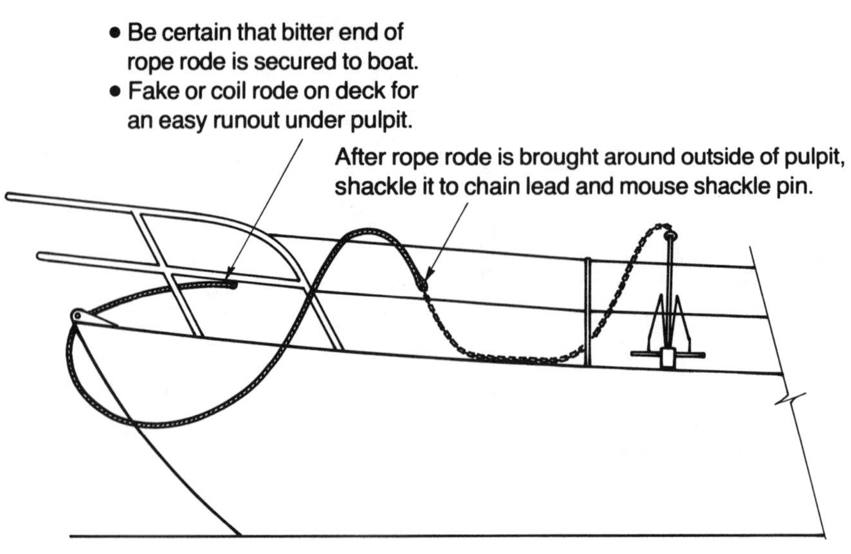

- Be certain that bitter end of rope rode is secured to boat.
- Fake or coil rode on deck for an easy runout under pulpit.

After rope rode is brought around outside of pulpit, shackle it to chain lead and mouse shackle pin.

Fig. 9-1. Preparing anchor and rode for deploying.

Just before reaching San Francisco, *Horizon* was knocked down on her beam ends in a gale. Inspection showed no major damage to the boat, but I had failed to look into the chain locker. The next time the boat was anchored was at Catalina Island where my son had taken friends for a week of scuba diving. *Horizon* was maneuvered into a tight anchorage, and the anchor let go. A few feet ran out before it snubbed up. A quick inspection revealed that the chain pile had tipped over on itself pinning the running chain in place. It was necessary to retrieve the anchor and maneuver the boat into clear water where time could be taken to clear the chain locker. Had this happened in a bad wind and sea condition, it could have been a greater problem.

The easiest way to prevent capsizing of the chain pile in the chain locker when weighing anchor is to have a crew person down below faking the chain down as it comes through the navel pipe. At least an inspection should be made of the chain pile before the next anchoring exercise is undertaken.

If you have any suspicions that the seabed may be covered with debris, abandoned cable or chain, or rocks that could entrap your anchor, you may want to consider putting a trip line on your anchor before letting go (Fig. 9-2). The simplest way is to bend the trip line to the crown of the anchor and put a marker buoy at the other end. It is very easy to affix trip lines to anchors with trip line eyes such as the CQR and Bruce. Others, such as the old-fashioned and Danforth, call for the trip line to be bent

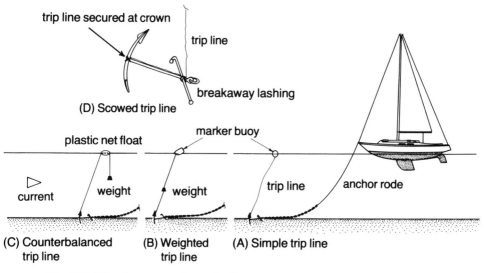

Fig. 9-2. Rigging an anchor trip line.

around the crown directly. This makes the trip line susceptible to abrasion on a rocky bottom and suggests the use of a short wire cable or chain shackled to the crown in a manner that will not interfere with the functioning of the anchor. Braided polyester rope makes the best trip line because it does not stretch and is quite abrasion resistant.

At low tide a trip line can become a menace to your boat or boats passing close aboard because of the loosely floating line. One solution is to put a sinker on the line (B) to hold it vertical. A better way is to use a counterbalance (C) to keep a moderate tension on the trip line independent of tidal changes. It is strongly suggested that you do not use a marker buoy that has any resemblance to mooring buoys.

There is a way to eliminate the marker buoy altogether and that is to run the trip line up the anchor rode, securing it in a few places with breakaway lashings. When you need to trip the anchor, strong tugs on the trip line will break the lashings and you will be able to retrieve the anchor, crown first, just as if you had used a marker buoy.

Old-fashioned and Northill anchors are very susceptible to fouling of the lazy arm by a slack trip line. This can be avoided by "scowing" the trip line to the shank of the anchor near the ring (D). The lashing should be light twine that will break easily when a firm tug is applied to the trip line.

Scowing the anchor rode itself is another way to prepare an anchor for use in a seabed that you suspect may foul your anchor. It is an old scheme used with the old-fashioned anchor but it can be used with any anchor. This technique (Fig. 9-3) calls for the anchor rode to be made fast to the crown of the anchor and the rode brought up alongside the shank past the ring but not through it. The rode is secured to the ring with a firm lashing which may even be light wire. The lashing, however, should not be stronger than about 20 percent of the rode's breaking strength.

Under normal conditions of anchorage, being held close against the shank by the tight lashings, the rode pulls as if it were secured directly at the ring of the anchor. Should your scowed anchor become fouled, you bring the boat to short stay and then heave away on the rode using bow buoyancy rather than back muscles. The lashing will break and then you can withdraw the anchor backwards from its snag using the rode as a trip line.

You should not depend on scowing, however, if the boat is being allowed to swing at anchor. A sideways pull could break the lashing, and the rode would then automatically upset the anchor. A scowed anchor is used for temporary anchoring where the reason is so overwhelming that an immediate search for a better seabed has to be delayed.

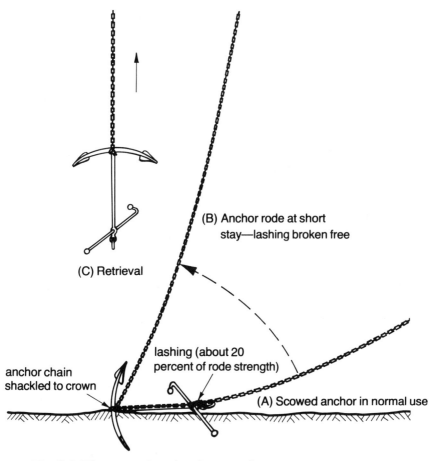

(B) Anchor rode at short
stay—lashing broken free

(C) Retrieval

lashing (about 20
percent of rode strength)

anchor chain
shackled to crown

(A) Scowed anchor in normal use

Fig. 9-3. The scowed anchor in operation.

LETTING GO THE ANCHOR

With the anchor hanging over the bow at ready, the foredeck crew will direct the skipper into the planned berth. The approach must account for wind and current, generally heading into the stronger element and crabbing into the other.

Proceed slowly into the anchorage until you arrive at your planned berth, then stop all way and either drift backwards or back down slowly. Let go the anchor in a controlled fashion, noting the depth marks as they pass over the bow. The trip line and its float are simultaneously cast over the side, clear of the anchor rode.

The foredeck crew signals when the anchor has reached bottom, and the boat is allowed to continue moving aft for a distance giving out a 3 to 1 scope. That is the earliest that any attempt should be made to snub up on the anchor for an initial set. You must remember that anchors, especially lightweight models, must be coaxed into the bottom. Do not use abrupt snubbing. Instead, gently tauten the rode until an initial set is obtained.

All anchors must drag a short distance to set themselves and that must be taken into account when positioning your boat in an anchorage. Little data exists on how far anchors actually drag before setting. French tests in 1992 (Table 6-1) indicate that boat anchors may drag as little as 16 feet or as much as 200 feet when setting efficiently in a sand seabed. It would be expected that anchors would drag significantly greater distances in mud seabeds. If you have anchored in light winds and later the winds become stronger, you can expect your anchor to drag as it sets further into the seabed. It is important to remember this and provide a sufficient margin of room from other boats or obstructions to leeward.

Assuming that your anchor has set, veer whatever remaining scope you need—4 to 1 for an all-chain rode and 7 to 1 for combination rodes. With the boat settled back head to wind on the anchor, belay the rode and finish the set with the engine. First back down at idle speed, add 200 rpm, then another 200 rpm until you are satisfied that the anchor is firmly set. The maximum power to be applied in reverse is about one-half throttle on sailing auxiliaries and no more than one-quarter throttle on powerboats.

When you are satisfied that the anchor is truly embedded in the bottom, then you can apply a technique known as power setting to assure the ultimate set. Possible wind loads on a boat which the ground tackle must counter can be estimated according to the methods of Chapter Two. These wind loads can then be simulated by propeller thrust, at least up to the capability of the installed powerplant.

Tests have shown that propellers can develop static thrust approximately as follows:

Hull type	Pounds of static thrust per horsepower
Displacement hulls	20
Semi-displacement hulls	15
Planing hulls	10

Thus, a 50 HP auxiliary engine in a sailboat can develop approximately 1,000 pounds of static thrust which equates to a 30 knot wind acting on a 37-foot sailboat. Twin 200 HP engines in a planing hull can develop as much as 4,000 pounds thrust equating to a wind load on a 60-foot boat in 42 knots of wind.

The anchorage at Kolonia, Pohnpei, where a loose mud bottom places great dependence on the holding power of a long chain rode in addition to the anchor.

Sailboats faced with storm conditions at anchor may want to seek the services of a powerboat to help them powerset their anchors before the winds arrive. It is to the advantage of everyone in an anchorage to powerset their anchors before the wind arrives. One boat insecurely anchored in a crowded anchorage can wipe out many other boats once its anchor begins to drag.

When anchoring in slippery mud or soft clay, don't try to set the anchor on short scope. Instead, lay out a 10 to 1 scope, and let the anchor and rode settle into the bottom. It may take hours or even days for the anchor to settle far enough down to get a bite in a hard bottom layer. Some soft bottoms have no hard strata at all, and your anchorage is chancy at best. Such is the small boat anchorage at Kolonia, Pohnpei, in the eastern Caroline islands. There the practice is to lay out 175 feet of rode (in 15 feet of water!) and then let the boat sit, hoping that the friction of anchor and rode in the mud will give it some holding power. Boats in this harbor have found that under gale conditions they have to run their engines to hold position.

To determine whether an anchor is holding or not, feel the rode with your hand or a bare foot while backing into the set. If it feels soft or slack, there is no set. If it is taut, but you feel irregular vibrations, the anchor is dragging. If no erratic vibrations are present, the anchor has taken hold. At this point you can finish your "power set" and then shut down the engine.

The anchor, however, has not finished its own setting, which takes place over a period of time. As the boat horses about its anchor, the alternate tugging and slackening of the rode will cause the anchor to wiggle its way farther into the bottom for a better grip, not unlike a little boy wiggling his feet into wet sand at the beach.

An anchor is not guaranteed to set simply because you have deployed it from your boat. There are many reasons why an anchor will not set and some of them are shown in Fig. 9-4. Unless the water is extremely clear and not too deep, you will not be able to see the anchor and ascertain its setting problem. In that case you will have to deduce why your anchor is not setting. Table 9-1 suggests some solutions to anchor-setting problems.

If you are having a continuing problem in setting your anchor, maneuver your boat out of the immediate area and make another ap-

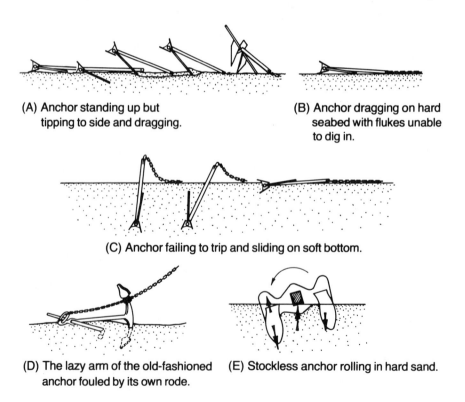

(A) Anchor standing up but tipping to side and dragging.

(B) Anchor dragging on hard seabed with flukes unable to dig in.

(C) Anchor failing to trip and sliding on soft bottom.

(D) The lazy arm of the old-fashioned anchor fouled by its own rode.

(E) Stockless anchor rolling in hard sand.

Fig. 9-4. Anchor antics in setting.

Table 9-1. Solving Anchor Set Problems

Symptom	Possible reason	Possible solution
Low constant drag load on anchor rode	Flukes not tripping	Try resetting anchor more carefully
"	Flukes fouled	Weigh and inspect anchor
"	Weeds	Change to hooking anchor
	Slippery mud seabed	{ Use larger or better burying anchor / Reset allowing anchor to settle for a longer time }
Sudden drop in drag load during setting	Anchor has rolled out of its set	Use more stable anchor—reset and snub up more gently
Erratic vibrations on anchor rode during setting	Anchor skipping across bottom	Change to hooking-type anchor
Steady high load on anchor rode but boat moves aft under high reverse propeller thrust	Inadequate anchor size for seabed	Use larger anchor—tandem anchors
Boat moves gradually aft after a good anchor set	Anchor loosening due to oscillating boat loads	Change type of anchor—Add a kellet (see Fig. 9-7)
"	Increasing wind	Set larger anchor, tandem anchors, or dual anchor systems
Boat moves aft quickly after a good set	Failure of ground tackle system	Re-anchor—replace failed components
"	Unreliable seabed	Seek new anchoring berth

proach with everything ready once again. If your anchor fails to bite a second time, you probably should consider a change in anchor or anchoring berth.

When the anchor is set and the engine shut down, it is time to clean up the foredeck. First belay the anchor rode permanently to the Samson post, bitt, or mooring cleat using the proper hitch. Put the excess rode back down the deck pipe or in the basket, or leave it neatly coiled up and secured to some permanent piece of foredeck equipment. Make a mental note of the amount of rode already paid out from the stem of the boat. Check to make sure that your trip line buoy is riding high with just enough slack to allow it to rise to the high water mark without putting a buoyant load on the anchor.

Your anchor chain should be stopped off with a chain riding stopper. Never let the anchor load lie to the windlass once your anchor is set. Excess chain should be run back down the deck pipe and the pipe capped.

Boats will tend to sheer back and forth (horsing) while at anchor, sometimes sweeping an arc of as much as ±30°, putting unnecessary loads on the anchor. This can be minimized by raising a riding sail aft. Ketches and yawls can use their mizzen sails with flattening reefs in them. Cutters, sloops, and schooners can set a small sail (try a storm head sail) on the backstay to accomplish the same goal. Powerboats with masts can also set a riding sail. A trick to use if you are anchored in a current is to apply full left or right rudder which will tend to hold the boat a bit across the stream and steady out the horsing.

If you are in water of swimming temperature, don your mask and snorkle and swim out over the anchor. Have a good look at it to satisfy yourself that it is, indeed, set and that there are no hazards like wrecks or coral heads within the swinging radius of your boat. If the water is too cold for swimming, use an underwater viewer and a dinghy. There is confidence to be had by seeing firsthand that all is in order with your anchor and rode.

CATAMARAN ANCHOR RODE ATTACHMENT

The catamaran poses a unique problem in anchoring because the twin hulls do not always provide a central location from which to lead the anchor rode. For light winds it is adequate to belay the anchor rode to a bitt or cleat near the stem of one hull and allow the boat to ride at an angle to the wind. Alternately, the rode can be belayed to a quarter cleat allowing the boat to ride stern to the wind for better ventilation.

For heavy winds, though, a catamaran must have a centerline rode attachment as far forward as the hull stems themselves. Catamarans with structural cross members at the hull stems can add a bow roller to the center of the strut and solve the anchor rode lead problem just as in a trimaran or a monohull. But the cross member must be able to take the vertical loading of the anchor rode (F_v in Fig. 3-1) when the boat pitches up over a wave.

Catamarans without structural cross members must resort to other ways of providing an equivalent centerline stemhead anchor rode attachment. One way is to use a snatch block on a pendant (Fig. 9-5). Although easy to do, it results in high inward loadings on the hulls. A better way is to set the anchor off of one hull and then bend a trimming line to it from the other hull. Adjust the rode-trimming lines to yield a 30° or smaller angle to keep the stem side loading less than one-quarter of the anchor rode load. Make the trimming line long enough so that if additional scope is desired, it can be run out at the same time the anchor rode is veered. Snatch blocks must be employed at the hull stems to minimize stretching wear on the rode and trimming lines.

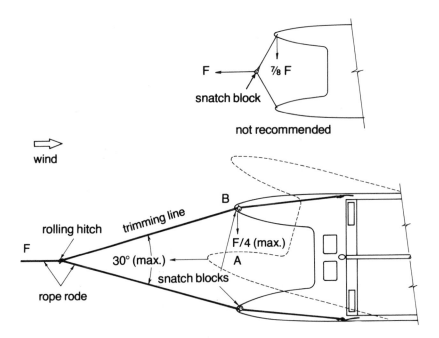

(A) Single hull rode attachment for light winds and small seas.
(B) Symmetrically bridled rode for stronger winds and higher seas.

Fig. 9-5. Anchor rode attachment for catamarans.

ANCHORING WITH OTHER BOATS

With your heart set on spending a night at a particular anchorage, you may have to shoehorn yourself in if you arrive after all of the best spots are taken. Sometimes you may find an opening in the midst of a group of boats that has been overlooked by everyone else and is yours for the taking. The problem is how to get into the spot safely and set a good anchor.

The first step is to proceed slowly through the anchorage, observing as you go how the other boats are lying. Note whether they are hanging on one anchor or two. You will want to do the same. Note the types of boats and their sizes to determine whether you will swing with wind and current in the same way they do. Assess the amount of scope they are using, ask them, while passing by, and note whether it is rope or chain.

When you get to your berth, slow down and estimate the room you have and what your swinging radius would be with reasonable scope. Note that boats can have overlapping swinging circles if they have similar characteristics and are anchored with the same scope (Fig. 9-6).

If your space is too small for adequate scope on a rope rode, put a kellet on it to give a shorter scope (Fig. 9-7). It is interesting to note that a 4 to 1 scope uses only one-third of the swinging room of a 7 to 1 scope.

In principle a whole fleet of boats could be anchored in the overlapping grid pattern. But in practice, it never works out quite that way because of differences in boat behaviors, ground tackle, anchoring techniques, and seabed variations.

The one natural phenomenon that gives you trouble with overlapping swinging circles is current. You will generally find it in rivers and estuaries but you can also find it in bights of land along ocean shorelines. Ocean currents running along the shoreline simply follow the inward-curving shoreline into the bight which may be your favorite anchorage.

Boats behave in different ways under the influence of wind and current. Keelboats will swing with the current (tide rode) whereas powerboats and multihulls tend to weathercock into the wind (wind rode). In an anchorage of mixed craft, the potential exists for anchored collisions (Fig. 9-8). The only solution to this is for everyone to lay out stern anchors or for the offending boat to leave. In the latter case, anchoring etiquette prevails: "He who anchors last, leaves first."

MOORING WITH ANCHORS

When a boat sets two anchors, it is said to be moored. The anchors may both be off the bow, or they may be fore and aft with the boat about midway between them (Fig. 9-9).

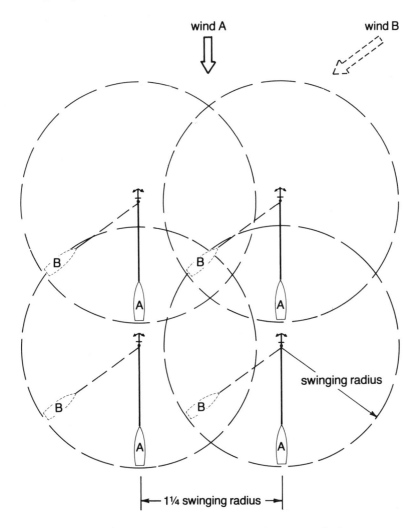

Fig. 9-6. Overlapping swinging circles with steady wind.

There are several reasons why a skipper would want to moor rather than simply to anchor. One is to reduce the size of the swinging circle so that more boats can be anchored in the same area. Another allows the boat to be moored in a narrow channel or close to a land mass. A third allows the boat to ride out a severe storm where excessive sheering or horsing of the boat may take place when riding to only one anchor.

Moorings are advisable when anchoring in a tidal river. In this instance, the boat on a single anchor would first ride in one direction and

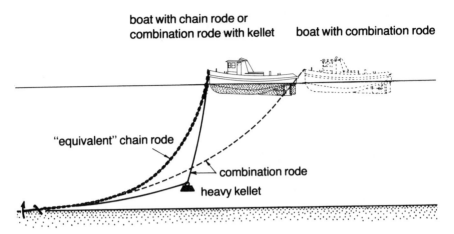

Fig. 9-7. Shortening scope on a combination rode. (See Fig. 10-1 for kellet rigging.)

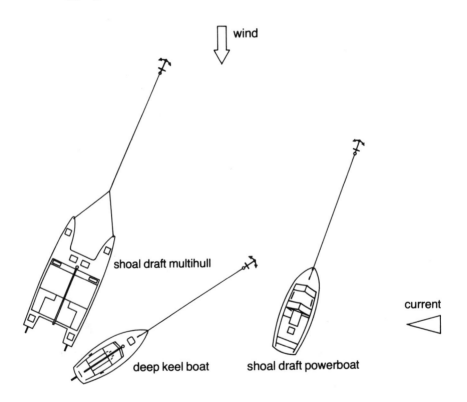

Fig. 9-8. Anchored boats lying to wind and current.

then turn with the tide to ride in the other direction. In the reversal, the boat ranges aimlessly for a period and could perhaps trip on its own anchor. Or, the anchor could break out with a 180° reversal in load direction.

It is not hard to visualize other examples for mooring instead of anchoring. If the bottom is a marginal holding ground or the shelter is limited, a second anchor can add substantially to the security of the boat. Or, if the owner is to leave the boat unattended for a period of time, two anchors would certainly be good insurance against bad weather as well as the simple failure of one of the anchor systems.

Unlike permanent moorings, all of the ground tackle for mooring with anchors is carried as part of the normal complement of the boat. This is another reason for carrying several sets of anchors and rodes.

Hammerlock Moor

This moor (Fig. 9-9 A) is designed to reduce the sheering motion of a boat in strong, gusty winds. In this situation neither a riding sail nor the use of the rudder can be expected to have much effect in steadying the boat while excessive loads are being put on the ground tackle and the anchor's set is severely tested. This sheering, tacking back and forth, is called "horsing" (Fig. 9-10 A). Much of the violent motion that occurs during horsing can be eliminated through the use of a second anchor which is dropped underfoot on short scope, putting a "hammerlock" on the horsing. This snubbing anchor will reduce the yawing considerably, resulting in less strain on the ground tackle. Fig. 9-10 B illustrates the hammerlock moor in action.

If the storm develops increased violence, you may want to consider raising the second anchor and redropping it at the limit of sheer but still on a short scope. You will now have a bridle to the bow which will minimize most of the undesirable horsing action of the boat. The main wind load will still be taken by the bow anchor. Should there be a significant change in wind direction, the snubbing anchor will, most likely, drag into a new position but will still tend to its job of controlling horsing. This is one of the few instances where a dragging anchor is part of your anchor plan. When an anchor is permitted to drag, it is called drudging.

Another use of the hammerlock moor prevents your boat from swinging into a hazard should the wind change and you do not have a complete swinging circle available.

In using the hammerlock moor, it should be clearly understood that the bow anchor takes the wind loads and the snubbing anchor prevents unwanted yawing of the boat. For this reason the snubbing anchor can be

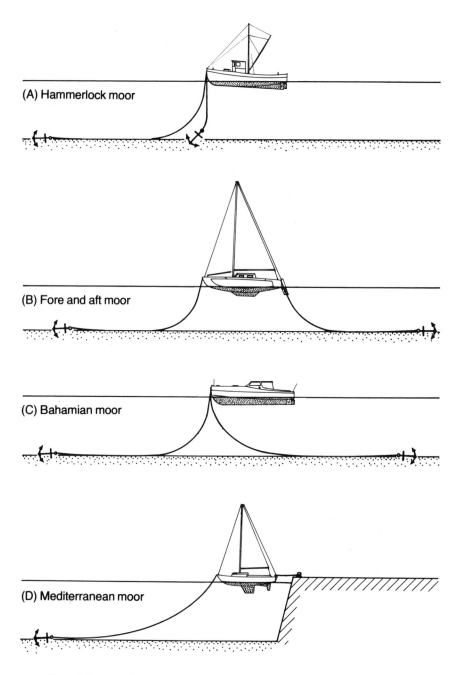

Fig. 9-9. Popular mooring concepts.

a smaller anchor, but it must be one that can set itself in the type of bottom you have since there will be no time to set it leisurely as you did with your bow anchor.

Fore and Aft Moor

When you wish to anchor in constricted waters where the wind and current are reasonably steady, you can use the fore and aft moor (Fig. 9-9 B). The bow anchor is set in a normal fashion, and then a stern anchor is set which prevents the boat from swinging sideways into other boats or into a hazard. It is not a good moor if there is a significant crosswind or crosscurrent because both elements meeting the boat broadside produce high loads on the ground tackle. One knot of crosscurrent or 15 knots of crosswind should be the maximum allowed for this type of mooring.

Laying the fore and aft moor can be done in the ordinary dropping moor (Fig. 9-11) or the flying moor (Fig. 9-12). The important factor in both moors is to pick your mooring slot carefully and fix in mind, using local reference marks, where you will place the bow and stern anchors so that the boat ends up in the proper position, C. Also, fully prepare both anchors ahead of time and be certain the crew knows the signals for letting

Moored fore and aft, the author's boat rides peacefully at Haka Maii, Marquesas Islands, between a rock reef to starboard and rocky cliffs to port.

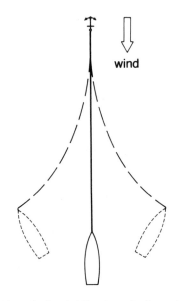

(A) Horsing of a boat riding to a single anchor

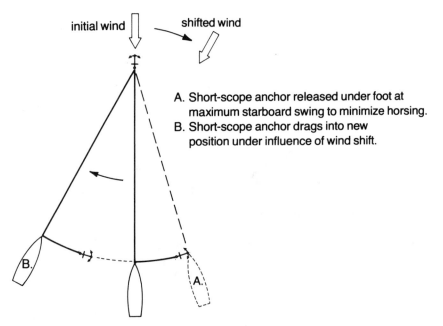

A. Short-scope anchor released under foot at maximum starboard swing to minimize horsing.
B. Short-scope anchor drags into new position under influence of wind shift.

(B) Use of a short-scope anchor to dampen horsing

Fig. 9-10. Hammerlock moor in action.

go and snubbing up. If you fail to set the anchors at the proper spots (A and B), you can end up with too little scope for them to be effective. In this moor the bow anchor is the larger anchor.

The flying moor calls for better coordination of the crew, but may be easier to do if your boat is one of those that does not back straight down no matter what you do. It is usually a more positive manner of anchoring in a narrow slot if you recognize the fact that any stern drag (from anchor and rode) can adversely affect your ability to control the boat while running ahead.

Sometimes you will have set a normal bow anchor in an uncrowded anchorage only to have late arrivals cut into your boat's swinging circle. When that happens, you have two options—remind the new arrivals of your status and that they should seek another anchoring location, or proceed quietly to lay out a stern anchor and ask your neighbors to do the same. Fore and aft moorings use anchorage space more efficiently allowing more boats into the anchorage.

There is an inherent hazard in setting a stern anchor, and that is inadvertently entangling a slack anchor rode with the rudder or propel-

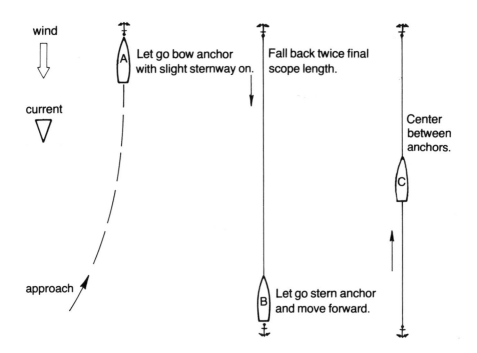

Fig. 9-11. The dropping fore and aft moor.

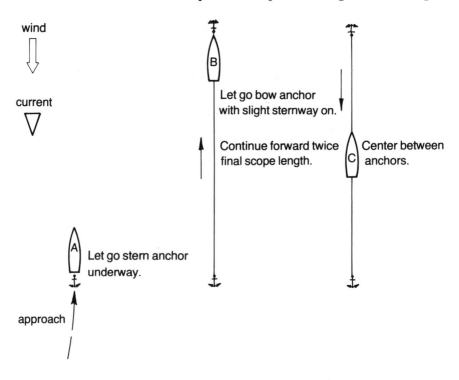

wind

current

Let go bow anchor
with slight sternway on.

Continue forward twice   Center between
final scope length.   anchors.

Let go stern anchor
underway.

approach

Fig. 9-12. The flying fore and aft moor.

ler. Where the tidal range is not great, the tension on the stern anchor can
be set initially and left alone. However, where the tidal range is great, the
stern anchor rode must be tended with each change of the tide.

Most of the boats caught in the Cabo San Lucas disaster (Chapter 12)
had employed a stern anchor shoreward to keep them from swinging into
their neighbors with normal changes in wind and current. But when the
gale winds hit and bow anchors started to drag, stern anchor rodes went
slack and got caught up in propellers as engines were started to take some
of the load off the dragging bow anchor. That was a significant factor in
the high losses sustained by the anchored boats.

The fore and aft moor can be used in rivers with significant currents
and with crosswinds blowing by running a slip line ashore (Fig. 9-13). In
this case you most likely would want to use the flying moor approach for
better control in the crosswind. The slip line can be taken ashore in your
dinghy or swum ashore if the current permits.

Boats that are lucky enough to be able to sail in the tropics will find
that many shorelines are steep and bordered with a fringing coral reef

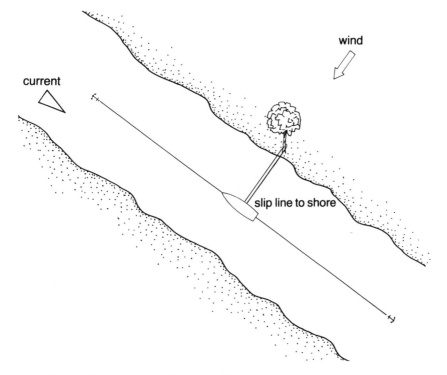

Fig. 9-13. Fore and aft moor with a crosswind.

that makes anchoring very difficult (Fig. 9-14). To solve this problem make a flying fore and aft moor, but don't take the flying part too seriously as you approach the reef. Let go the stern anchor in deep water and snub it up so that you know it has set. Have someone take the bow anchor ashore where it will be set by hand in the sand.

Your selection of anchors for the shore mooring is different than that for a straight fore and aft moor. Put your working anchor on the stern rode so that you will have good holding power to keep you off the reef. The bow anchor system will then use the lighter stern anchor or even a separate kedge anchor. Whatever combination you use, be ready to slip the bow anchor if the weather deteriorates. Don't hesitate to sacrifice a small anchor to save the boat.

Bahamian Moor

When a vessel must anchor in waters characterized by a strong reversing current, it is essential to set two anchors—one up current (the riding anchor) and one down current (the lee anchor) (Fig. 9-9 C). In this

manner when the current reverses itself, the original riding anchor becomes the lee anchor and the original lee anchor, the riding anchor.
Nominally, both anchors should be of the same size although in some
rivers and channels there is a dissimilarity in ebb and flood strengths. If
your boat is outfitted with a storm and a working anchor, it would be
natural to make the larger anchor the riding anchor for the stronger
current direction. The Bahamian moor is also known as the ordinary
moor for large vessels.

Besides providing a secure riding anchor for either current direction, the Bahamian moor also restricts the size of the swinging circle of
your boat (Fig. 9-15). With only current and no wind, your boat would
assume either positions A or B and have a nominal swinging circle. If
there is a crosswind blowing, however, a substantial side load could be

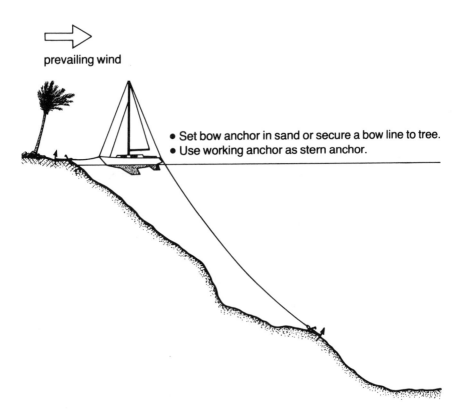

Fig. 9-14. An atoll mooring.

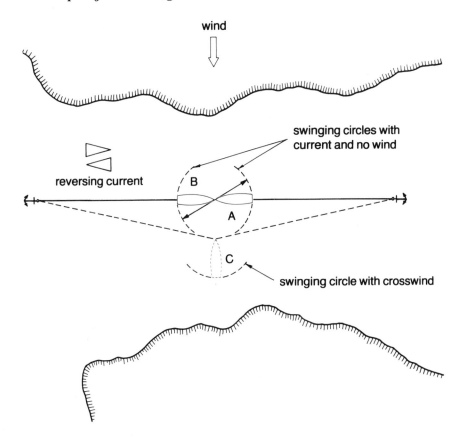

Fig. 9-15. Swinging circles to the Bahamian moor.

created, causing both anchors to take up crosswind loads for which the mooring is not intended.

The Bahamian moor can be laid using either the "dropping" or "flying" moor. When both anchors are set, the stern (lee) rode is brought forward and secured at the bow (Fig. 9-16).

Two problems can possibly occur with this moor. One is illustrated in Fig. 9-17 where the leeward rope rode drifts idly under the boat. When the boat swings in a current reversal, the rode may snag the keel and prevent the boat from freely swinging to the new current direction.

To counter this, the rodes are bridled together at deck level by either a rolling hitch (rope rode bent onto chain rode) or seized together with twine. The combination is then allowed to run out a number of feet to put the rope rode below the bottom of the keel. If one rode is chain, the combination will settle by itself. If both rodes are rope, it will be necessary to add a kellet to ensure that the bridle will drop.

Boats that often use the Bahamian moor equip the chain anchor rode with a shackle at the proper depth to which the rope anchor rode can be easily attached. Of course, once you have made a bridle of the two anchor rodes, you can no longer adjust them independently for position or scope.

The other problem with the Bahamian moor develops as a result of the boat always turning in the same direction with the current change. This will cause the anchor rodes to twist themselves together, shortening the scope and causing undesirable wear on the rodes. If you intend to leave your boat on a Bahamian moor for an extended period of time, it is best to fashion a bridle with swivel and a single heavy chain to the deck gear.

Mediterranean Moor

In many parts of the world the rise and fall of the tide is relatively small, making it possible to moor stern (or bow) close against a quay (wharf) so that persons can walk a short gangway from boat to quay (Figure 9-9 D). This is the situation in the Mediterranean Sea and in a few other places, including Tahiti. Besides the convenience of direct boarding, it is possible to increase the number of boats that can be moored along a given length of quay since each boat nominally takes up only a beam width of quay rather than a boat length. In practice, about three times as many boats can be accommodated along a quay using the "Med" moor instead of conventional side-to docking. The Med moor is known as the Tahiti moor in the Pacific.

The Med moor is not an easy moor to implement because you must back your boat into a narrow slot between other boats. Twin-screw powerboats can do quite well, but single-screw boats, keelboats in particular, have great trouble. Of course, the worst part of Med mooring is that it is done in popular cruising and tourists spots so that you always have a quayful of onlookers to watch your performance. But rest assured, wherever you have to make a Med moor, the delights of visiting the area will far overshadow any problems.

Several schemes for making a Med moor are illustrated in Fig. 9-18. The single bow anchor moor without a crosswind is the one you pray for but rarely get. With help from the adjoining boats, who will want to save their topsides, you can also make a crosswind moor using either a hammerlock anchor or a skewed bow anchor set.

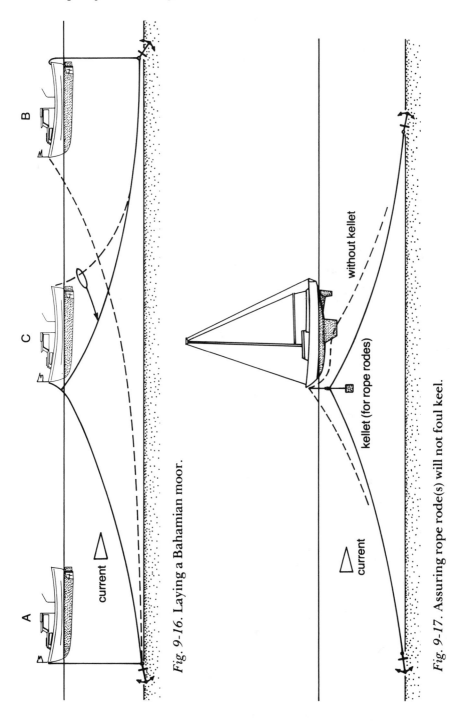

Fig. 9-16. Laying a Bahamian moor.

Fig. 9-17. Assuring rope rode(s) will not foul keel.

Boats from all over the world moor Med style at the quay in Papeete. The small tidal range allows the use of a stern boarding plank.

Preparation for the Med moor starts with getting the bow anchor ready. It should be a big anchor. Put out the storm anchor (my preference so that I can tauten the anchor rode after the stern is secured and be certain that the vulnerable stern of the boat does not touch the quay). Then get spring lines and stern lines ready, having the spring lines long enough so that they can be heaved ashore to helping hands on the quay. Position all your fenders along the stern quarters where initial contact with adjacent boats may take place. They will have to later be moved forward when the boat is settled in position.

Let go your bow anchor in the predetermined position, allowing for the use of storm scope rode lengths—5 to 1 for chain and 8 to 1 for rope rodes. Back down in the direction of the available slot paying out the bow rode and snubbing it up to set the anchor as you go. When you approach your slot, heave the spring lines to adjacent boats or to helping hands on the quay who will warp you in the remaining distance. Go slowly as you near the key and snub hard on the bow anchor in time to avoid hitting the quay. Then adjust all of your lines, relocate the fenders, and place your stern gangway ashore.

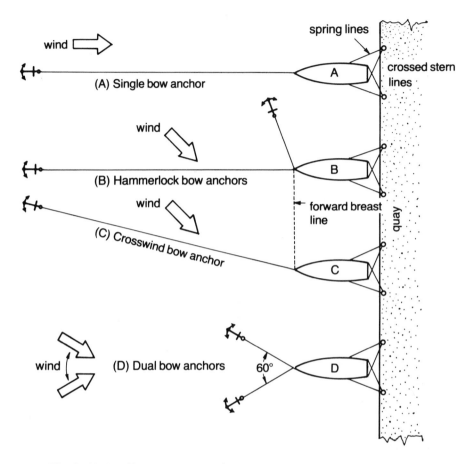

Fig. 9-18. Mediterranean (Med) moor.

If your boat does not back down with any degree of control, which *Horizon* does not, or if the crosswind is really strong, a different approach should be tried. Head the boat into the wind and at the proper drop point let go the anchor and allow the boat to settle back, gently snubbing the rode to set the anchor. Let out slightly less rode than the distance from the anchor to the bows of the other boats. Take a warp ashore in the dinghy and manually warp the stern of your boat into position at the entrance to your slot from where it can be further warped into the quay as before.

Some precautions: position your boat fore and aft so that your spreaders or outriggers do not tangle with those of the adjoining boats; put sufficient load on your bow anchor so that your vulnerable stern appendages cannot strike the quay; if the crosswind is strong, do not depend on leaning against your leeward neighbor, set a hammerlock anchor to windward with its rode under the bow anchor rode of your windward neighbor; when letting go your bow anchor, be certain that you have not crossed anyone else's rode; don't let a falling tide slack your bow rode so that the stern can strike the quay; and lash your stern gangway in place on the boat and let it move on the quay.

ANCHORING IN CORAL

Tropical boating is more than balmy breezes, moonlit nights and sparkling seas, it is sailing in an area of extreme ecological sensitivity. When anchoring over a tropical coral seabed, you must come to grips with it in the most gentle manner possible. Every day of the year someone carelessly drops an anchor on coral beds someplace in this world. Individually, the damage may be only a localized scratch on the coral's surface. Collectively, though, it amounts to a terrible and unforgiving amount of damage to these delicate works of Nature's most amazing animal, the tiny coral polyp. Enough scratches and chipping and coral reef growth has been set back for decades, if not killed off entirely. This is of particular concern in high-trafficked anchorage areas such as where charter boats operate, cruising boats congregate, or dive boats anchor to show their passengers the wonders of the underwater world.

The protection of the living coral in an anchorage area starts with a careful eyeball examination of the seabed before anchoring. In all probability it will reveal patches of sand in 20 or 30 feet where an anchor can be set. Maybe someone already anchored in the area has done the survey and can guide you into a sandy area where an anchor can securely set itself without destroying the surrounding coral growth. It is not enough that the anchor alone finds a way to set in a coral sand patch, there must be a sand fairway in which your anchor chain can ride without it tearing at the living coral as your boat swings with wind and current during your stay. If the chosen sandy patch has an occasional coral head in it, consider buoying the anchor chain to lift it over the coral patches as you swing at anchor.

If you can't find sand patches at shallow depths, back off to deeper waters in the neighborhood of 100 feet or more which are free of coral growth. Use your depth finder to locate a sandy shelf beyond the coral growth. You may need a total of 400 feet of rode to anchor at this depth, but it can be made up of nylon and chain in a fifty-fifty ratio alleviating the weight of an all-chain rode.

Peace of mind at anchor certainly does not include the hideous wrenching and rumbling sounds that come when your anchor chain grinds against living coral. In a purely mercenary sense, remember that when you hear the anchor chain rumbling, the coral is also grinding away the precious galvanizing on the anchor chain. The long term solution to protecting the living coral in popular areas while still giving boats access to them is to install coral moorings. This is discussed in Chapter 13.

WEIGHING ANCHOR

There is only one way to weigh anchor and that is with patience. The anchor that held you so securely throughout the night will not of itself give up its firm grip on the bottom and it will have to be coaxed and cajoled to let go. As the skipper you have at your disposal a whole bag of tricks to convince the anchor to let go, should it not break out easily. Try them in order (see Chapter 10).

This neat ground tackle installation on the *Sis W* from Chicago includes two saltwater wash down spigots near the bulwarks. The anchor windlass foot switch is located beneath the electric motor making it difficult to trip it accidently when walking on the foredeck.

Before weighing anchor, ascertain that your boat is ready to go. Clean up the decks, belay all lines, have your engine warmed up or your sails ready to hoist, and instruct your crew on the method of anchor retrieval that you will use.

If your boat has been moored instead of anchored, the first step is to "single up." Usually you will retrieve the leeward anchor first while hanging on the windward anchor. If you have set dual bow anchors, retrieve the smaller one first, or that anchor which tends to be leeward. Once you have singled up, proceed with weighing the remaining anchor.

Bring the boat to "short stay" to accomplish the preparatory cleanup work. (Short stay means to reduce the scope of the rode by about one-half). Keep a wary eye on your position, because if you had a poor set in the first place, short stay may break it loose before you are ready.

Once ready, the foredeck crew will heave in on the rope anchor rode or crank in on the anchor windlass which at the same time pulls the boat forward. If the boat is large, the helmsman should put the engine in forward idle and ease up to the anchor while the crew hauls in on the rode. Do not overrun the rode in motoring forward. The rode should be heaved in smoothly, as it becomes slack, right up to the point where it becomes vertical. The rode is then said to be "up and down" and the anchor is said to be "apeak." All way should be taken off, and the boat allowed to bob freely which, in most cases, will free the anchor from its grip on the bottom.

As soon as the anchor breaks free, the foredeck crew calls "anchor aweigh" to the helmsman and proceeds to haul in the remaining rode and anchor. The helmsman will get steerageway on and stay clear of other boats and hazards.

One danger to getting underway with the anchor still suspended is the possibility of the anchor "kiting" or planing back under the boat menacing hull and rudder. Lightweight, pivoted-fluke anchors such as the Danforth, Fortress, and Benson are most noted for this. Even the Bruce will sometimes kite, but upside down.

When the anchor breaks surface, it is said to be "at the hawse." Clean it well before taking it on board. A foredeck washing hose, buckets of water, or a brush and muscle power will do the job. A dirty rode inside the boat presents a distinctive odor in a matter of hours.

Chain is really the most difficult to clean, especially if it has been lying in mud. One way to clean it as it comes aboard is with a boat hook. Hook the chain with the boat hook as far down as you can reach and alternately lift it up and let it drop back, swishing it off in the seawater.

Finally, bring your anchor on board and place it home in its chocks or bow roller where it is normally carried. Lash it down securely. Run the complete rode down the deck pipe to the chain locker and seal off the opening. When you have completely squared away the ground tackle and foredeck, head the boat out into open water.

RETRIEVING THE CORAL PICK ANCHOR

The coral pick anchor has been developed for use in deep water (to 100 fathoms) and over coral or rocky bottoms, both of which pose special problems in retrieval. But the wily fishermen who use these anchors in the Pacific have developed a simple procedure for retrieval. The secret lies with a retrieval buoy that is nothing more than one of the boat's heavy-duty dock fenders.

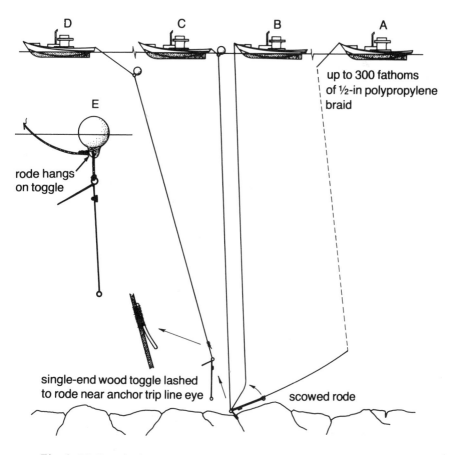

Fig. 9-19. Retrieving the coral pick anchor.

The procedure is as follows and as shown in Fig. 9-19:

A. Fishing boat is anchored in deep water over a rocky bottom. Polypropylene rode is scowed to the anchor ring.

B. The anchor rode is brought "up and down" over the pick, freeing scowed rode.

C. The rode is then moved aft on the boat, threaded through the eye of a large fender, and belayed near the transom.

D. The boat moves slowly forward, extracting the anchor from its set. Drag of the submerged buoy causes rode to pull through eye, thereby automatically bringing the anchor to the surface.

E. When the wood toggle passes through the eye of the fender, towing is stopped, and the anchor rode hangs back on the toggle. The rode is then handed into the boat, and the anchor is lifted aboard.

The skipper of the commercial fishing sailing catamaran *Keaouhi* from Kailua-Kona, Hawaii, proudly displays one of his coral pick anchors.

CHAPTER TEN

Anchoring Tricks

It is really not a case of if your anchor drags, but rather of when it drags, for all seamen who have engaged in the anchoring game have found that an anchor will drag in spite of the quality of the product, or the expertise of the crew. And, dragging always occurs at night after the cook has prepared a superior evening repast, and the crew is peacefully asleep in their bunks.

When dragging occurs, there is a change in the boat's motion. No longer does it horse about the anchor, alternately heeling to one side and then to the other. The whistling in the rigging tends to be a steady pitch instead of the undulating tone associated with a boat sheering back and forth while riding to a well-set anchor. No longer is there a pitching motion as the bow rides over the crest of a wave. Instead, you feel a rolling of the boat and a tendency for it to heel continuously in one direction. Missing are the slap of the waves at the bow and the hiss of the disturbed water running alongside the hull. An eerie silence takes over which awakens you as much as the change in motion.

No one needs to tell the experienced seaman what has happened. You are instantly on deck and your observations only confirm what you had already sensed—the anchor is dragging. Your one connection to terra firma has taken leave and your boat sits crosswind in the troughs of the waves.

WAYS TO STOP ANCHOR DRAGGING

Your first action is an almost instinctive look astern to ascertain how much distance you have to the lee shore or the nearest boat. Given sufficient distance, which translates into time to act, you can pay out more scope on the anchor rode. Do it slowly and use some of the clearance distance up before you begin to snub gently on the rode, looking for a new anchor set. At some point you must commit yourself with a firm snub because it's your last chance to set the anchor and belay the rode firmly. Check bearings on surrounding objects to fix your new position. If you have succeeded in getting a new set, pay out additional rode for insurance, and then set an anchor watch until dawn.

If your scope should pass the 10 to 1 mark (rope rode), and you have not gotten a positive anchor set, it is probably time to start your engine and take some of the load off the anchor. Possibly you can hold your position under power until dawn when you can weigh anchor and seek a new location. If there is adequate space in the immediate area to set a second anchor, motor forward and to one side and set a second (temporary) anchor.

When using your engine to help a dragging anchor, be certain that all lines from rigging, etc., are on board and that you don't overrun your bow anchor rode. If you were being steadied by a stern anchor, clear that rode away from the propeller. Since use of the engine is usually a last resort measure, don't hazard a failure of it by carelessness under stress.

The propeller performs two functions when the engine is used to assist the anchor. One is to thrust against the drag of the wind, and the other is to provide propeller wash over the rudder so that you can steer the boat, keeping the bow to windward. Running the engine will buy you time to take other, more positive actions, but it is only a temporary measure by itself.

The dedicated sailor without auxiliary power will, at this point, be glad that he took anchorage in a more open part of the harbor where he can quickly weigh anchor and make an exit under sail. His will be a very limited time to correct a bad situation.

Sometimes your available anchorage area may be just too small or the water too deep to let out all of the scope that you really need for the occasion. This situation will arise more frequently with the combination rope-chain rode than with the all-chain rode. The solution is to place a concentrated weight along the anchor rode that tells it to behave like a heavy chain rode. This weight is called a kellet or sentinel and it may be made from materials on board (Fig. 10-1).

The function of the kellet is to steepen the initial drop of the rode and to flatten out the rode on the sea bottom to decrease the anchor lead angle. A kellet should weigh about 25 to 30 pounds for a 40-foot boat, and it should be so located that it is about halfway along the rode from bow roller to anchor ring. If better anchor holding is what you want, place the kellet closer to the anchor. If more cushioning of surges is needed, place the kellet slightly higher on the rode. The best location is determined by the conditions of your anchorage which may change with time. It is possible to set up a resonant condition between boat and kellet where the kellet will bounce with every surge of the boat. This can be avoided by moving the kellet up or down the rode, or changing scope.

The kellet can be slid down the anchor rode after the anchor is set and the need established. A large shackle can be used as the rider for a chain

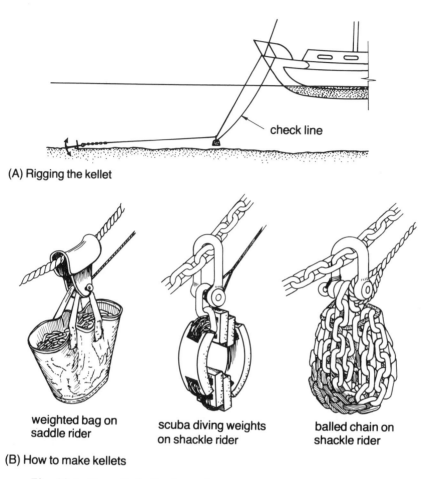

(A) Rigging the kellet

weighted bag on
saddle rider

scuba diving weights
on shackle rider

balled chain on
shackle rider

(B) How to make kellets

Fig. 10-1. Use of a kellet in anchoring.

kellet, but a properly designed saddle must be used for a rope rode to minimize abrasion.

The checkline controlling the kellet's position is secured to the kellet rider and belayed to a cleat on the foredeck. Do not let the kellet checkline go slack as it may drift aft and foul keel, rudder, or propeller.

SETTING TANDEM ANCHORS

A very elegant way of improving the holding power of your single bow anchor system is to put two anchors on it in tandem. The conditions under which this works successfully are quite specific but worth considering when you are preparing to ride out a storm in poor holding ground. In straight line pull tests, the U.S. Navy has shown* that tandem anchors set in mud can yield a 20-30 percent improvement in holding power over the sum of their individual holding powers. In sand, the holding power of the combination is only slightly greater than the sum of the two anchors singly.

No test data is available to illustrate the holding power of the tandem anchors under a veering situation, just as little test data exists for single anchors in the same situation. Experience with using tandem anchors in small boats has been variable dependent on type(s) of anchors used and the composition of the seabed. These factors can be summarized as follows:

Anchor types

Stock-stabilized, pivoted fluke anchors are far and away the preferred choice. The greater the anchor stability in roll, the better the chances are of the anchors staying embedded or being able to rebed after rolling out of a set under veering loads. Unfortunately, makers of these anchors have not provided a standard ring-in-crown for attachment of the backing anchor. The tripline eyes on the "crown" of the CQR and Bruce anchors are too "high" to make a suitable attaching point for backing anchors. Tests using this eye as a backing anchor attachment have generally resulted in the anchors rolling out of their sets under veering loads.

Seabed Characteristics

While the U.S. Navy's carefully executed tandem anchor tests showed that they could be set in both sand and mud, the value of this idea lies in improving the holding power of a single anchor rode system in mud. Chapter 6 summarized the holding power of various anchors in sand and mud. In general, the anchors developed three to seven times more holding power in sand than in mud. By designing the anchor system for use in sand, it comes up wanting when the seabed is mud.

One solution to closing the holding power gap between sand and mud is to carry a much larger anchor for use in mud; another would be to consider the use of tandem anchors to narrow the holding power performance gap. Weight and stowage considerations would favor the latter approach. Ex-

---

*R. J. Taylor and G. R. Walker, "Model and Small-Scale Tests to Evaluate the Performance of Drag Anchors in Combination." (Washington D.C.: U.S. Navy Technical Note CEL N-1707, October 1984), and R. J. Taylor, "Single and Tandem Anchor Performance of the New Navy Mooring Anchor: The NAVMOOR Anchor." (Washington D.C.: U.S. Navy Technical Note CEL N-1774, July 1987).

perience under poorly controlled conditions by small boat operators has shown that there are fewer problems and more reliability when setting tandem anchors in mud than in sand. It would seem, therefore, that the use of tandem anchors in small boats is a technique best considered when anchoring in mud bottoms. (The tandem anchor trick now seems most appropriate to solving the problem of anchoring at Kolonia, Pohnpei, as discussed earlier on page 223.)

The design criteria for tandem stock-stabilized, pivoting fluke anchors are illustrated in Fig. 10-2. In action, the forward anchor behaves as an independent anchor and sets in about eight fluke lengths of drag distance. The back anchor also acts as an independent anchor until it drags into the seabed disturbed by the forward anchor where, initially it unloads a little, then penetrates deeper than normal, adding to its holding power. This occurs after about 10 fluke lengths of drag distance.

ROWING OUT AN ANCHOR

Rowing out a kedge anchor from your boat is one of the saltier things you can do in this world. With most boats having engines in them, it

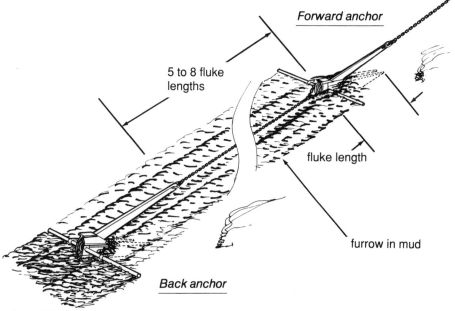

Note: The back anchor chain should be shackled to the crown of the forward anchor and not to its ring.

Fig. 10-2. Tandem anchor system design.

is rare that the occasion arises for you actually to set an anchor after your boat has come to rest. But there can be instances when it is easier to set a second anchor from a dinghy than to try to maneuver your boat around one anchor to set another.

I recall one such instance in Papeete Harbor where *Horizon* was soundly moored to the quay when an unusual crosswind sprang up. We set the 20-pound Danforth Hi-Tensile anchor to windward by rowing it out in our Avon inflatable dinghy and making a hammerlock moor. Our crewman at the time was a superb seaman and showed great satisfaction in using old-fashioned seamanship to solve a problem that has been around since man first took to the water.

To make the job simple, you have to do a bit of planning. First decide where to set your kedge anchor; then decide which anchor you will use. The old-fashioned anchor was the original kedge, but few people carry one on today's sophisticated boats. It is a pity not to have an old-fashioned anchor aboard for it is probably the most versatile of all anchors. Next best is the Danforth whose early years were engaged in doing nothing but kedging landing craft off of World War II beaches. You most likely have one of these for a stern anchor or a working anchor. Whichever anchor you choose, it should not be a heavyweight.

The kedge rode should be a rope-chain combination matched to the anchor used. An all-chain rode is an impossible thing to carry out in a dinghy.

It takes two people to row out a kedge anchor, although I have seen it done by single-handers when necessary. The dinghy crew stows the anchor and rode for the ride and furnishes the propulsion. The boat crew directs the dinghy to the drop point and takes in on the rode when the kedge is let go. These actions must be coordinated with arm signals since voice does not carry well in the wind. Preparation for rowing out the anchor is illustrated in Fig. 10-3.

The length of rode to put into the dinghy is the scope desired plus one added depth. The reason for the additional amount is that when the kedge is released from the dinghy, it will tend to draw the rode straight down initially, with the remaining rode following in a long flat arc because of the water drag on it. If you don't provide an extra "depth" of rode length, the kedge will pull up short, and you will not get the desired scope.

Although your dinghy crewman with a macho display of oarsmanship may say that he can drag the rode of the boat with no trouble, don't believe him. It is far easier to row and control the dinghy direction when you do not have the problem of the rode dragging off the boat. With the rode in the dinghy, you are, essentially, laying it out rather than dragging it out.

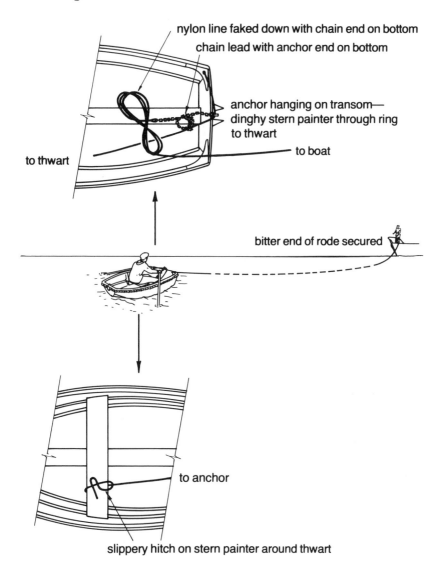

Fig. 10-3. Rowing out an anchor.

With everything in readiness, the dinghy crew rows away from the boat, and the rode is allowed to unfake slowly from the dinghy. When the rode has all run out, the dinghy crew frees the slippery hitch letting go the anchor. The boat crew allows time enough for the anchor to reach bottom, and then hauls in easy on the rode to set the anchor.

While rowing out an anchor with a rope anchor rode is not particularly difficult, rowing out an anchor with a chain rode is another matter. This has to be done in two steps. First row out a small anchor with a light rope rode attached to it and set it beyond where you want your new anchor set. Then return to the boat and hang the new anchor on the dinghy transom holding it in place with the dinghy stern painter, à la the rope rode method previously described. Now, instead of rowing the dinghy out to the new anchor's target location, pull yourself and dinghy hand over hand along the light anchor rode until in the proper position to drop the new anchor. Don't expect to shuttle too large an anchor and chain out by this method, but for small stern anchors or a small anchor in a kedging operation it can be manageable.

KEDGING

Before the advent of auxiliary power and tugboats, sailing vessels would move themselves about in a harbor by kedging. While this is not part of anchoring, it uses the same ground tackle and the skills learned in rowing out an anchor. Two anchors are generally used for kedging—a heavy one on a chain rode for short scope anchoring and a lighter kedge for rowing out.

The boat is allowed to swing to the heavy anchor on as short a scope as possible. The kedge is then rowed out as far as it can go and is set. The heavy anchor is weighed, and the kedge anchor rode is heaved in, moving the boat forward. When the kedge is on such short scope that it drags, the heavy anchor is let go underfoot to hold the boat's position while the kedge is weighed and again rowed out in the dinghy.

THE BUOYED-ANCHOR RODE

Anchoring with a buoyed rode is a trick used by West Coast fishermen when they anchor in areas of poor protection from waves and swells. It is essentially a single anchor moor which uses a buoy to cushion the shock of large waves (Fig. 10-4).

The buoy is a large fishing float, 24 or more inches in diameter. A normal scope of chain anchor rode is paid out but instead of securing the rode to the boat, it is first secured to the buoy with a shackle or heavy lashing. Another 50 to 100 feet of rode is then paid out as a pendant and the rode then belayed to the boat in its proper place.

When the wind is light, the boat will ride to the buoy just as in a mooring. As the wind increases, the boat tugs harder at the buoy, tending to sink it. If a big wave comes along, the anchor rode catenary is flattened out at the same time the buoy is dragged under the surface, giving an

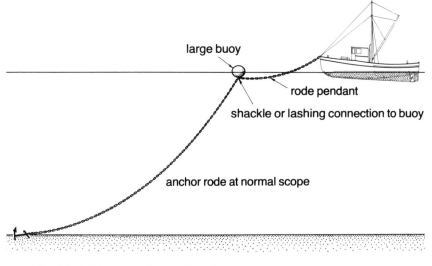

large buoy

rode pendant

shackle or lashing connection to buoy

anchor rode at normal scope

Fig. 10-4. Rigging a buoyed anchor.

increased instantaneous scope to the system, forestalling any significant increase in anchor loading, or change in the anchor lead angle. The anchor rarely senses any change in the pull on the rode because the buoy is cushioning the sharp impact of the waves.

The buoyed anchor rode has particular value in anchoring in waters with coral heads because the anchor rode (sometimes foreshortened) rides over the tops of these hazards. The float carries the vertical load of the chain, taking much weight off of the bow of the boat, allowing it to rise more gracefully over the incoming waves.

ANCHORING ON THE BANKS

Before his untimely death, I had the opportunity to exchange ideas with Peter Tangvald (*L'Artemis de Pytheas,* 49′ gaff cutter) [*] regarding anchoring on ocean banks. Few people have had any experience in this form of anchoring and we put together the following ideas.

The issue of banks anchoring is not the depth of the water, per se, which may be as little as 10 or 15 feet, but the steepness of the seas which generate in shoal water. We agreed that while the selection of anchor and rode are still determined by the nature of the seabed, the factor of greatest importance seemed to be the scope.

---

[*] Private communication from Peter Tangvald, 9 March 1991.

Because of the steepness of seas over shoal areas, the boat will be experiencing more rapid and severe pitching. The need then becomes apparent for a large scope—possibly as much as you can put out. Certainly 10:1 would not be unreasonable. If the seabed is rock or coral, chain rode is important for that part that will be lying across the bottom, but a nylon spring line also needs to be incorporated to cushion surge loads. If the seabed is sand or mud, then less chain and lots of 3-strand nylon would make sense. It is important to minimize the weight hanging off the bow (or lying in the bow) which would prevent the boat from riding over the waves.

One thing of concern in anchoring (or even sailing) in shoal waters is that as the waves steepen due to shoaling, the crests become higher and troughs lower.[*] When wave heights reach the order of 15 to 20 feet in shoal water, there is a distinct possibility of the boat hitting the bottom in a trough with subsequent damage, especially if it repeatedly hits the bottom. The problems of anchoring in shoal water with an unlimited fetch suggest that it is better to plan your passage to avoid such areas in stormy conditions.

STERN ANCHORING

This technique for minimizing the amount of sailing that a boat will do at anchor may not be perfectly obvious until you try it. Most sailboats and powerboats have high windage forward of the center of lateral resistance which makes them horse when at anchor, taking up valuable anchorage space, and exposing first one side and then the other to the wind. In nominal winds and seas the solution is to anchor from the stern which not only cuts down on boat motion but improves interior ventilation.

Narrow-beamed boats can use a quarter cleat to belay the anchor rode, but broad-beamed boats should consider a bridle between quarter cleats if a central bitt is not present. Stern anchoring is a temporary technique for use while fishing, swimming, or just plain loafing which is a permissible facet of boating. If you intend to leave the boat unattended, switch back to a bow anchor.

Stern anchoring is *not* to be used by outboard or inboard/outdrive boats carrying a large percentage of their weight near the transom. Nor should it be used by boats having low freeboard or cutaway transoms. Strong wave action or the movement of passengers aft could bring about a swamping of the boat. Such boats should only be anchored by the bow.

---

[*] Earl Hinz. "The Ups and Downs of Water Depths," *Cruising World*, November 1991.

SIDE BRIDLE

Rolling of a boat at anchor is usually due to the swell coming from a different direction than the wind. In harbors and bights this is not an unusual situation, for the swells coming down the coast tend to wrap around the headlands and come at the anchored boat from an angle. Some degree of relief from this can be obtained by orienting the boat at an angle to the wind which minimizes the roll without preventing the boat from having a natural swing.

Fig. 10-5 illustrates how to rig a bridle, making it adjustable for any combination of wind and swell directions. The bridle is made with a rope pendant that is twice as long as the boat and to which is bent a block to ride along the anchor rode. If the rode is chain, a rope pendant is bent to it with a rolling hitch, and the length of the pendant and deployed rode are adjusted together to get the proper riding angle for the boat.

Two critical areas of chafe must be watched—at the bow where the rode is bent sharply back on itself and at the point where the pendant snatch block rides on the rope rode.

USE OF A DROGUE IN A CURRENT

Should your boat be anchored in a strong current with an opposing wind coming from the stern, it will have a tendency to stand forward on the anchor rode and do more than a little horsing in the stream. One way to eliminate this problem is to deploy a drogue over the stern, getting added current drag to hold the boat firmly against the anchor rode (Fig. 10-6).

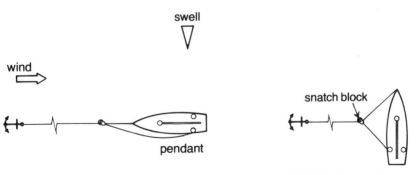

(A) Rigging bridle

(B) Bridle trimmed to swell

Fig. 10-5. Use of bridle in cross-swell anchoring.

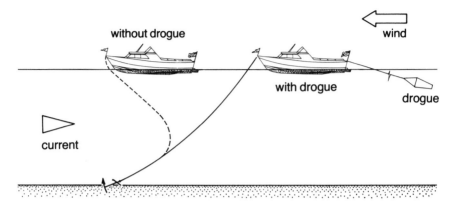

Fig. 10-6. Use of a drogue in opposing wind-current situation.

BEACHING MULTIHULLS

One of the advantages of multihulls is their ability to be deliberately beached for repairs or, simply, to land the crew. Beaching a multihull should be preceded by the laying out of a stern anchor or kedge to ensure that the boat can be unbeached as well as to stabilize it while on the beach.

When approaching the beach you must have knowledge of the range and state of the tides. This knowledge is necessary because if you beach the boat at a very high tide, you cannot get it off except with great difficulty until the next high tide comes along. When you are about 75 feet off the beach, set a kedge anchor over the stern. Although old-fashioned anchors are the best, multihulls rarely carry them. They do carry Danforth lightweights, though, which were the anchors used for beaching landing craft during World War II.

Approach the beach slowly with daggerboards up and crew weight aft. Try to slide gently onto the sand without damage to hull bottom. When the boat has come to a halt, run out a bow anchor or place a line ashore to a tree. Then take in on the stern rode to hold the vessel straight into the beach.

When leaving, simply remove the bow line, gather the crew aft, and heave in on the stern rode and kedge yourself off of the beach into deep water.

ROLL DAMPERS

You may have found the perfect anchorage, fully protected from the wind, a good holding bottom, and plenty of swinging room, only to discover that swells keep finding their way into it. And, of course, a boat tends to align itself with swells in such a way that dishes and canned goods slide and roll around in the lockers and your favorite bottle of spirits glides off the galley counter onto the cabin sole. There is a way to minimize this rolling problem and that is to set out roll dampers.

The diagram of Fig. 10-7 illustrates methods for powerboats and sailboats to reduce rolling at anchor. The amount of roll damping which these devices can provide is proportional to the area of the drag device times its distance from the centerline of the boat. The secret is, therefore, to make them as large in area as practical and hang them as far out from the boat as practical.

The flat plate flopper-stoppers are the kind that you make at home. They are about two feet square and have hinged flaps on top which control the direction of water flow and, hence, drag. Some experimentation will be necessary to get them to open and close symmetrically and to prevent them from skating sideways when being lowered in the open

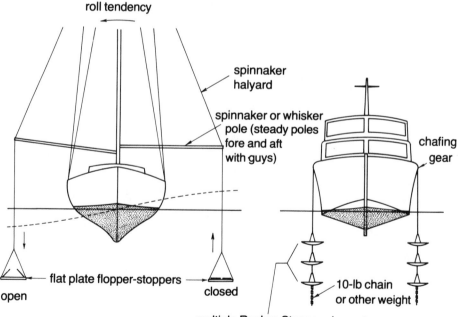

Fig. 10-7. Flopper-stoppers to minimize rolling at anchor.

position. Ballast or vertical edges of four inches or more in depth are two ways to prevent skating.

The sailboat method of rigging flopper-stoppers is easy and effective, but places considerable stress on the rigging. The pole should be rigged perpendicular to the mast and guyed fore and aft before deploying the flopper-stopper and the topping lift must be stronger than that for normal sailing use. If the swell-induced rolling is particularly severe, you may want to retrieve the flopper-stoppers and seek a quieter anchorage.

BREAKING OUT THE STUBBORN ANCHOR

There will be times when you are attempting to weigh anchor and it will not come loose from the bottom and your patience is becoming shorter. Save your ulcers by using your head, for there are a number of tricks that you can use to break out a stubborn anchor.

The Pelican Flopper Stopper is an effective means of reducing rolling in an anchored boat. Two six-vane units attached to the midship cleats of a 42-foot powerboat effectively reduced rolling to a minimum. Four-vane units are recommended for boats to 30 feet and six-vane units for larger boats. Courtesy: Pelican Products, Inc.

The first thing to do is to take maximum advantage of the lifting power of the bow of the boat. With the rode "up and down," snub it in with each dip of the bow in the swells, tautening the rode so that subsequent waves or swells will apply full bow lift to the stuck anchor. This is a very persuasive technique, and most anchors not hooked on rock or coral will usually give in gracefully. Even more bow lift can be gained by first having the whole crew move to the foredeck while you snub the rode short. Then everyone moves aft as far as possible levering the bow up and the anchor with it.

Should the anchor still be winning the game, pay out about a 1½ to 1 scope and continue forward under power. This action tends to back the hook out from whatever is holding it. If this fails, pay out more rode to give a 2 to 1 scope and then start circling the anchor, keeping the rode as taut as you can. A change in the angle of pull may just free the hook from its rock captor.

But there will be times when no amount of gentle persuasion will break out the hook, and then you must resort to more drastic measures. What you do depends on how well you can assess the problem. If you are in swimmable water, don a bathing suit and snorkle gear, and have a look at your problem. If there is no way to see the problem, then you will have to deduce the most likely cause—rocks, debris, another anchor chain or, maybe, a utility cable. The action to be taken will depend on the reason for fouling.

To free an anchor fouled on a chain or cable, first try lifting it high enough off the bottom to slip a sling line under the offending cable. Then shake your anchor free and bring it on board. Drop the cable off your sling line and proceed to clean up the foredeck.

USING AN ANCHOR CHASER

If you cannot lift the chain or cable off the bottom with your anchor, you can try an anchor chaser, assuming your fouled anchor is a stockless or stock-in-crown design, namely, a CQR, Bruce, Danforth, or Northill. A chaser is made from a short length of chain shackled together in a loop around the anchor rode. It should be a very loose fit so that it can slide down over shackles, anchor ring, and anchor shank. The messenger line should be at least a ⅜-inch diameter braided dacron rope which will not stretch under load and snap back when the anchor frees itself.

Lower the chaser down the rode (Fig. 10-8), jiggling the messenger line to get it to clear the shackles. The more vertical the snagged anchor's rode is at this time, the easier it will be to lower the chaser. If the anchor

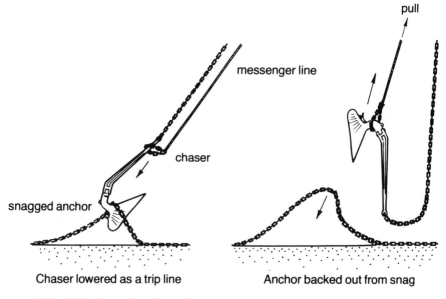

Fig. 10-8. Use of anchor chaser.

rode is all chain, you will be able to feel the chaser slide over the links. If there is any doubt that the chaser has descended all the way and slipped over the anchor shank, visually inspect it.

If still in doubt, row the messenger line out in your dinghy in a direction opposite to the boat and pull and jiggle the messenger line to draw the chaser over the shank of the fouled anchor. Then take the messenger line back to the boat and make your move to pull the anchor free with this jury-rigged trip line.

Some anchors will resist even this technique; so carry it one step further. Cast off the shortest length of rode that you can from the fouled anchor and buoy it in the water above the fouled anchor. Maneuver your boat to a position 180° from where it was and apply power away from the anchor, pulling hard on the messenger line to break the anchor out backwards (Fig. 10-9). Do not use nylon rope for the messenger line because the elasticity could cause it to snap back viciously if it should break. Use braided polyester line for maximum safety.

Getting the chaser over the fouled anchor's shank is the biggest job in this method of retrieval. If the previous techniques do not produce results, try the following: after you have put your chaser around the rode of the fouled anchor, bend your kedge anchor to the rode with as short a scope as possible; bend a trip line and buoy to the crown of your kedge anchor; and then cast off the fouled anchor's rode and the kedge anchor so that the kedge is set ahead of the fouled anchor (Fig. 10-10). With the kedge anchor set, maneuver the boat over the fouled anchor, drawing in on the messenger line so as to slide the chaser along the fouled anchor's rode and over the fouled anchor's shank. Then hoist away on the messenger line to retrieve the fouled anchor. After the fouled anchor is free, retrieve the kedge anchor and buoy and be on your way.

GRAPPLING FOR THE SNAG

If all else fails, you can try your hand at grappling to free the anchor. Equip your grapnel with a sturdy trip line to the crown and then drag for the offending cable (Fig. 10-11). If you are lucky enough to hook the cable, you can lift it off the bottom and free your anchor. The grapnel is then retrieved with the trip line. To send the grapnel down without a trip line is to risk losing it also.

SLIPPING THE ANCHOR

Occasionally nothing works and you have to leave the anchorage because of weather or your schedule, and you have in mind coming

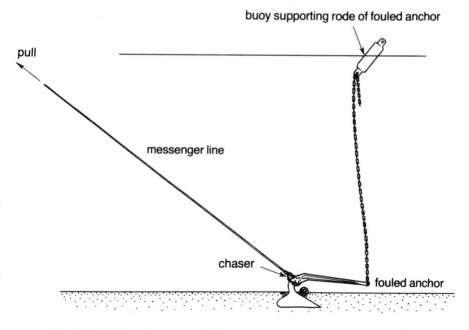

Fig. 10-9 Using boat to pull free a badly fouled anchor.

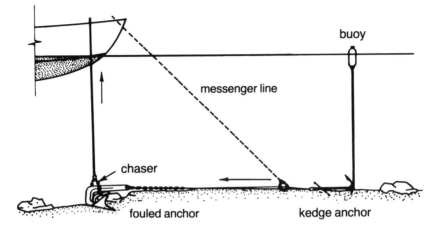

Fig. 10-10. Using kedge anchor for placing chaser.

back later or getting a salvage outfit to recover your ground tackle. The thing to do then is to slip the anchor gracefully, buoying the rode so that it can be later found and recovered. In order that you will have some claim to your property at the later time, your buoy should be clearly identified with your boat's name. Make a pendant equal in length to the depth of water that your anchor is in. Bend the pendant between your marked anchor buoy and the anchor chain at the waterline. Then cut the chain taking as much of it along as possible.

If time does not permit the luxury of partial salvage of your chain, cut the lashings holding the bitter end of the chain to the boat and buoy the bitter end with a stout line at least as long as the depth of the water. Let the entire chain rode sink to the bottom to await your return. In the case of a rope rode, sever it close to the water and buoy it short so that there is a minimum of loose rope floating around possibly to foul your or someone else's boat. You may cry a little when you leave hundreds of dollars of ground tackle behind, but look at the bright side—you have saved your boat and you might get your ground tackle back. Many antique anchors found today on the bottoms of bays and harbors are anchors that were slipped by the old windjammers when the weather turned sour and they had no choice but to put to sea to save themselves.

SLIDING RING ANCHORS

The one problem common to all anchors is the possibility of fouling when set. No anchor is immune from hooking the bill of a fluke under a rock or a coral head and wedging it in so tightly that it cannot be

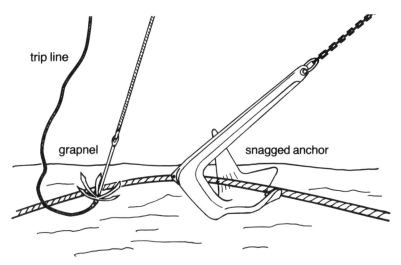

Fig. 10-11. Grappling to free a snagged anchor.

There are many manufacturers of sliding ring, stock-stabilized, pivoting fluke anchors. This one is a Keepers. All sliding ring anchors must be tended if the wind changes in direction. The slotted shank is not able to take large side loads and, if the ring slides to the crown, there is a possibility that the anchor will be upset. Do not leave a boat unattended on a sliding ring anchor. Courtesy: *Sea.*

retrieved by normal means. Some anchors like the CQR and Bruce are equipped with a trip line eye near the crown.

Another approach to the problem is to give the anchor ring the freedom to slide down the shank towards the crown so that it can be used to pull the anchor out backwards using the anchor rode. Typical of these anchors are the Huntley, Danforth Sure-Ring, and the Benson Snag-Proof. The shanks of these anchors are slotted providing a track for the ring to slide from head to crown.

While the principle of the sliding ring anchor is good, in practice it can be fraught with danger. Consider the circumstances of a 180° shift in the wind and current causing the pull of the rode to change its direction so that the ring is pulled down the shank until it reaches its limit of travel at the crown. Any further pull on the rode will then back the anchor out of its set with the result that the boat is no longer anchored. For this reason the slotted shank anchor is used primarily for a lunch hook or fishing anchor where it can be watched and where easy retrieval is a virtue.

CHAPTER ELEVEN

Rights and Responsibilities

In our crowded world of recreational boating, commercial shipping, and naval operations, nothing is simple any longer; and maritime law has grown, along with the number of lawyers in the practice. No longer does one simply "throw the anchor out," for there are legal rocks and shoals which can constrain, confuse, and condemn many an anchoring practice. But take heart, the responsibilities are not so overwhelming as to cause you to think of "swallowing the anchor" and seek simpler pleasures on the golf course or tennis court. On the contrary, there are more than enough rights to go along with the responsibilities to make anchoring an attractive alternative to seeking a marina slip every night.

Every vessel has a right to anchor. In an emergency that vessel may even anchor in an active channel or fairway. But don't take anchoring rights too literally, or you will become enmeshed in maritime law up to your bow roller. The reason for this is that there are multiple agencies who regulate and enforce the law in the coastal waters of the United States.

Recreational and other boats under 20 meters in length have been provided with many "special anchorages" for their own use in which they are not required to exhibit anchor lights, day shapes, or sound fog signals as required by the Inland Rules. These special anchorages should be your first choice where they exist.

If there is not a special anchorage in your area, seek local advice on where it is, or where it is not, permissible to set your hook. Local governments have been given the right by the federal government to regulate their harbor waters, and they have created the post of harbormaster whose job it is to run the harbor. The harbormaster is the one you should talk to regarding a proper place to anchor. Almost universally harbormasters monitor VHF (Channel 16), and you can pose your question to them by radio as you enter their harbors. Most harbors are also policed by patrol boats and if you have anchored in a forbidden area, you most certainly will hear a thump on your hull and be asked to move to a proper anchorage.

I recall our own first entry into Hilo (Hawaii) harbor after a sail from French Polynesia. Since we had no VHF radio, I did the next best thing and carefully read the latest Sailing Directions which identified an anchorage area off tiny Coconut Island. We anchored there for the night wondering where all the boats were. We were aroused the following morning by the harbormaster who had come out in a Coast Guard skiff which gave him plenty of authority. He politely but firmly asked us to follow him into the small boat harbor hidden behind the Matson Lines container terminal. There we moored, Med style, to the container wharf. It was not only a more protected anchorage, but it had toilet and shower facilities and easy access to town.

The case for anchoring in a channel or navigable waters has all sorts of ramifications. First, a narrow channel, like a harbor entrance that is frequented by large ships, is no place for a boat to stay longer than it takes to transit that channel. But there are also wide channels and vast expanses of shallow, navigable waterways that make excellent cruising, gunkholing, and anchoring at the end of the day. Among these are the thousands of

The harbormaster at Hilo, Hawaii, directs all cruising boats to moor in Radio Bay rather than anchor out in the designated anchorage of Hilo Harbor. The shoreside conveniences are well worth the move to this snug harbor.

miles of the Intracoastal Waterway, the whole Chesapeake Bay, the broad rivers of the Middle West and Great Plains states, and the enticing waters of Puget Sound. Along the Eastern Seaboard and the Gulf of Mexico are waters shallow enough for you to anchor in many places. What. then, are the rights and responsibilities of anchoring a boat "out in the open" in these navigable waters?

The rights are simple—you can anchor in any location that is not a designated channel or marked fairway unless it is an emergency. Then you can anchor anyplace, but you must make every effort to solve your emergency quickly and move out of the channel as soon as possible. Obviously, while anchored you must display the proper lights and day shapes plus taking such other actions required of anchored vessels.

On the other hand, some channels are so wide that vessels can anchor off to the side without violating local regulations. To take that right means

Boats attending the annual meeting of the internationally known Seven Seas Cruising Association anchor along the Intracoastal Waterway at Lantana, Florida. Although local authorities, more often than not, tend to discourage boats from anchoring along their shorelines, a skipper has every right to anchor in coastal waters provided he does not impede traffic or present a hazard. Even then, if his vessel is in trouble, he has the right to anchor temporarily for his own safety at any location.

you must also take the responsibility for proper anchor lights and shapes, and a capable lookout and sound signals if visibility becomes restricted. You must also ensure that your boat will not swing farther into the channel should the wind or current change; that no obstruction will block the view of your boat by an approaching vessel; and that if your boat drags its anchor, it will not move farther into the channel. In short, you cannot willfully or accidentally impede or obstruct traffic in the channel in which you have anchored without becoming responsible for the results. While an anchored boat normally does not have to take unusual precautions to avoid collisions with moving vessels, if you are anchored in a channel, you must exercise an extra measure of good seamanship.

If you are anchored in navigable waters which clearly are not part of a channel or fairway, then you have the right to anchor, paying only normal attention to anchor lights and shapes and sound signals. The boat should not be left unattended as a constant lookout is one of the prerequisites to safe anchoring in all navigable waters. If you plan to leave your vessel unattended, then you should, by all means, move it to a special anchorage where neither lights, shapes, nor sound signals are required.

There is one place that you do not anchor and that is over a submarine cable. The locations of submarine cables are shown on charts (Fig. 11-1) and large notice boards are posted on the shoreline where the cable enters or exits the water. These may be telephone or electric cables and the shock you can get from an 11,000 or so volt electric cable is only exceeded by the legal expenses if you are apprehended while dragging your anchor and damaging a cable.

CONFLICTS OF JURISDICTION

The people of the United States have a constitutional right to free navigation in navigable waters of the United States for the purposes of transportation, commerce, and recreation. Navigation includes the right to anchor in those waters free of interference from local laws. While local governments might impose laws pertaining to the health, safety, and welfare of people using those waters or living on adjacent land, paramount authority over the use of navigable waters of the United States remains with the federal government.

In recent years, many municipalities and states have placed restrictions on the anchoring of boats in federal navigable waters. These restrictions have grown to crisis proportions in such states as Florida, California, and Hawaii, forcing local boaters to band together and fight these repressive measures enacted by local governments. On an individual basis, boaters who have challenged local anchoring laws that conflict with federal jurisdiction usually have won their cases in the local courts, but the basic issue of state versus

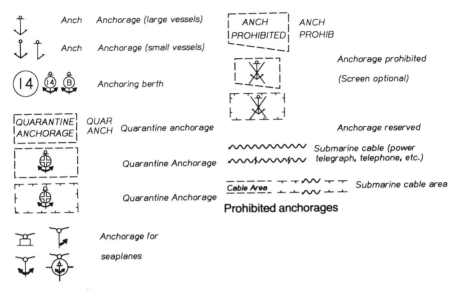

Fig. 11-1. Chart symbols for use in anchoring (from Tables G and P in *Chart No. 1: United States of America Nautical Chart Symbols and Abbreviations*, Eighth Edition, 1984).

federal authority remains unresolved. What is needed is a uniform national anchorage policy that addresses the concerns of local governments regarding environmental preservation of the local waters while retaining the constitutional right of the people to navigate in those waters.

Action at the federal level has been taken in two states. An aggressive initiative by a group of Florida boaters in 1991 brought forth a clarification from the Coast Guard, seventh district, reaffirming federal supremacy over navigable waters in that state. In 1992 a lawsuit was filed in U.S. district court by the Hawaii Navigable Waters Preservation Society to overturn state regulations restricting anchoring in federally controlled navigable waters around the Hawaiian islands.

The U.S. Coast Guard has attempted for years to stay aloof from the controversy. A spokesman for the Coast Guard, fourteenth district (Pacific Islands), said: "We cannot, as a federal agency, intervene between citizens and state government." To the recreational boater, this, however, appears to be more of a case of state and local governments usurping federal authority, which happens to be under the jurisdiction of the Coast Guard. Other federal agencies, such as the Environmental Protection Agency and the

Corps of Engineers, have shown no such reluctance to correct states when they infringe on their jurisdictions.

In 1992 the national boating organization, Boat/US, made a formal request on behalf of all recreational boaters to the Commandant, U.S. Coast Guard, for a uniform Coast Guard position. As a result, the Coast Guard's legal counsel undertook a review of various state and local regulations affecting freedom of navigation. The review was completed in January 1993 and the Commandant replied, thusly:

"The states through their inherent police powers have concurrent authority with the federal government over navigable waters of the United States within their respective state borders. This exercise of state police power is, however, limited in two ways. First, if Congress enacts a federal statute that conflicts with state law, federal law preempts the conflicting state law. Second, the exercise of state law in this area is directly limited by the power reserved to the federal government to regulate interstate commerce. Even where Congress fails to act, state regulation cannot unduly burden interstate commerce.

"Thus states do have the authority to enact anchorage regulation as long as their regulation does not actually conflict with federal law. The Coast Guard designates anchorage areas, usually at the request of local municipalities, solely for the purpose of exempting vessels of less than 65 feet from the Federal requirement of exhibiting anchor lights and sounding signals while anchored in the designated anchorage area. Concurrent state or local regulation within these areas has been a long standing practice which the Coast Guard has encouraged and that the courts have upheld. The Coast Guard's primary concern regarding anchoring is that navigation safety is not compromised and commerce is not restricted.

"While the regulations promulgated by the states may be unpopular with the recreational boater, the Coast Guard has no authority to impose limits on state regulation when Congress has not specifically intended to prevent state regulation of navigation. The status of state anchorage regulations as an undue infringement upon the right of navigation has not been clearly determined by case law and is a question more properly directed at the courts by individual boaters. Our nations' waterways serve a multitude of competing interests. As these waterways become more congested and environmental resources threatened, coordinating this multiple use becomes imperative. How to manage waterway use to preserve and enhance navigability is a question that cannot be answered solely at the federal level."

This Coast Guard policy cannot be expected to be the end to the controversy. Nor can one expect the results of the suit by the Hawaii Navigable Waters Preservation Society to end the Hawaii controversy and set precedent for other states. Court appeals are certain to follow, and they in turn will be followed by attempts to change federal law. Boaters are advised to keep current on the status of anchoring laws in the vicinity where they operate their boats.

(Current information on the anchoring controversy can be obtained from: Boat Owners Association of the United States, 880 South Pickett St., Alexandria, VA 22304; Concerned Boaters, 601 West 1st Street, Stuart, FL 34994; and Hawaii Navigable Waters Preservation Society, 24 Sand Island Road, #27, Honolulu, HI 96819.)

ETIQUETTE OF ANCHORING

Weekends and holidays find literally thousands of boats slipping their urban moorings to seek solitude in isolated coves where the peace and quiet of nature can be enjoyed. But the growing numbers of boats are straining the capacity of the limited accessible coves posing new social problems. Yachting people are not only gregarious in nature but many are newcomers to the sport and tend to gather, seeking the security of more experienced boaters. What may spell trouble in an anchorage is the neo-phyte or the aggressive individual trying to shoehorn into a limited space giving all of the other mariners a trying time at anchor.

While much has been said about the technology and techniques of anchoring, a proper attitude towards the etiquette of anchoring is essential if everyone is to enjoy collectively the pleasures of available anchorages. Since you can't always escape to uninhabited islands in the South Seas, you must learn to get along with other boaters suffering the same restrictions.

Although everyone has a right to anchor, no one has a right to infringe on the berth of a boat already at anchor. The old maxim, first come, first served, was never truer than in an anchorage. The first boat into an anchorage is entitled to choose the best spot which usually means the best shelter, holding ground, access to beach, etc. Subsequent arrivals are then committed to the next best locations so as not to foul the berths of those who were there first.

Newcomers who are unsure how to apply their limited anchoring knowledge should be particularly careful. Giving a wide berth in anchoring not only shows respect for the boats who got there first, but should wind or current change, it will give the novice breathing room and not expose his inexperience.

The first come, first served rule for anchoring has a legal precedent that you will quickly learn should your boat damage another that was

One of the joys of cruising is to find a secure anchorage where yours is the only boat. This is Jaluit atoll in the Marshall Islands.

anchored first. It places the blame for collision on the later vessel to arrive that has anchored too close to the first so as to foul her when swinging. The first vessel to anchor is not only the privileged vessel, but it also has the right to warn off later arrivals who appear to be anchoring so close as to possibly foul its berth.

When you arrive at an anchorage, study the potential berthing areas carefully so that you can put down your hook where it won't foul another berth. Observe the general scheme of previously anchored boats—one anchor or two, all-chain rode of short scope or rope rodes of long scope, and the locations of anchors and anchor markers. Also, take into account the size and design of boats, and anchor with your own kind so that you will swing in like circles.

Those who anchor first should not just sit back with beverage in hand and smirk at others trying to set their anchors. Particularly in a difficult anchorage, the first-comers should lend a hand to others to help them pick a good spot and set a secure anchor. It can be a worthwhile defensive act.

On our first Pacific cruise we entered the harbor at Neiafu, Tonga, with little idea where to anchor, knowing that the bottom was a montage of coral heads and coral sand. The boat *Rigadoon* from Miami was already anchored with the crew enjoying the tropical environment. The skipper, on seeing us come in, boarded his dinghy and came over to guide us to a clear sand spot where we set the hook and stayed for a week. All of us who have anchored in difficult situations have come to appreciate help that is offered by others already anchored.

The worst side of boating people comes out when they are a part of a flotilla spending a weekend together. I am sure you have seen it. By sheer numbers the group takes over the anchorage, literally pushing others out by anchoring too close, shouting between boats, running dinghy races in the anchorage, and keeping auxiliary generators running into the wee hours of the night. It is an unfortunate but true aspect of the boating scene. In an open anchorage there is little that you can do about it but pick up your own hook and move to a more secluded anchorage. In a controlled anchorage a complaint to the local authority might bring some relief although most likely a compromise will be suggested and you'll inevitably be the loser. Although you have the right to your anchoring berth, it is better to move than risk damage to your boat and your nerves.

The Isthmus Cove at Catalina Island has always been a favorite spot for the Los Angeles boating fraternity. But as the years went by, more and more moorings were placed in it so that the open area for anchoring had to move into deeper water. One Fourth of July we had anchored our 29-foot sailboat just outside the last row of moorings in about 60 feet of water. Along came a small fleet of outboard powerboats to anchor outside of us in still deeper water. This anchorage was in water so deep they must have fully expected to hang safely on a 1 to 1 scope with their inadequate rodes. The quiet evening brought no difficulty but when the onshore wind came up the next day, anchors started to drag, and soon seven boats including ours were entangled. My boat and a neighboring one were well set, and we formed the backstop to the others. Some of the skippers tried to motor out of the melee, adding further to the tangle. When we got the propellers stopped, I put on fins, mask, and snorkle and took a knife over the side and started severing anchor lines wound around propellers, handing them back to the surface. By this time the owners of the dragging boats were so mortified in the presence of the large holiday crowd that they gladly accepted their severed anchor rodes and departed when freed. Don't let the euphoria of simply arriving at an anchorage impair your anchoring judgment.

I recall another incident in Matauwhi Bay, New Zealand, that points out the too-eager-to-get-ashore problem. A 40-foot ketch from Coos Bay, Oregon, motored into the anchorage and took up a berth almost directly to leeward of us and before the boat could complete its initial swing after the anchor took hold, the crew was in its dinghy flailing at the oars to get ashore quickly. Gusty winds are the norm in this area surrounded by many hills. When a particularly severe gust hit, guess whose boat started to drag its anchor? The Oregon boat was headed inexorably for the shore until we boarded her and increased the scope of the rode to get the anchor to bite. I don't think the crew ever noticed that their boat had moved or that the anchor rode had been belayed in a manner different than their usual practice.

Give some thought to the consequences of a dragging anchor—either yours or a neighboring boat to windward. Whichever boat drags becomes the burdened vessel regardless of the first come, first served rule, and the burdened boat is responsible for damage to any boat with which it collides. Of course, if the boat goes on the rocks, and it is yours, you have an immediate recognizable loss on your hands. If all the boats drag due to an unexpectedly strong wind as in the Cabo San Lucas disaster, then it is an Act of God and individual claims become difficult to pursue in a court of law. Nevertheless, even in the Cabo San Lucas disaster the owner of the Alden 45 yawl, *Gemini,* filed suit against the large powerboat, *Caprice,* claiming inadequate ground tackle as the reason for the defendant's boat being dragged down on the plaintiff's boat resulting in both boats being lost.

SIGNALS WHILE ANCHORED

A vessel at anchor has a clearly spelled out responsibility to display certain signals and take other precautions to minimize the chances of a collision from a boat underway in its vicinity. The rules which govern the conditions for anchoring in inland waters of the United States (which encompass a goodly share of all harbors, rivers, and lakes) were established in the Inland Navigational Rules Act of 1980 which took effect on 24 December 1981. The new Inland Rules unified the old Inland Rules, the Western Rivers Rules, and the Great Lakes Rules.

When outside the inland waters of the United States or in foreign waters where no special inland rules exist, the rules which govern the conditions for anchoring are those promulgated in the International Regulations for Preventing Collisions at Sea, 1972, more commonly known as the Rules of the Road or often referred to simply as COLREGS. The most recent amendments to COLREGS took effect 1 June 1983. The

Coast Guard publishes these rules in a book entitled *Navigation Rules, International-Inland,* available from the U. S. Government Printing Office.

The right of way of vessels that are moving versus those that are not moving are specifically called out in both the Inland Rules and COLREGS. A vessel that is underway and moving is presumed to be at fault if it collides with a vessel that is underway but not moving or one that is not underway but anchored. But (and this is a big but), if the vessel anchored displayed improper lights or other signals or was in an improper location for anchoring, it, too, is deemed to have contributed to the collision and can be held jointly liable. When marine accidents involving two or more vessels occur, liability is apportioned on the basis of adherence or lack of adherence to the rules by each party.

In all cases the skipper is responsible for the practice of good seamanship to prevent a collision from happening. The Rules state:

> Nothing in these Rules shall exonerate any vessel, or the owner, master, or crew thereof, from the consequences of any neglect to comply with these Rules or of the neglect of any precautions which may be required by the ordinary practice of seamen, or by the special circumstances of the case.

In other words, you must not only follow the Rules in anchoring but you must also take whatever additional precautions are warranted, and possible, to avoid a collision between a boat underway and your own anchored boat. Boats anchored outside of special anchorage areas and in times of reduced visibility must certainly take extra precautions.

It has been clearly established through centuries of maritime litigation that an anchored boat does have a responsibility to avoid collision by a boat underway. An anchored vessel has the responsibility to display proper lights or other signals; sound such warnings as appropriate; maintain an anchor watch if not in a designated anchorage; and not anchor (except in an emergency) in a narrow channel or fairway, where other traffic is liable to collide with the anchored vessel, or in traffic separation zones. The use of proper signals while anchored is fundamental to avoid collisions. The boat operator is referred to the current Rules of the Road for legal specifics on all manners of signals required for boats on inland and international waters.

During nighttime and at periods of reduced visibility, an anchor light is to be exhibited from an elevated part of the anchored vessel in all but special anchorages. The visibility or distinctive character of the anchor light should not be impaired nor should other lights be displayed that may imply a different anchoring situation. Figs. 11-2 and 11-3 illustrate current Coast Guard anchor light requirements for powerboats and sailboats under 50 meters (164 feet) in length.

During day in unrestricted
visibility:
   Daymark—black ball on
   halyard

At night in unrestricted visibility:
   All-around light (360° -
   32 points) visible for 2 miles

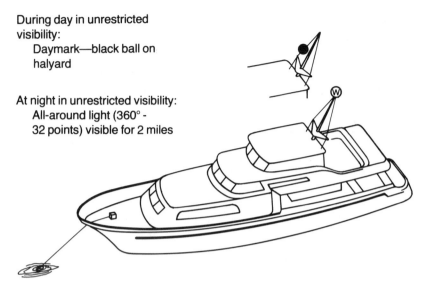

In fog and restricted visibility:
   In addition to the day and night signals shown above, vessels should also have
   a bell mounted forward which is rung rapidly for 5 seconds out of every minute.

Fig. 11-2. Anchor signals for powerboats under 50 meters in length
(164 feet).

Nonelectric lights, such as kerosene lights, are acceptable as anchor
lights, and their intensity should, as far as is practical, be the same as for
electric. The all-round light is required to be a steady white light. Strobe
lights are not legal for this purpose as the Coast Guard recognizes them
only as distress signals.

Although lights are thought of normally as nighttime signals, they
are also required to be used during periods of restricted visibility such as
fog, rain, and snow, dust storms, and the like. An anchor light may also be
shown at any other time while at anchor when it is deemed necessary.

Two special situations exist which negate the need for showing an
anchor light or a day shape on a small boat at anchor. These are:

> In inland waters when a vessel of less than 20 meters in length
> (66 feet) is at a special anchorage.

> When a vessel of less than 7 meters in length (23 feet) is at
> anchor not in or near a narrow channel, fairway, anchor-
> age, or other area where other vessels would normally
> navigate.

During day in unrestricted visibility:
Daymark—black ball on forestay or flag halyard

At night in unrestricted visibility:
All-around light (360° - 32 points) visible for 2 miles, either at masthead or alternatively on forestay or flag halyard

In fog and restricted visibility:
In addition to the day and night signals shown above, vessels should also have a bell mounted forward which is rung rapidly for 5 seconds out of every minute.

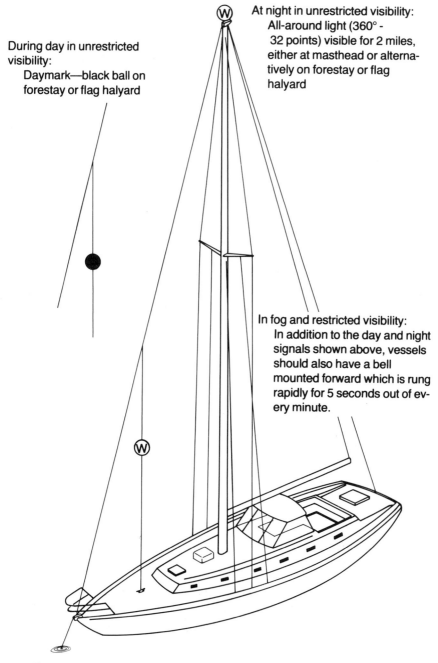

Fig. 11-3. Anchor signals for sailboats under 50 meters in length (164 feet).

The proper day shape for an anchored small boat is a black ball suspended where best seen, preferably in the forepart of the vessel. The ball should have a diameter of not less than 0.6 meters (2 feet) except that for a vessel of less than 20 meters in length, a shape of lesser dimension but commensurate with the size of the vessel may be used. Inflatable balls of approximately 1½ feet in diameter are available. The minimum size to be used on any boat probably should not be smaller than one foot in diameter. These can be made from children's beach balls that are painted black.

Vessels at anchor are required to have the capability to make sound signals on a bell and, optionally, also, on a horn or whistle. Sound signals are to be used to supplement anchor lights and day shapes when the visibility becomes restricted.

The distance at which visibility becomes "restricted" is not specified but reasonably can be taken to be the distance at which an anchor light or day shape can be seen in clear weather. For boats under 50 meters in length the distance would be 2 miles.

A vessel at anchor in restricted visibility should ring its bell rapidly for 5 seconds out of every minute. In vessels under 100 meters in length (328 feet), the bell should be sounded in the forepart of the vessel.

In addition to a bell, a vessel at anchor may sound three blasts in succession on a horn or whistle. The pattern of sounds is one short, one long, and one short. This additional warning is particularly useful if your lookout spots by sound or eye another vessel approaching your anchorage on what could become a collision course.

A vessel of less than 20 meters in length when at anchor in a special anchorage is not required to sound fog signals.

A vessel of less than 12 meters in length need not give either the required bell signal nor the supplementary whistle signal provided that it gives some other efficient sound signal at intervals of not more than 2 minutes.

Flags are a traditional method of signaling requests or actions while in a harbor. The U. S. edition of the *International Code of Signals* (H. O. 102) is the basic guide to signals to be used for visual, sound, and radio communications. Other signals have been developed on the yachting scene and their use must be restricted to yachting events or areas.

The following one- and two-letter flag signals from H. O. 102 are particularly applicable to small boat anchoring, especially in commercial harbors and on the international scene:

Flag	Meaning
Y	I am dragging my anchor.
P	This vessel is preparing to put to sea within 24 hours.
Z	I require a tug (or a tow).
QT	You should not anchor. You are going to foul my anchor.
QU	Anchoring is prohibited.
QX	I request permission to anchor (to harbormaster).
RD	You should weigh anchor immediately.
RE	You should change your anchorage. It is not safe.

It is recommended that boats traveling internationally carry a full set of signal flags as well as a copy of H. O. 102, not only to be able to converse at anchor but for communication purposes enroute and in moving about harbors.

CHAPTER TWELVE

Storm Anchoring

To discuss storm anchoring is to think about the unthinkable. Too many sailors would like to forget the whole subject on the assumption that it could not happen to them. That may be true for the majority of boat owners who do not expose themselves to severe weather, wisely staying near the fire when the storm warnings are flying. But for those out cruising and, especially, fishermen plying their trade, a storm can come along most unexpectedly, and it is only the boat's on-board resources that can handle the problem. The 45 anchored boats at Cabo San Lucas that were hit by the unexpected short-lived gale in December 1982 had no inkling that the weather would turn on them in the normally mild seasonal weather of the cape.

Nor did the big cruising fleet anchored in the peaceful lagoons of French Polynesia during the southern hemisphere summer of 1982-1983 think that they would be facing five hurricanes in as many months when French Polynesia had not seen a hurricane in 23 years. But the two events did happen, and over 50 boats were lost while at anchor. Many more were saved due to good ground tackle and better survival tactics. I have cruised both of these areas and my stomach knots up at the thought of the boats lost. But at the same time it has given me inspiration to write this chapter on storm anchoring.

A viable storm anchoring system requires good ground tackle consisting of a proper anchor, an elastic rode, and adequate chafing protection. The anchor is the simplest element of the three to provide. You select that design suitable to the seabed and of storm size and have it deployed before the storm hits. In Chapter 7 I discussed in detail the selection process for both seabed compatibility and size governed by boat requirements. Make your choice carefully because when the storm hits, it is the dug-in anchor at the end of the rode that is going to save your boat and not the one you have stowed in the bilge.

The important thing is to have the proper anchor ready. If you have advance warning of a storm, you may have time to replace your working

Most famous of all cruising boat wrecks is that of the brigantine *Yankee* whose bones lie rusting on the fringing coral reef at Rarotonga, Cook Islands. The boat was originally owned by Irving Johnson, a well-known *National Geographic* magazine contributor, who used it in the 1950s as a school ship for teaching sailing on world circumnavigations. The subsequent owner had it in charter in the South Seas and was anchored off the village of Avarua, Rarotonga, when a northerly gale arose making the reef a lee shore. The crew was unable to hold the *Yankee* off the reef and there she perished with no loss of life. Be wary of shifting winds.

anchor with your storm anchor. But if you are out cruising and reliable weather reports are not available or the storm is an unexpected monster, you have to have your storm anchor already in place on the bottom.

Day cruisers, coastal cruisers, and sportfishers normally operate in areas that are well supplied with weather warnings and can get by keeping only a working anchor ready. Fishermen and blue water cruisers, on the other hand, venture into areas where weather forecasts are not available, unreliable, or unintelligible at best (a foreign language, for instance). They should be ready at all times with their storm anchor which means carrying it as the bow anchor even though it adds permanent weight at the bow.

On *Horizon*'s Pacific voyages, the 60-pound CQR has always had the position of honor on the bow roller and has been used for all anchoring chores even though it meant more sweat at the windlass when weighing anchor. The suddenness of the storm at normally placid Cabo San Lucas did not allow any time for the boats to improve on their ground tackle, in fact, some boat crews could not even get to their boats before the storm struck. No amount of paper insurance could help these boats, the only insurance of value to them was their already deployed ground tackle. At final count 23 boats had good insurance policies, and 22 boats did not.

The second critical element in your storm anchoring system is an elastic rode. Surprising to many will be the fact that an all-chain rode is not an elastic system for purposes of storm anchoring. You saw in Chapter 5 how quickly the catenary (sag) of a chain rode disappeared with only moderate end loads. When that sag is gone, there is no more cushion to the system, and shock loads due to surge are applied directly to the rode. Think of it this way—the wind stretches the chain out removing the catenary, if the waters were calm, this would be just a static load well within the capability of the chain. But, waters are not calm in a storm, and the boat will surge, pitch, and gyrate in an unbelievable fashion, applying sudden and sharp loads to the chain already stretched taut. A chain that is stretched taut and then given an additional sharp load is a candidate for failure.

Three tragic examples of chain anchor rodes failing during storms all occurred in 1981 in the Cook Islands archipelago in the South Pacific. One occurred in Penrhyn atoll, and two occurred in Suvarov atoll. Winds in all cases were 50 to 60 knots and shelter was minimal at best. The problem was simply that the strong winds stretched out each anchor chain to the point where there was no catenary left to absorb surge loads or wind gusts. The chains parted, and the boats went on the reefs.

Van Dorn (see Bibliography) presents an analytical approach to designing a practical storm anchoring system that is well worth reading although a bit technical for the lay person. He says:

> Chain is an essential element of an optimum storm anchoring system, but it might better be viewed as a flexible, abrasion-resistant weight, that is already at hand on most vessels, and that can be used to considerably reduce the scope of an elastic nylon rode.

One does not need to be a mathematician to assimilate Van Dorn's theory on storm anchoring. Since he, too, has done blue water cruising, his arguments are sound. Some can be summarized as follows:

> The rode should be made up of equal lengths of chain and twisted 3-strand nylon rope, both of good quality.

> The rope and chain should be joined with a special eye splice made around a chafe-proof thimble of Van Dorn's own design.

Excessive scope need not be used. As the water depth increases, less scope can be used.

Both chain and rope in the rode can be designed to work at half their breaking strength to accommodate storm surges, but they should be in good condition.

Chafe is the primary adversary in storm anchoring, and Van Dorn suggests the use of a special eye splice and thimble to solve that problem where the rope is joined to the chain. Unfortunately, such a unique thimble is not a stock item in chandleries and has to be made to order. There are alternatives, though, such as the Newco thimble and the Samson Nylite connector shown in Chapter 5. With these the rope is well protected from chafe and the thimble cannot slip out of the eye.

The other point of critical chafing concern is where the nylon rode passes over the bow of the boat, whether over a roller, through a chock, or simply rubbing over the toe rail or gunwale cap. You cannot have too smooth a roller or too large a diameter to prevent chafe. Supplementary chafing gear is a necessity in storm anchoring. Leather, fire hose, and reinforced rubber hose are the primary candidates for chafe protection, but heavy canvas can help, if nothing else is available. The problem is to fasten it securely to a rope that is alive—jumping, weaving, and thrashing around like a thing possessed. If bow roller and bits are separated by several feet, the rope will be stretching a foot or more in between them at the same time. I cannot overemphasize the potential difficulty and the adverse circumstances that accompany such a simple a task as wrapping chafing gear around an ordinary rope when the storm is in progress. But it has to be done.

Some of the best advice on the design of chafing gear for anchor rodes comes from the experience of the Houston Yacht Club in surviving cyclonic storms which threaten their cruising fleet every year. By 1983 when hurricane Alicia struck, they had perfected many survival techniques* among which was a successful method of preventing rope chafe through the use of concentric hoses as shown in Fig. 12-1. This chafe guard can be fabricated from readily available material in the off-season and be ready for use when the hurricane threatens. Boats using larger or smaller storm anchor rodes can proportionately increase or decrease the diameters of the corded neoprene hoses.

---

*Hurricane Preparedness Plan, Houston Yacht Club (P. O. Box 1276, LaPorte, TX 77571, 1985).

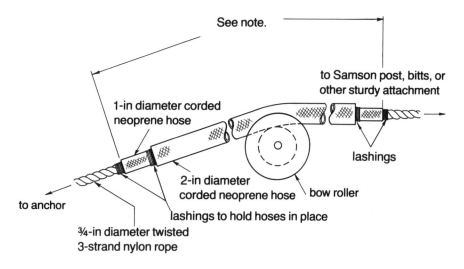

Fig. 12-1. Chafing gear for hurricane anchoring as devised by the Houston Yacht Club.

Even with chafing gear, you cannot depend 100 percent on not getting some wear on your rode at the bow of the boat. For that reason you must be ready to pay out another foot or two of line frequently to distribute the wear. This, of course, will require you to reposition the chafing gear immediately. The game appears to be endless, but every storm eventually blows itself out, and if you have properly tended your ground tackle, seemingly against insurmountable odds, you will most likely see the dawn of a new day from your boat.

CYCLONIC STORMS

Call them what you will—hurricanes, cyclones, typhoons —they all produce the same disastrous winds and seas. A hurricane is defined as a cyclonic storm with winds in excess of 63 knots but if the winds are 63 knots or less, it is a mere tropical storm. Gusts, though, can increase the instantaneous wind speed by as much as 25 to 50 percent. With a minimum hurricane wind speed of 64 knots, the top gust speeds may reach 90 knots. Since sustained wind speeds can easily reach 90 knots or more, the gusts can attain fantastic speeds of 135 knots or more. If the speed of the wind doesn't scare you into careful preparation, remember that the actual aerodynamic force of the wind increases as the square of the wind speed. A 90-knot wind has twice the force of a 64-knot wind, and a 135-knot gust has four times the force of the 64-knot wind. Therefore, prepare your ground tackle for the gusts and not for the lower sustained wind speed.

To complicate the problem further, a cyclonic storm rotates around an eye—counterclockwise in the northern hemisphere and clockwise in the southern hemisphere. If you are caught anywhere within the circle of gale radius (about 200 miles from the eye), you will experience changing wind directions as the storm moves over or past you. This demands that your ground tackle be able to take winds from any direction.

Obviously, winds of hurricane speeds will produce horrendous waves, especially if there is a long fetch. It is essential, therefore, to get your boat into a refuge where it will be partially protected from severe wave action.

Regardless of where you are in sheltered waters, you will have to face tidal or storm surge which can reach heights of 10 feet or more above the normal tide levels. This surge usually precedes the storm arrival and is amplified like all waves as it slides up the coastal slopes into shallower water. It is the storm surge that inundates shoreline land areas making them impassable during a hurricane. Hence the need for completing all shoreside preparations before the onslaught of the full hurricane.

Choose your storm anchorage carefully with due regard to the presence of other boats and, especially, with consideration of what might take place if other vessels break loose during the storm. Hurricane Klaus unexpectedly bore down on the U.S. Virgin Islands in November 1984 resulting in the loss (sunk or severely damaged, some beyond repair) of upwards of 100 boats. While the wind was the direct cause, it was barges breaking moorings, and a cruise ship not under control that physically wiped out dozens of private and charter yachts. You cannot choose your neighbors too carefully in a storm anchorage.

DUAL ANCHOR MOOR

If you at all suspect that the weather is going to turn nasty with increasing winds, you should consider setting dual bow anchors ahead of time instead of having to rely on the hammerlock moor set after the winds arrive. The dual anchor moor not only prevents the boat from sheering side to side but adds insurance through a second anchor, giving increased holding power, and serving as a backup should the first anchor system fail for any reason (Fig. 12-2).

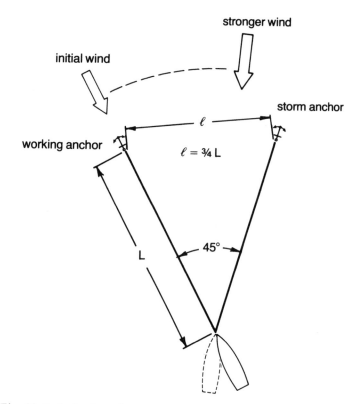

Fig. 12-2. A dual anchor moor.

In a typical blow, due to the passage of a cold front, you can expect the wind to shift as the front passes. And with the passage of the front may come increased wind speeds. Therefore, when laying the dual anchor moor, it is best to set your storm anchor so that it will take the larger wind load.

The same reasoning applies to the positioning of anchors in anticipation of a hurricane. Determine from which direction the maximum winds will come and then lay your storm anchor in that direction. This dual anchor moor is called a "hurricane hawse" in Caribbean waters because local boats use it to ride out hurricanes.

To lay the dual anchor moor, proceed as in laying a single anchor to the prevailing wind. Select either the storm or working anchor for the first lay depending on whether the prevailing wind direction will have the stronger winds or not. Set the first anchor to port or starboard depending on where you want your boat to ride finally under the dual anchors. Put a marker float with this first anchor as a reference for laying the second anchor.

To lay the second anchor, note the compass heading of the first anchor lay and then, under power, motor ahead at 45° to the first anchor lay until you have traveled a distance equal to the first anchor's rode length (L). At this point let go the second anchor and fall back on it, snubbing lightly to establish a good set. The two anchor rodes are then adjusted so that your boat rides comfortably between them.

You might prefer to lay the second anchor in a somewhat different manner if the winds and currents are light. Let go the first anchor at the desired spot and then motor at right angles to the wind (laying out the first rode as you go) a distance (ℓ) that will give you the 45° lay between anchors after settling back. Let go the second anchor at this point, and settle back into the apex of the V, adjusting the scope of the two rodes as necessary. In a 45° moor, the distance between anchors (ℓ) is about three-quarters of the scope length (L) of the equal anchor rodes. Scopes should be 4 to 1 for chain, and 7 to 1 for combination rodes.

The matching of rode scopes is easy if both rodes are made up the same, i.e., all-chain or rope-chain combinations. If you have different rode makeups, then you have to set the anchors asymmetrically, giving the rope rode a greater length (scope) to develop the full holding power of its anchor. Selection of the initial and expected final lay directions of each rode is particularly important as is the matter of swinging room.

The advantage of laying the dual anchor moor in a 45° configuration, initially, is that it can easily be converted to storm configuration if needed. In the 45° configuration the swinging circle is greatly minimized. When the winds pick up, you can veer additional scope on both rodes, yielding a 30°-included angle which is recommended for gale conditions. This, then, is the best of both worlds.

If you use the dual anchor moor for an extended period of time in which the winds shift around the clock, you may find that the two rodes have wrapped themselves together. If one of the rodes is rope, it is an easy matter to cast it off, unwind it from the chain rode, and then belay it back in position. If you have both chain rodes, the task is more difficult, and it may be easier to motor around in a circle to unwind them. The use of a bridle connection with a large swivel to correct this problem is not recommended.

STORM MOORING

When a hurricane does threaten, move your boat immediately into an area of refuge. Take a hint from aviators who always have a landing field in mind in case an emergency landing is required. You should have a hurricane refuge in mind whenever you are sailing in hurricane-prone waters during the local hurricane season.

Rivers or channels are the best places to seek refuge especially if they are surrounded by hills or mountains or have heavily forested shorelines. If a narrow river or channel is selected, think in terms of mooring your boat in the center of the stream, headed into the expected direction of the wind and ultimate waves. If the channel or inlet is too wide to allow simultaneous mooring to both shorelines, choose the shoreline that will put your boat in the lee of the land and use a combination of shoreline mooring on one side and storm anchoring on the other.

The channel moor assumes that the maneuvering area is too small for the boat to swing with the wind, hence it must be secured fore and aft and take the wind on the beam as best it can. A minimum of 6 mooring lines should be used—2 forward, 2 abeam, and 2 aft as shown in Fig. 12-3. Your strongest lines should be put on the bow which faces into the predicted wind and wave. They can be fastened to your normal foredeck ground tackle fittings with plenty of chafing gear. The lines abeam can be run

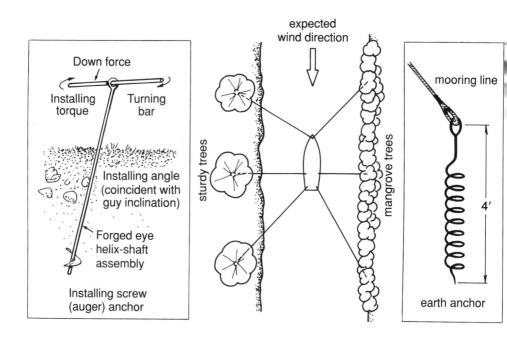

Fig. 12-3. Hurricane mooring in a narrow channel or river.

around the mast at cabin top level if, and only if, the mast is keel stepped. Otherwise, secure the lines to other strong points located amidships. The aft mooring lines should be secured to the cleats used for stern anchoring or to any substantial fitting aft that can take the loads without failure. Each of the paired lines should be tied across the vessel to help share attachment loads.

The shore ends of the mooring lines should be attached to firm anchors which might be healthy trees with a deep root system or posts or pilings set to great depths. If mangroves line the bank, you are in good shape. Mangroves are well anchored to the bottom and passing a line around a clump of them will give you a firm tie to the land. But you must restrain your mooring line from sliding up and off the trunks.

A special screw-type earth anchor can also be very useful where no other attachment means exists. These are made for a similar purpose of tying down airplanes and mobile homes in high winds.

The small boat refuge at Saipan is a narrow winding channel lined with mangroves and ironwood trees and a number of unreliable pilings of old wharfs. With no other protection on the island, a boat could possibly survive a passing typhoon (but not a direct hit) by employing storm moorings in this channel. Although only one boat was moored in the channel at the time of this photograph, when a storm threatens, many small boats, both recreational and charter, take shelter here with considerable crowding.

Once all of your mooring lines are in place, double up on them with whatever rope you have left, which should not be skimpy. Try to use boat and shore attachments that are not already in use to gain an independent system. Your mooring lines should be orderly, not haphazard, with each line doing its share of the work. Failure of any one or two lines (most likely it will be due to chafing) should not put your boat in jeopardy. At this point your boat may look much like Gulliver who was trussed in place by the Lilliputians with a multiplicity of lines. If done correctly, your boat, like Gulliver, will live to see another day.

One last word on mooring lines: they should be long enough to accommodate the tidal surge that accompanies a hurricane. While it is not recommended that you leave too much slack in them for this purpose, you may have to because you do not want your boat so restrained that it takes water over the bow and eventually becomes submerged. I have, however, heard of instances where boats have been deliberately sunk in shallow water and anchored in place on the bottom, protecting them from wave action although the boat furnishings were written off as near total losses.

A TAHITI HURRICANE

The years 1982 and 1983 were notable for their unusual weather in the Pacific basin. These were the years of the most severe El Nino* activity that has ever been recorded. Trade winds disappeared; the equatorial countercurrent broadened into an immense river of warm water flowing from the western to the eastern Pacific; the schools of anchovies off of the Peruvian coast fled the warm water; game fish like yellowfin tuna and marlin were caught as far north as the Oregon coast; a general drought set into the western Pacific while torrential rains drenched the west coast of the Americas; 17 million sea birds on Christmas Island took flight to find drier nesting places and better foraging; and we sailors found baffling winds throughout the Pacific.

The infamous gale at Cabo San Lucas was believed to be a product of El Nino as well as the hurricanes that struck French Polynesia. The islands of French Polynesia are out of the normal hurricane belt and hadn't experienced a hurricane since 1959. In fact, there had been only 20 hurricanes since record keeping started in 1825. But 1982 and 1983 were to be different—5 hurricanes plus 2 tropical storms pummeled the area.

---

*Near the end of every calendar year, a weak southward-flowing warm ocean current develops along the coast of Peru and Ecuador. Because it comes near the Christmas season, the local residents call it "El Nino," "The Child," referring to the Christ child. The 1982-1983 event was so severe that there is some question whether it was simply the annual event or something else, but the name has held.

The damage to the islands of French Polynesia was severe, and overseas cruising boats, as well as local boats, suffered considerable losses. But out of it came stories of fights to survive, some successful and some not so successful, but all of them telling how to (or how not to) survive a hurricane at anchor. The most succinct and dramatic of these stories was told by Jack Ronalter. Jack, a single-hander, sailing a Golden Gate 30 sloop, *World Citizen*, had just missed the Cabo San Lucas gale and the preceding 4 hurricanes in French Polynesia only to be caught in hurricane Veena, the last and meanest of the El Nino hurricanes to strike French Polynesia in 1983. Jack not only described the drama of the event, but detailed his tactics to save his anchored boat—choosing an anchorage, preparing the boat, fighting chafe, and using multiple anchors and rodes. All of the good and bad of the anchoring game were encountered, but let Jack tell the story in his own words.*

The first variable in the equation is the anchoring location. I decided to try my luck at Maeva Beach, a decision which was controversial at best since Maeva Beach was hit hard and suffered the most casualties. My logic for picking that spot was based largely on the reports that Papeete Harbor had become a virtual zoo during the previous hurricane. This was because many boats had left the quai and anchored close together with poor ground tackle in the middle of the harbor. I didn't want any part of that bump and grind contest a la Cabo San Lucas.

The next two possibilities I considered were Beachcomber Bay and Maeva Beach Bay. Beachcomber Bay had a little better protection than Maeva and, reportedly, good holding ground. However, it was crowded when I got there, so I ended up at Maeva.

Maeva Beach Bay is wide open to any winds that come from the northwest through southwest, but the barrier reef provides fair protection from the seas. It also, reportedly, has good holding ground. But above all it was the *least* crowded. I wasn't completely happy with it because of the marginal protection, but in my opinion it was the least of the three evils. Essentially, I was betting that given room to maneuver, my good ground tackle would make up for some of the shortcomings of the anchorage.

I found my way away from the other boats, out in the middle of the bay, in about 45 feet of water. I anchored with my regular bow hook arrangement, a 22-pound Bruce and 200 feet of 5/16-inch chain.

---

*By permission. Jack Ronalter's letter was first published in *Latitude 38*, July 1983. Most of that letter is reproduced here.

Compare the serenity of this scene of Maeva Beach Bay, Tahiti, with the untamed violence of hurricane Veena which Jack Ronalter survived at the same location. The island of Moorea is in the background.

Next I shackled a 300-foot length of 1/2-inch nylon to the end of the chain and payed out about 100 feet.

Next I took my 35-pound CQR with 50 feet of chain and 300 feet of 1/2-inch nylon and dropped it over the bow, letting only about 30 feet of chain out. I brought the rode back to the cockpit winch and set it up so that I could drop the CQR to the bottom from the cockpit. Now I was ready to pay out the main anchor rode if more scope was needed, to change the chafe point, or to set the CQR as I payed out the main anchor or if I started to drag.

For backup I had a 13S Danforth with 15 feet of chain and about 120 feet of nylon ready to go over the side—I planned to use this for a steadying or stern anchor. Also a 22H Danforth with 15 feet of chain and 200 feet of 9/16-inch nylon, and lastly a 16.5-pound Bruce with miscellaneous lengths of dock lines that could be bent to it if things got really bad. So I had five anchors in all, one set and the rest held in reserve. I did not set more anchors at the time for fear that the rodes would badly tangle.

After the anchors were prepared, I stripped the boat. I took down the dodger and weather cloths, removed the spinnaker halyards. I deflated my Avon dinghy and stowed it below with the Seagull outboard motor. Essentially, everything topsides got stowed below except my life raft. Some boats went so far as to remove their main booms. I elected to leave mine in place because there wasn't any more room below. But I did wrap about 50 feet of line tightly around the mainsail to reduce windage that would be caused by a flapping sail cover.

The night before the storm I went to sleep about 2100 with a little help from a good dinner and a bottle of wine. *Veena* was packing sustained winds of 100 knots and heading for Tahiti, but there were still hot, humid winds where I was. Even at this point I didn't *really* think we were going to get hit hard. I woke up around 0100 to the unmistakable sound of wind—lots of wind! By 0200 it was screaming and the seas were building. Almost right away I realized that "fight the chafe" was the name of the game. I had rubber hoses and leather for chafe gear. Still hanging on one hook, I fought to keep my main anchor rode from being destroyed.

As the seas continued to build, the chafe problem got amazingly difficult to cope with. The anchor rode was like a wild snake, avoiding all my efforts to keep chafe gear attached. Time wore on as the wind continued to scream and shriek at an ever more deafening volume. The boat was pitching, rolling, and yawing all at the same time, and the crazy snake of a rode continuously destroyed my chafe gear.

At 0400 the job seemed to be impossible, the seas were now about 6 feet, and the wind was taking the tops of the waves clean off, filling the air with a thunderous white wall. Because of this, I could no longer stand up nor could I face into the wind. All work at the bow had to be done by Braille. I spent at least 20 minutes putting one piece of leather in place only to return to the bow 10 minutes later and find that the wild snake was free of it once again. When I bent over to reattach it, solid green water started washing over my head, completely submerging my body. I was ingesting mouthfuls of water, and trying to time my breathing with the dunkings I was taking.

There didn't appear to be any way to deal with all of these problems at once. First I would have to hang on constantly so I couldn't tie knots with two hands; then I couldn't see; and now I couldn't breathe. This definitely could no longer be listed under the heading of "fun."

It was confirmed later that at this point in time the airport, which was about two miles downwind of where I was anchored, was recording sustained winds of 96 knots and gusts near 132 knots.

Back in the cockpit I let out about ten feet more of scope on the CQR so that it would now just touch bottom. I was very worried that if the main rode snapped I would be drifting so fast that the 35-pound

CQR would not be able to set itself, so I also let the 13S Danforth go to the bottom and payed out all of its meager 135 feet of scope. I didn't think it would do much good in these conditions, just slow the boat down a little and give the CQR a chance to set.

With that work finished I started to think of what an awful fix I was in. My big plan wasn't working very well. I couldn't control the chafe on my main anchor rode with chafe gear. I couldn't pay out more scope on it to change the chafe point because another boat, which had to slip its first set of ground tackle, was now too close to me and getting even closer as the wind started to veer to the west. I began to face the fact that after the night was over I may have to get a new boat to continue my cruising trip.

My spirits were pretty low by now, but before they could get any lower, the worst happened. My main anchor rode parted. I heard a faint snap from the bow and then the screaming wind took my boat off toward the reef. I dived for the winch and quickly started paying out the 35-pound CQR rode. I looked over my shoulder to make sure that all the Danforth's scope was out. Within seconds I had about 220 feet out, and I started to take up on the strain slowly. My heart was pounding. Will it dig in? Will it set? Slowly the bow came around and into the wind as the anchor dug in. I couldn't see the boat that I had been next to before so I didn't know how much ground I had lost, but I wasn't on the reef and I wasn't close to any other boats. I was holding. My plan was working! I was still safe.

I rushed to the bow with new energy. I started again at the impossible task of fighting chafe, now on two anchor rodes. The difference was now my spirits were up, and it wasn't impossible anymore. I was finding ways to fight back. I even found comfort in the fact that when the waves would break over me, I would be completely under water, there was no more wind!

I worked like a madman dragging my 22H Danforth to the bow and lowering it over the side the same way I had with the big CQR— just off the bottom, in reserve. I bent the remainder of the parted bow rode to my 16-pound Bruce and added dock lines, sheets, and whatever else I could find. I brought the Bruce to the bow, lowered it over, and hung it just off the bottom. I made up my mind that I wasn't going on the beach until every bit of ground tackle that I had was put to use. I even eyed my dinghy anchor a few times.

I think it became light around 0500 but due to that incredible wall of white around me, my first glimpse of the beach wasn't until almost 0600. Just in the Maeva Beach area I counted 11 yachts on the beach or reef and only 9 still floating. About an hour later I was able to get out the binoculars and I counted 17 boats beached or reefed and it wasn't over yet. To the best of my knowledge the final count for the entire island was 47 boats either sunk, beached, or reefed. Of the 47 at least 30 were cruising yachts.

The hurricane damage to my boat was certainly less than it could have been. My masthead wind direction vane had blown away. I lost a large amount of dried foods that were stored forward in compartments that had gotten flooded due to enormous amounts of water going down my deck pipe. Two weeks after the storm my windlass froze up. I discovered that the Simpson-Lawrence 510 windlass is not designed for continuous underwater duty, since it had gotten full of salt water. On the brighter side I found my main anchor ground tackle while scuba diving, so I still have my normal complement of five anchors.

Two days after the storm, as part of an emergency assistance dive team, I worked to find and dig up ground tackle lost by other boats at Maeva Beach. The picture was almost the same on all of the ground tackle we found: anchor well buried, chain still attached, a good length of line—and then that sick-looking ragged end of the line that had gotten chafed through. Some anchors took as much as 45 minutes to dig out; they weren't going anywhere. The big problem was holding onto the ground tackle, controlling chafe. That may sound simple, but as I found out in these ultimate conditions, the problems are complex. One boat's bow roller got torn completely off and the boat went on the beach after lines chafed through on sharp edges. Another boat's heavy duty stainless steel bow roller was twisted 70° from the enormous strains. Another boat's windlass (wildcat) broke into pieces when the chain snubbers parted and the chain was still in the wildcat.

If nothing else, riding out Hurricane *Veena* was one h—— of a learning experience for me. Also, I would like to think that even though I wasn't in Cabo during that disaster, I did learn a lot from it by arriving just after it and seeing the destruction and talking to the people. Although no two storms are alike and the conditions are never the same, I hope that something in these notes proves to be of value for someone who reads them and ends up in the "ultimate condition," a hurricane.

Little can be added to Jack Ronalter's story. He had equipped his boat with the appropriate ground tackle, and he showed immense ingenuity in deploying it during the height of the hurricane. It came through loud and clear that chafe was his number one problem and the violent pitching motion of the boat made it almost impossible to combat. While chain would have done away with chafe, would it have stood up to the surging of the boat in that violent sea?

THE CABO SAN LUCAS DISASTER

There is much to be learned from the experiences of others regarding storm management at sea or at anchor. Only a relative handful of people survive major storms and getting the facts out after such harrowing experiences proves difficult but not impossible. The Cabo San Lucas disaster became well documented in writing and interviews, and, when some of the surviving boats arrived in Hawaii, I was able to verify certain anchoring situations at Cabo San Lucas that bear on the subject of storm anchoring in general.

Weather was obviously the principal factor but it was the quickness with which the storm developed and changed direction that was the real culprit. About 1600 on 8 December 1982, the first Weatherfax report came through showing that a front with 30- to 40-knot southwest winds was due before midnight. Cabo San Lucas anchorage is well sheltered from southwest winds so few of the crews were concerned. (Four boats took the weather report very seriously and departed the anchorage to their everlasting satisfaction.) Around 1800 the wind shifted suddenly to the southeast exposing the entire anchorage to onshore winds with a fetch of several hundred miles. The winds quickly built to 30 knots and by 2000 they were howling into the open anchorage at 50 to 60 knots. Seas built rapidly and by 2100 they were estimated at 12 to 15 feet.

Now there wasn't a boat there that could not have withstood 60-knot winds and 15-foot seas in the open ocean. But these boats were anchored on a shelving bottom. They had sought the convenience of being close to the beach and in doing so they had put themselves inside the surf line of storm waves. They were battered and jerked about until 28 of them were on the beach either from upset anchors, parted rodes, or broken deck gear.

I can recount a similar event which I witnessed many years ago on an August cruise to Smuggler's Cove at Santa Cruz Island off the coast of Southern California. Smuggler's is also a shallow open roadstead and the surf breaks far offshore tending to make boats anchor quite a distance from the shoreline. The weather was good but southerly swells were coming in from a hurricane off Baja California. While most boats anchored well offshore, one Cal-24 anchored inside the rest. I thought nothing of it and at every anchor check through the night I saw its anchor light bobbing up and down in the blackness until near dawn when it disappeared. At daylight we saw the boat lying on its side on the cobbly beach. Low tide had set in and the surf line had moved farther away from the shore putting this boat in the breaking surf where no boat should be. In this case there was little wind and it was simply the breaking waves that caused the trouble.

Meanwhile back at Cabo San Lucas things steadily got worse. Several boats in an outer row (80- to 90-foot depths) were able to get free and put out to sea leaving their ground tackle behind. The buoyed ground tackle plus free-floating lost ground tackle was making it impossible for other boats to motor out since props were getting wrapped and engines stalled. Five boats who attempted to motor out stalled their engines. Some then tried to sail out, but there was inadequate tacking room and floating gear fouled rudders.

Floating anchor rodes and other debris added to the troubles of those who elected to ride out the storm at anchor with engine power. The floating debris fouled their props and rudders preventing them from using the engines to help steady the boat. Engine overheating also became a major problem due to bottom sand churned up by the breaking waves getting into the cooling system.

Collisions were rampant among anchored boats, drifting boats, and boats attempting to make a run for it. The reason behind it was the gregarious nature of the cruisers which led them to anchor in a dense pack formation in a small bight of land. They were so closely anchored that stern anchors were required to keep the boats from going bump in the night under just normal conditions. More than one drifting boat literally tangled with another still anchored and dragged it along to the beach.

One boat was successfully riding out the storm when its mainsail and jib were whipped free of the sail bags adding to the windage. The ground tackle was overpowered and the boat ended up on the beach.

The storm abated after midnight but the waves kept rolling in until dawn. Then the true measure of the disaster was apparent. Of the 45 boats that had been enjoying the hospitality of this small Mexican port, 28 of them were on the beach and, of these, 22 were written off as total losses.

There are several messages that come out of this disaster that can help the rest of us anchor our boats safely:

> Have plenty of ground tackle on board—3 or 4 complete sets, at least.

> Note that chain rodes can break when the boat pitches violently against a taut anchor rode. Use a nylon rope spring in the anchor rode.

Dense pack anchoring ends up in dense pack wreckage, as shown along the shoreline of Cabo San Lucas after the surprise gale of December 1982. Courtesy: *Latitude 38.*

Choose an anchorage with plenty of swinging room and in depths that are still reasonable from a scope standpoint but not so shallow that storm waves can break where you are located.

Watch the weather closely, and, at the first sign of a storm, take appropriate action. It is better to be a cowardly sailor with a boat than a macho sailor without one.

Use plenty of chafing gear.

Prepare your boat for the storm by stripping it of all topside canvas and loose items that could go astray.

Always have an escape plan in mind and your boat ready to go. Do not even sit down to happy hour after an arrival until you have made certain that your boat is ready to evacuate the anchorage on a moment's notice.

The remarkable thing about the Cabo San Lucas affair is that no lives were lost although many blue water cruising dreams were shattered. This unfortunate experience of others should make all of us more wary in choosing an anchorage just for convenience.

PART III

THE MECHANICS OF MOORINGS

A comprehensive guide to designing and fabricating a variety of permanent boat moorings and some of their limitations.

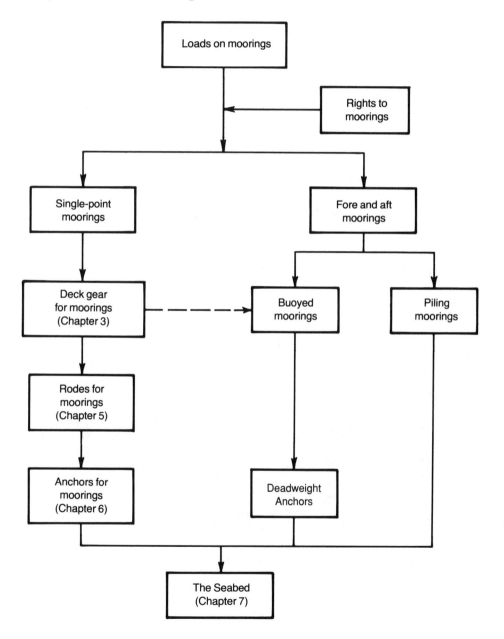

CHAPTER THIRTEEN

Permanent Moorings

Permanent moorings are variations on the anchoring theme wherein the boat is secured in place by means of ground tackle which is normally not a part of the boat's on-board equipment. Permanent moorings are generally used in protected waters and where it is not feasible to build slips for boat moorage. A permanent mooring shows a degree of "ownership" of an area of water which is much less apt to be appropriated by someone else in your absence than if it were simply an open anchorage area.

Single point moorings are provided by the Marianas Yacht Club for members and visiting cruising boats. Deep water in the Apra, Guam, commercial harbor and a fringing coral reef make simple anchoring a difficult and insecure task. When typhoons threaten, boats take refuge in the nearby mangrove-lined Piti channel.

MUSHROOM ANCHOR SINGLE POINT MOORING

The single point mooring concept is similar to anchoring in that the boat is allowed to swing with wind and current, but it has the convenience of your not having to handle heavy ground tackle on board the boat. The basic variations in the single point mooring concept lie in the manner of anchoring which, in its simplest form, consists of a single omnidirectional mushroom anchor and in its more sophisticated form may utilize multiple patent anchors.

Bottom conditions favoring a mushroom anchor are cohesive soils like mud or clay, soft enough to allow the anchor to bury itself well. A mushroom anchor is inherently easy to handle and rig, and it has great

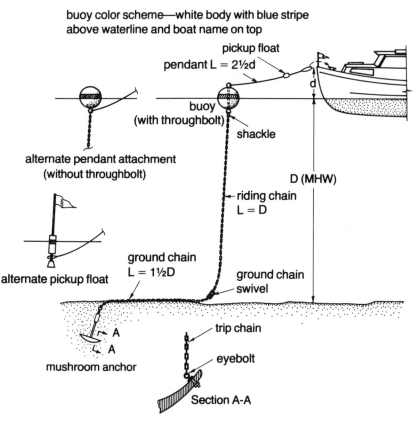

Fig. 13-1. Elements of a mushroom anchor mooring.

Table 13-1. Permanent Mooring Design Loads

Critical dimensions[a]			Horizontal mooring load—lbs[b]		
LOA	Beam—feet		ABYC[c]	Hurricanes: Wind speed	
feet	Power	Sail	Wind speed = 52 knots (Beaufort 10)	= 64 knots (Beaufort 12, Category I)	= 100 knots (Beaufort 12, Category III)
10	5	4	480	720	1,150
15	6	5	750	1,130	2,500
20	8	7	1,080	1,630	3,600
25	9	8	1,470	2,220	5,000
30	11	9	2,100	3,170	7,000
35	13	10	2,700	4,080	9,000
40	14	11	3,600	5,440	12,000
50	16	13	4,800	7,250	16,000
60	18	15	6,000	9,060	20,000
70	20	17		10,900	24,000
80	22	19		12,800	31,200

[a] Use LOA *or* beam of boat, whichever produces the larger load. Houseboats should use the load for the next larger powerboat size.
[b] Assumes freedom to oscillate and moderate shelter from seas proportionate to hull size.
[c] Source, American Boat and Yacht Council, Inc., P. O. Box 806, Amityville, New York 11701.

reliability. When it is well dug in and the pull is steady, it can resist great forces because of the weight and suction of the cohesive soil bottom. If the pull is sharp and repetitious, it is possible that the mushroom anchor will creep, but it will probably not break its set.

The components and geometry of the single point mooring system using a mushroom anchor are illustrated in Fig. 13-1.

The wind and sea loads generated on a mooring can be estimated by the same means as is done for anchored boats in Chapter 2. The American Boat and Yacht Council has established its recommendations for moorings in winds to 52 knots. Table 13-1 presents these loads along with higher loads that could be expected from hurricane force winds. Again, if your vessel is not of common proportions as represented by the ABYC nominal boats, it may be best to calculate the wind loads as was done for anchors in Chapter 2.

Having established the magnitude of the loads on the mooring, a proper size mushroom anchor can be selected compatible with the nature of the seabed. Fig. 13-2 relates anchor size to holding power for cohesive soil seabeds where mushroom anchors are at their best. One manufactur-

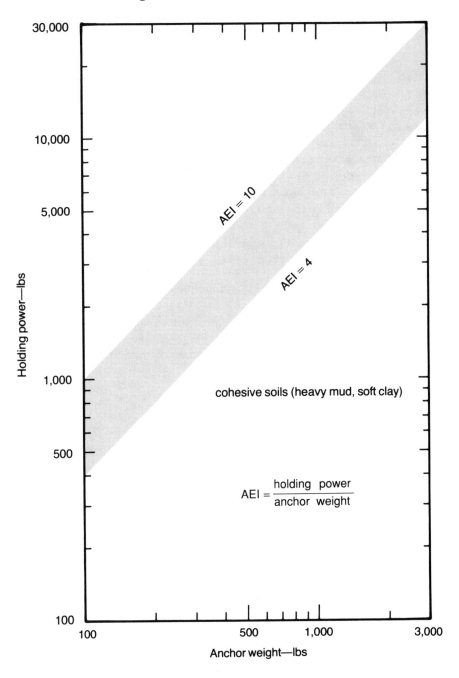

Fig. 13-2. Holding power of a well-silted-in mushroom anchor.

er's recommendations are listed in Table 13-2. These appear compatible with the ABYC loads for an anchor efficiency index (AEI) of 10.

While the weights of the recommended mushroom anchors may seem high when compared with the weights of patent anchors of the same holding power, the price of a mushroom anchor is but a fraction of that of a patent anchor. Where seabed conditions are compatible, the mushroom anchor will make a very suitable and economical permanent mooring anchor.

The components of the mooring system that connect the anchor with the boat are also of extraordinary size for two reasons. First, they are heavy in weight to provide short scope movement of the boat at the mooring. Second, they are large in size to minimize the possible dangers of wear and abrasion on the parts when left unattended for long periods of time with a valuable boat at tether.

The rationale for the sizing of the permanent mooring rode is as follows:

> The mushroom anchor holding power equals 10 times its weight.
>
> Riding chain breaking strength equals 2 times the anchor holding power.
>
> Ground chain diameter equals 2 times the riding chain diameter.
>
> Rope pendant breaking strength equals 4 times the anchor holding power. .

Table 13-2. Mushroom Anchor Sizes for Single-Point Moorings

For wind speed = 52 knots
Maximum anchor efficiency

LOA—ft	Powerboat	Mushroom anchor weight—lbs	
		Racing sailboat and multihulls	Cruising sailboats
up to 15	100	100	100
20	150	100	150
25	250	150	200
35	300	200	250
45	400	300	400
55	500	400	600

Source: Sea Spike Anchors, Inc., Farmingdale, New York.

Suggested sizes for the rode components of a permanent mushroom anchor mooring based on the above rationale are listed in Table 13-3. The lengths of the various components were specified in Fig. 13-1.

Several questions arise on the selection of materials for the rode components. For one, should the ground and riding chains be galvanized or left in their natural state? The consensus is that they need not be galvanized because they are heavy enough to suffer some rusting without endangering their strength. Furthermore, through one or two seasons of use they most likely would lose their galvanizing anyhow.

Although the rope pendant can be made of any natural or artificial fiber, polyester braid-on-braid rope is highly recommended. The pendant is so short that neither elasticity nor cost are significant in its selection. The strength, resistance to sunlight, ability to absorb abrasion, and its resistance to internal friction all favor polyester braid-on-braid rope for this purpose.

Stainless steel pendants are not recommended for permanent mooring installations. The reason is twofold—stainless steel cable repeatedly immersed in water tends to corrode internally, making it difficult to inspect by visual means and, second, steel cable with its relatively small diameter and the constant movement of the boat will "saw" through most chocks, fairleads, or rollers during the course of a season.

Moorings should be equipped with two pendants of equal size and construction, one being the primary pendant and the other a safety pendant. The safety pendant should be 25 percent longer than the primary pendant.

The other components of the mooring rode such as anchor shackle, swivel, buoy shackle, through-bolt, and pendant shackle must be of sizes compatible with the intended load capability of the mooring. Needless to

Table 13-3. Suggested Sizes of Permanent Mooring Rode Components

Mushroom anchor weight—pounds	Riding chain size—inches	Ground chain size—inches	Pendant size—inches Rope diameter[a]
200	1/4	1/2	5/8
300	5/16	5/8	3/4
400	3/8	3/4	7/8
600	7/16	7/8	1-1/16
800	1/2	1	1-1/4
1,000	5/8	1-1/4	1-1/2
1,200	5/8	1-1/4	1-5/8

[a] Polyester

say, so should the cleats, Samson post, or bitts on the bow of your boat. Shackles must be properly safety wired with galvanized steel wire.

The buoyancy of the mooring buoy should be 50 to 100 percent greater than the combined weight of the suspended components of the rode in the water (riding chain and pendant assembly). Do not paint the bottom of the mooring float with copper-based antifouling paint because of possible electrolysis problems with the galvanized steel parts in adjacent components.

Normally the heavy ground chain by itself will suffice to keep a good catenary in the combined chain rode. Should you want to further minimize swinging room, you can hang a kellet of 25 to 50 percent of the anchor weight at the chain juncture swivel.

The very fact that the mushroom anchor can bury itself effectively in soft bottoms means that it will be difficult to retrieve for inspection. One solution to that problem is to attach a trip chain to the edge of the anchor bowl (Fig. 13-1). Lead it along the ground chain far enough so that it won't be buried in the bottom. Wire it to the ground chain and it will be available for upsetting the mushroom anchor when the time comes for the inspection.

Many mooring installations use a deadweight anchor or sinker in place of a mushroom or patent anchor. The reasons may be cost or availability, but more importantly, a deadweight anchor can provide holding power in seabeds not compatible with other anchors, i.e. hard clay, packed sand, or gravel. They have another distinct advantage over patent anchors in that if they do start to drag, their efficiency is not materially reduced, whereas a patent anchor's efficiency becomes nil once it has started to drag.

The horizontal holding power of a deadweight anchor depends on how much friction it can develop resting on the bottom. Deadweight anchors depend on their immersed weight and not their weight in air. Immersed weight for various materials is as follows:

Material	Percent of weight in air
Concrete	55
Granite	64
Iron	86

Commonly used deadweight anchors are made of concrete whose holding power is about equal to 50 percent of their weight in air. A well sanded-in deadweight anchor can produce somewhat more holding power. To improve the holding power significantly, especially on harder seabeds, shear keys or fences can be cast into the bottom of the deadweight. (See R. J. Taylor. *Interaction of Anchors with Soil and Anchor Design.* (Washington, D.C.:

U.S. Navy Technical Note CEL N-1627, April 1982). Railroad wheels and automobile engine blocks can develop holding power to about 85 percent of their weight in air. As a rule of thumb, a deadweight anchor can develop holding power equal to its immersed weight. Compared to well silted-in mushroom anchors, a deadweight anchor should be made ten times as heavy to do the same job.

Scope is also important to both mushroom and deadweight anchors, although in a manner quite different from patent anchors. For patent anchors, large scope is desired to enhance the penetrating capability of the flukes of the anchor. For mushroom and deadweight anchors, large scope is desired to eliminate the lifting force on the anchor, which tends to make it less effective. Table 13-4 shows the vertical (lifting) force on these anchors as a function of the amount of scope in the rode.

Table 13-4. Short Scope Lifting Forces on Mooring Rodes (Per 1,000 Pounds of Horizontal Force)

Scope	1-1/4:1	1-1/2:1	2:1	2-1/2:1	3:1	4:1	5:1	8:1	10:1
Load on rode-lb	1,667	1,342	1,159	1,100	1,061	1,033	1,021	1,010	1,005
Lift - lb	1,333	900	575	425	350	250	200	124	100

Bitter experience gained from Hurricane Bob, which struck the northeast United States Coast in 1991 showed that virtually all moorings in use at that time were inadequate to cope with the hurricane force winds, wave, and surge. Wind forces alone in a 100 knot wind are almost four times those of the 52 knot winds used for the ABYC design loads for gales (Table 13-1). Wave heights grow and the surge adds 10 to 12 feet to the water's depth. Obviously, the standard gale mooring needs to be enhanced if your boat is to survive hurricane winds while on its mooring. Some of the ways recommended to do this can be found in Michael Taylor's *Moorings—A Discussion of the Problems and Solutions* (CIGNA Loss Control Services, Inc., Harvard, MA, Technical Paper, 1992), and are as follows:

> Locate mooring where it will give the boat freedom to swing on long scope and not interfere with other boats.
>
> Plan on setting oversize mushroom or deadweight anchors beforehand.
>
> Shun jury-rigged mooring anchors such as drums of concrete, bathtubs, engine blocks, and clusters of mushroom anchors.

Increase the size of chain and fittings used in the rode.

Extend the rode to yield a 7:1 minimum scope.

If rode cannot be lengthened, plan on adding a kellet to the rode to improve the catenary shape and help absorb surge loads.

Increase size of polyester pendant and provide extensive chafing gear. Install a backup safety pendant.

Reinforce boat deck hardware to take the added stress.

Inspect the mooring carefully before the hurricane season sets in and repair all deficiencies.

SCREW ANCHOR MOORINGS

A very useful bit of mooring anchor technology has come out of offshore oil pipeline developments. These are the screw anchors (Fig. 13-3). Unlike the smaller screw or earth anchors recommended for use as part of storm anchoring in Chapter 12, these screw anchors come in a variety of large sizes. The holding power of screw anchors is determined by number and diameter of helices welded to the shaft and, of course, by the competency of the seabed. A 150-pound screw anchor with a 1¼-inch diameter steel shaft has demonstrated a holding power equivalent to a 40,000-pound concrete sinker. They are hot-dip galvanized to minimize rusting in the marine environment.

These large screw anchors are installed with an hydraulic motor powered by an hydraulic pump on a surface barge. (The size of the equipment requires the assistance of an experienced underwater installer such as Energy Structures Incorporated, 10101 Chickasaw, Suite B, Houston, TX 77401.) A diver positions the screw over the desired location and then the hydraulic motor is activated, literally screwing the anchor into the seabed like a self-tapping screw. During installation, the anchors do not "dig holes" but, instead, they screw themselves into the soil at a rate of 5 to 8 feet per minute. The torque necessary to drive the screw is also a measure of the competency of the seabed and the anchor's resulting holding power.

Like the coral mooring eyebolt anchor (pages 323-25), the screw anchor installation equipment and personnel requirement is large enough to make the concept practical only for mooring clusters. Using screw anchors instead of concrete sinkers or mushroom anchors could be a very cost-effective design for a new mooring field. The cost of diver, installation equipment, and anchors appears significantly less than placing individual sinkers or mushroom anchors and it is considerably faster.

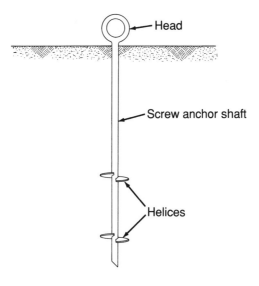

Fig. 13-3. The screw anchor for moorings.

MULTIPLE ANCHOR SINGLE POINT MOORING

It is entirely feasible to make a single point permanent mooring system using multiple burying or hooking anchors instead of one large mushroom anchor. In fact, if the seabed of your mooring area will not permit complete silting-in of a mushroom anchor, you had better think about using an anchor design that is compatible with the nature of the bottom.

In place of the single mushroom anchor you can set two or more of your favorite anchors (on chain rodes) equally spaced in a circle. Three, four, or five anchors may be considered. Three seems to be the most popular number holding the swinging circle to a minimum while still not involving too great a financial outlay. The three ground chains positioned 120° apart are brought together at the center of the circle and individually shackled to the swivel at the bottom of the riding chain. With the three anchors dug in symmetrically, the load on any one anchor never exceeds its capability as a single anchor under the same conditions (Fig. 13-4).

Criteria for selecting an anchor for the multiple anchor mooring concept differ from that of your boat's ground tackle because it has only to render service in one type of bottom and does not have to be easily handled nor conveniently stowed on board your boat. Therefore, it can be a specialized anchor design. Anchor compatibility with various types of bottoms was discussed in Chapter 7.

Experience has shown that the Danforth Standard LWT anchor works well in this application but one must not overlook the fact that the simpler Bruce anchor originated in this type of service.

Anchor size will depend on the weather expected in your intended mooring area. If storms do not produce winds over 30 knots and the area is protected from heavy seas, you can select working-size anchors for this application. However, if an occasional gale sweeps through, or you are near the path of seasonal hurricanes, you should choose storm-size anchors for the mooring.

The all-chain riding system is made in a way similar to the previously described mushroom anchor mooring system, in fact, it is identical, from the ground chain swivel up through the pendant. Below the ground chain swivel, it is different because there are now three ground chains to connect. Each ground chain should be made equal to the size of the riding chain (Table 13-3) and with sufficient length to yield an overall scope of 3 to 1 for your mooring to withstand a 30-knot blow.

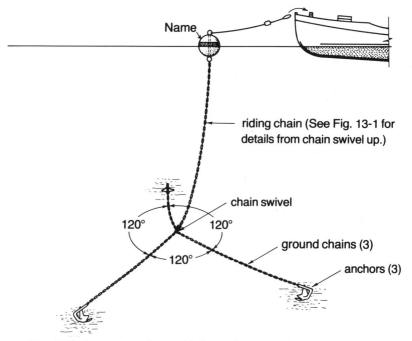

Fig. 13-4. Geometry of a multiple-anchor mooring.

The single-arm old-fashioned anchor used for multiple-anchor, permanent moorings has changed little through the years. *Above,* an anchor from the eighteenth or nineteenth century recovered from Pensacola Bay, Florida and *below,* a modern version in use in Hawaii. The crown eye permits the anchor to be lowered by a crane so that the active arm can engage the seabed. The stock keeps it from rolling out of its set when the vessel veers.

If you are going to use storm-size anchors, you will want to increase the scope available to 4 to 1 or more and, in order to preserve a small swinging radius, possibly hang a kellet on the chain swivel.

Retrieving the anchors of a three-point chain mooring can be done either using the services of a diver or by dragging for them. Which choice you make depends on your resources as well as the seabed. If you are a good free diver or a scuba-qualified diver, I would suggest using that technique since you probably also set the mooring by the same means.

Dragging for the individual ground chains using a grapnel is not all that difficult. Once you have hooked one chain and upset its anchor, the other two will come fairly easy. You are working blind, though, which is a disadvantage of this retrieval method.

FORE AND AFT BUOYED MOORINGS

Fore and aft moorings are employed where it is desirable to restrain the swinging of the boat caused by either wind or current, thereby making use of a narrow mooring slot or being able to pack a number of

This homemade 400-pound concrete deadweight anchor utilizes a short length of stud link chain cast into the concrete as the mooring ring. A swivel is fitted between the mooring ring and the riding chain.

Fore and aft moorings have reached a high level of development at Santa Catalina Island off the coast of Southern California. Fiberglass buoys and pickup wands are used, and concrete sinkers are replacing engine blocks as "anchors." This winter scene shows relatively few boats in this cove, but during the summer there is a turn away crowd.

moorings into a given area. It is only feasible where crosscurrents or crosswinds are not strong. Besides increasing the side loads on the mooring for which they are not designed, crosswinds and crosscurrents can bedevil you as you try to bring your boat into a densely packed fore and aft mooring situation. And when you are moored, the cross elements will set up an uncomfortable rolling of the boat. But there are situations where no other mooring is practical.

One of the foremost examples of fore and aft moorings is the array of them that literally surround Catalina Island off the coast of Southern California. With a boating population of more than 30,000 units only 25 miles away in Los Angeles, the fore and aft mooring concept has provided boaters with a maximum number of mooring slots in a limited area. They have saved embarrassment to thousands of novice boaters who come out every year with no experience in deep water anchoring. But to a number of old-timers who like to anchor in the coves now dotted with moorings, they are a noxious intrusion on our freedom to navigate.

The value of a Catalina mooring is its utility. It can handle boats with a wide range of lengths and can accommodate the nominal 6-foot range of tides. Also, it is easy to use by the weekend boater (Fig. 13-5).

The Catalina mooring has been improved over the years to enhance security, flexibility of use, and durability at a low cost, but it is still a fair weather mooring which is compatible with the normal boating season weather in the area. At times when fringes of hurricanes pass by or when the winter gales blow, use of the moorings is discouraged. When bad weather is anticipated, as for instance when the vicious offshore Santa Ana winds blow, the several Catalina harbormasters shoo everybody off of the moorings. The reason for this is clear when you consider that the moorings use deadweight anchors in a variety of concrete and iron shapes and are attached with short scope rodes. The pendants and the rope portions of the rigging are made from polypropylene rope which at the end of the season look pretty ragged.

The riding chain of the fore and aft buoyed mooring is usually made oversize and short to minimize the wandering of the buoy with wind and current. The buoy itself can be made from a cutoff hot water heater tank although more sophisticated installations now use fiberglass buoys. Bow and stern pendants are made of ¾-inch diameter or larger polypropylene

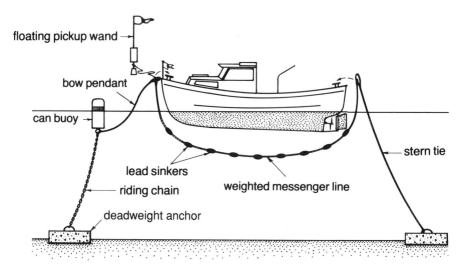

Fig. 13-5. Geometry of the Catalina mooring.

Handling even small deadweight anchors (400 pounds) requires skill and industrial size equipment.

rope which is good for one season. The rope messenger line is weighted with lead sinkers to cause it to sink quickly on release so that it does not foul rudder or propeller when the boat moves off the mooring.

FORE AND AFT PILE MOORINGS

There is another fore and aft mooring system that is popular in areas where pilings can be easily driven into the seabed. This system uses a pair of pilings that are spaced far enough apart to position a boat between them with, say, 10 feet of fore and aft clearance. The pilings are aligned with the current if in a river, or to the prevailing wind if in a large body of relatively still water. Usually the pilings will have spikes driven in a few feet above average water depth so that the slip lines will not drop all the way down the piling. You can then adjust the slip lines fore and aft to keep the boat centered between the pilings allowing sufficient slack to counter tidal height changes (Fig. 13-6).

I was introduced to pile moorings at the mouth of a New Zealand river where tidal changes were in the neighborhood of 12 feet and the current reversed itself with the tides. After a day of experimenting, I was

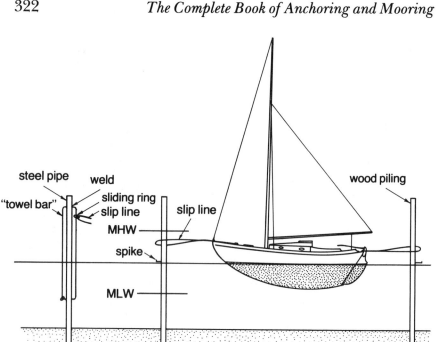

Fig. 13-6. Fore and aft pile moorings.

satisfied that the bow and stern slip lines were properly adjusted and I was free to leave the boat through any number of subsequent tidal changes.

Pilings leave much to be desired in a cosmetic sense in the sterile shoreline evolution that is taking place. But they are cheap to install, very serviceable, and lend themselves to densely packed arrangements.

A variation of the piling mooring is the post mooring made up of a pair of large diameter steel pipes driven into the seabed at the proper spacing to accommodate a boat between them with fore and aft clearance much like the pile mooring. To each post is welded a vertical "towel bar" (one on each side if the post serves two moorings) on which slides a steel ring. You secure your boat to these steel rings with slip lines in a manner similar to the pile moorings. But in this case the rings slide up and down along the towel bar, taking all of the wear and saving your slip lines. At high tide the sliding rings may not be visible when you arrive because gravity has taken them to the bottom of the towel bar. You can retrieve them with a boat hook.

The author's boat moored between pilings in the Waitangi River, New Zealand, where flood and ebb currents reach 3 to 5 knots. The rocky bottom (as indicated by the foreshore) adds to the difficulty of conventional anchoring.

Obviously, the mooring post will be more expensive than the piling approach, but if teredos and other wood-destroying organisms are abundant in your local waters, the additional cost may be offset by the longer life obtained.

CORAL SEABED MOORING DESIGN

As our ocean recreation population has increased dramatically over the past years, so has our concern for protecting the scenic coral reefs of the tropics. Boat anchors and chain rodes have been especially damaging to coral reefs in highly popular areas of the tropics to the detriment of the living coral. Ecologically-sensitive water enthusiasts now think in terms of preserving this great aesthetic and marine resource by using unique mooring designs for boats instead of anchoring.

The Key Largo National Marine Sanctuary in Florida was a pioneer in this effort. Based on their demonstrated success with installing moorings in coral reefs, the University of Hawaii further developed a technique usable by local dive groups for installing moorings at minimum cost and effort.

Setting coral moorings is not a single person task. There is equipment to procure and multi-manning of it during the setting process. It is best done by a cadre of experienced scuba divers who are prepared to set a whole series of eyebolts in a relatively small area. Having them manufactured, procuring the grouting, renting (or buying) the hydraulic equipment, and bringing the gear out to the site all require manpower and dollars which can best be justified in the placement of several moorings at one time. Exclusive of the hydraulic equipment, the cost of materials for a mooring is about $100 per mooring eye with labor provided by volunteer scuba divers interested in preserving the ecology of their diving domain.

The Hawaii design (see Fig. 13-7) starts with a ⅞-inch diameter 12-inch deep hole drilled into the the bedrock. A ¾-inch chevron-pointed carbide tip drill in a Stanley HD-45 rotary-impact hydraulic drill (or equivalent) can drill a ⅞-inch hole, 12 inches deep, in solid lava in under 10 minutes. In porous lava or cemented ash the drill time is 5 minutes and in dense solid coral it is only about 30 seconds. Such a piece of equipment is easily handled underwater by a competent scuba diver with the power unit in a boat on the surface.

Mooring eyes are made from ¾-inch diameter type 304 stainless steel rod with an eye on one end of a 12-inch straight shank. The straight shank is then threaded its full length to provide increased shear strength. The full 12 inches of the threaded shank is eventually immersed in the grout with only the eye exposed.

Grouts recommended are Quickcrete No. 1126 hydraulic cement or Quickcrete No. 1245 anchoring cement. The quick-setting cement is mixed with fresh water into a thick slurry on the dive boat and then injected by the diver into the hole (from the bottom up) using a homemade 2-inch diameter PVC syringe. The eyebolt is then inserted into the fluid grout, sinking slowly until the neck of the eye is flush with the top of the hole. It is gently rotated two or three revolutions to thoroughly wet the bolt shank. Setting time is a nominal 30 minutes to initial hardening and 24 hours to final cure.

The rigging of the mooring from eyebolt to float and pickup pendant is similar to anchor or sinker-type moorings. The entire mooring should be inspected regularly as with other moorings. The coral mooring is not a storm mooring and boats should vacate it on signs of approaching bad weather.

It would appear, offhand, that the overall cost of the coral eyebolt mooring is no more than that of a conventional mud mooring using a mushroom anchor and it is far less destructive to a coral seabed than the anchor of a boat. To be able to preserve, protect, and still use our wonderful tropical marine habitat is a fortuitous union of man and nature.

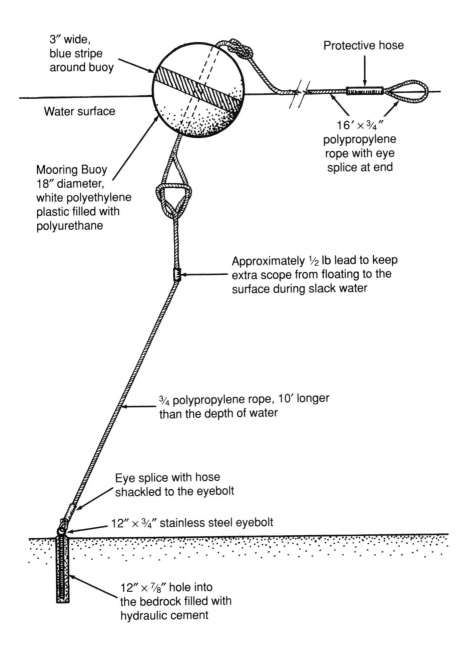

3" wide, blue stripe around buoy

Protective hose

Water surface

16' × ¾" polypropylene rope with eye splice at end

Mooring Buoy 18" diameter, white polyethylene plastic filled with polyurethane

Approximately ½ lb lead to keep extra scope from floating to the surface during slack water

¾ polypropylene rope, 10' longer than the depth of water

Eye splice with hose shackled to the eyebolt

12" × ¾" stainless steel eyebolt

12" × ⅞" hole into the bedrock filled with hydraulic cement

Fig. 13-7. Schematic of coral mooring design.

MOORING MAINTENANCE

Little maintenance but much inspection is required of a properly made mooring system of the types just described. When first set, sufficient time must be given for the mushroom anchor to sand itself in place. A visual check of its buried state should be made, if possible, before placing full reliance on it. Similarly, the anchors of a multiple-anchor mooring must each be initially well set. All shackles must be safety wired. The pendant should be checked frequently for wear and replaced when it shows severe wear or deterioration. No rope likes the rays of the sun, much less the steady diet of sun, salt, and sand that a mooring pendant gets.

Substantial chafing gear should always be used if the boat is left unattended for a long period. Leather and corded hose give good chafing protection when held securely in place. If there is any chance that the pendant will lift free of its chock or cleat, lash it in place. A boat adrift is not only a loss to the owner but could become a hazard to other boats in the area.

In a way you are lucky if your mooring has to be removed every year because it provides an excellent opportunity for inspection, and the whole winter to correct any problems. A mooring should not be left in the water longer than two years before refurbishment, and it should be inspected carefully every year.

Your yearly checklist of in-the-water components should include the following:

Corrosion and electrolysis. A little rust won't hurt anything but at some point the rusted part may become dangerously weakened. Chip a little rust off and see how much actual metal remains to hold your mooring together.

Wear of shackle pins, chain end links, swivel bails, and other such joining elements. Too much wear could cause them to give up rather suddenly.

Condition of the riding chain. Sun and warmer surface water seem to cause troubles with chain nearer the surface than at the lower reaches. Therefore, extra care of chain within 6 to 10 feet of the water's surface is recommended.

Maintenance of the multiple anchor mooring system is similar to the mushroom anchor mooring, but it is recommended that the anchors be retrieved at the end of the season. Since conventional anchors are easily broken out, and they represent a much bigger investment than a single mushroom anchor, it is best not to appear to have abandoned them.

Groups of moorings should be given special attention after a blow because one or more of the moorings may have been dragged out of position and their boats could foul other moorings. Moorings in a cluster should not be closer than one and one-quarter times the total scope (ground chain plus riding chain plus pendant) plus the overall length of the boat using the mooring. If the distance becomes less than that, it is time to reset one or more moorings.

Every mooring buoy should have some kind of identification on it, preferably the owner's boat's name. But it could also have the name of the yacht club and an identifying number. If the mooring is solely for the use of guests, it should say "guest." Boaters will be more careful in the use of a mooring if they know that it, indeed, has an owner. Reflective tape added to the buoy topsides will make it easier for the user to find it at night.

RIGHTS TO MOORINGS

In a superficial sense, there is nothing more comforting after a hard ride at sea than to come into a harbor and see an unoccupied mooring buoy beckoning to you. But is it really available to you? Every mooring was set by some person or organization who intends to use it for their convenience and at their whim. That person may be on the boat entering the harbor behind you, or, more than likely, the person will be on the boat that arrives after midnight when you are having a happy dream about how accommodating the boating community really is.

If you do not own the mooring that you are looking at, seek out the owner for permission to use it. Yacht clubs usually have port captains to assign moorings. Commercial moorings are usually controlled by a harbormaster who gets very indignant if you take up a mooring without first seeking an assignment.

But what if you can't find the owners or managers of the moorings? What then? You just take your chance, if it meets your needs. But if the rightful owner or lessee shows up, cast off your mooring line gracefully and thank the owner for the interim use.

In many ways abandoning the mooring may be the best thing you could do because you really don't have the slightest idea whether the mooring is safe or not. You have no idea what kind of anchor it used, how large (or small) the ground and riding chains were, nor when the underwater components were last inspected and renewed. All you know is that the buoy was afloat. The immediate convenience of an unfamiliar mooring should not be substituted for the known security of your boat.

Appendix

ANCHOR MANUFACTURERS AND IMPORTERS

A&B Industries
1261 Anderson Drive
San Rafael, CA 94901
(plow, old-fashioned)

Benson Marine Products Div.
1387 Fairport Road, #800
Fairport, NY 14450
(grapnel)

Avon Seagull Marine
1851 McGaw Avenue
Irvine, CA 92714
(CQR, Delta)

A. B. Chance Co.
210 North Allen Street
Centralia, MO 65240
(screw anchors)

Creative Marine
P.O. Box 2120
Natchez, MS 39121
(The MAX)

The Crosby Co.
183 Pratt Street
Buffalo, NY 14240-1083
(stainless steel SSPF)

Euro Marine Trading, Inc.
8325 #D, S.W. 107th Ave.
Miami, FL 33173
(FOB)

Haft Marine Products, Inc.
P.O. Bos 11210
Bradenton, FL 34282-1210
(Delta)

Hans C-Anchor, Inc.
P.O. Box 66756
St. Petersburg, FL 33736
(Hans C-Anchor)

High Seas
4861 24th Avenue
Port Huron, MI 48060
(SSPF)

Imtra
30 Sam Barnett Blvd.
New Bedford, MA 02745
(Bruce)

Paul E. Luke
P.O. Box 816
East Boothbay, ME 04544
(Old-fashioned)

NAV–X Corporation
1386W West McNab Road
Fort Lauderdale, FL 33309
(aluminum SSPF)

S.A.K. Anchor, Inc.
P.O. Box 595
Port Huron, MI 48060
(modular SSPF)

Pekny Industries, Inc.
300 2nd Ave., S.E. #69
St. Petersburg, FL 33701
(Northill/Pekny)

Sea Spike Marine Supply
994 Fulton St.
Farmingdale, NY 11735
(SSPF, grapnel)

Rule Industries
Cape Ann Industrial Park
Gloucester, MA 01930
(plow, SSPF)

U.S. Anchor Mfg. Inc.
503-A Selig Drive
Atlanta, GA 30366
(SSPF)

Sailors Outfitting Service
13613 Gulf Blvd.
Madeira Beach, FL 33708
(Barnacle)

West Marine Products
500 West Ridge Drive
Watsonville, CA 95076-4100
(SSPF)

WINDLASS MANUFACTURERS AND IMPORTERS

A&B Industries
1261 Anderson Drive, Suite C
San Rafael, CA 94901
(ABI/manual)

W.H. Denouden
P.O. Box 8712
Baltimore, MD 21240
(Vetus/electric)

Avon Seagull Marine
1851 McGaw Avenue
Irvine, CA 92714
(Simpson-Lawrence/
    manual and electric)

Fleming Marine Inc.
P.O. Box 60500
San Diego, CA 92106
(Fleming/electric)

Galley Maid Marine Products
P.O. Box 10417
Riviera Beach, FL 33419
(Galley Maid/electric
    and hydraulic)

Benson Marine Products, Inc.
125 Mount View Lane
Colorado Springs, CO 80907
(Hydra-Cap/hydraulic)

Good Automatic Windlass
Box 357
Barnegat, NJ 08005
(Good/electric)

Ideal Windlass Co.
P.O. Box 430
East Greenwich, RI 02818
(Ideal/electric)

Imtra Corporation
30 Barnet Boulevard
New Bedford, MA 02745
(Lofrans/electric)

International Marine
P.O. Box 308
Guilford, CT 06437
(Lewmar/electric)

Lighthouse Mfg. Co.
2944 Rubidoux Blvd.
Riverside, CA 92509
(Lighthouse/electric
    and hydraulic)

Lunenburg Foundry
    and Engineering
P.O. Box 1240
Lunenburg, Nova Scotia
Canada B0J 2C0
(traditional manual)

Maxwell Winches, Inc.
629 Terminal Way, Suite #1
Costa Mesa, CA 92627
(Maxwell/electric and
    hydraulic)

Nordic Machine and
    Manufacturing Co.
4700 Ballard Avenue N.W.
Seattle, WA 98107
(Nordic/hydraulic)

Plastimo, USA
6605 Selnick Road, Route 100
Business Park
Baltimore, MD 21227
(Plastimo/manual and
    electric)

R.C. Plath
5300 S.E. Johnson Creek Blvd.
Portland, OR 97222
(Plath/manual and electric)

Powerwinch Co.
810 Union Avenue
Bridgeport, CT 06607
(Powermate/electric)

South Pacific Associates
4918 Leary Avenue N.W.
Seattle, WA 98107
(Muir and Lofrans/electric)

Simpson-Lawrence USA
3004 29th Avenue East
Bradenton, FL 32408
(Simpson-Lawrence/
    manual and electric)

Wilcraft Marine
28 Bremen Street
Rochester, NY 14621
(Wilcraft/electric)

Bibliography

American Boat and Yacht Council. *Anchoring, Mooring, Docking, Towing, and Lifting. Project A-5.* Amityville, N.Y.: ABYC, 1978.

American Practical Navigator (Bowditch). H.O. Publication No. 9. Washington, D.C.: U.S. Government Printing Office, 1977.

Bates, Robert L. and Julia A. Jackson, eds. *Dictionary of Geological Terms.* 3rd. ed. Garden City, N.Y.: Anchor Press/Doubleday, 1984.

Kinney, Francis S. *Skene's Elements of Yacht Design.* Rev. ed. New York: Dodd, Mead & Co., 1973.

Moriarty, James R. and Neil F. Marshall. *The History and Evolution of Anchors.* Occasional Paper #3. San Diego, Cal.: University of California at San Diego (San Diego Science Foundation), 1965.

Ogg, Robert Danforth and Donald C. Linnenbank. *Anchors and Anchoring.* Gloucester, Mass.: Rule Industries, 1977.

Shepard, F. P. *The Earth Beneath the Sea.* Baltimore: The Johns Hopkins University Press, 1967.

Smith, Robert A. *Anchors—Selection and Use.* 2d. ed. Portland, Ore.: Robert A. Smith, Naval Architect (1825 N.E. Fremont St.), 1983.

Sverdrup, H. V., et al. *The Oceans.* Englewood Cliffs, N.J.: Prentice-Hall, 1942.

Tate, William H. *A Mariner's Guide to the Rules of the Road.* 2d ed. Annapolis, Md.: Naval Institute Press, 1982.

Van Dorn, W. G. *Oceanography and Seamanship.* 2d. ed. Centreville, Md.: Cornell Maritime Press, 1993.

Index

Anchor stowage: improper on bobstay, 34; Bruce, 36; stock-stabilized,
pivoted-fluke, 36-37; Danforth
LWT, 36-37, 43, 44; CQR (plow),
36, 38; old-fashioned, 39; hanging,
39, 40, 41; in well, 39, 41-43, disassembled, 42, 43; old-fashioned on
motor cruiser, 42

Anchor well, 39, 41-43

Anchor windlass: capstan, 72, 73, 74;
description and types, 72-74; features, 74-75; mounting failure, 75;
proper use, 75; installation, 75, 82,
87, 89; positioning, 77, 78; maintenance, 92, 94-95; failure, 299

B

Billboard, 68, 69

Bitt: making fast, 7; bolt-on, 53-54;
twin, 53-54; hollow, 54; defined, 56;
disappearing, 56, 57; metal, 56-57;
twin, hitch, 60

Boat motion, 15-17

Bollard, 56

Bow roller: failure, 3, 28, 299; stemhead, 27-30, 38; loads, 29; design, 29,
193; restraining rode, 29-30

Bowsprit roller: metal tubing sprit, 32;
loads on, 33; riding stopper, 119

Bridles: catamarans, 227; crosswind
anchoring, 259

Buoy: mooring, 5, 300-2, 307, 318, 319,
323-25; on trip line, 219; on anchor
rode, 256-57

Burying anchor: Fortress, 43, 147, 149,
163, 165, 167, 170, 171, 178, 194;
Hall stockless, 68; description, 140-
41; CQR, 142, 163, 165, 170, 172-75,
178, 179, 194; Bruce, 143-44, 163,
165, 170, 171, 172-74, 178, 194;
Delta, 143, 165, 194; stock-stabilized,
pivoted-fluke, 144-48, 180; Danforth
LWT, 144-48, 147, 163, 165, 166, 172-
74, 176, 177-78, 194; MAX, 145, 169,
170; Danforth Deepset, 146, 148,

163, 165, 178; Wishbone, 148, 150;
Navy stockless, 149-50, 151, 170, 194;
Babbit, 159; Britany, 171; FOB, 171;
sliding ring, 181, 267, 268; matched
to seabed, 186-87, 191; selection of,
191-92, 194, 195, 196, 197-98; stockless patent, 192; Keepers, 267

C

Cable, 7

Cabo San Lucas disaster: bow roller
failure, 28; windlass attachment failure, 75; human failure, 200-1; fore
and aft mooring, 232, 233, 235-37;
dragging anchor, 278; weather, 284,
285-86, 300; lessons learned, 301-3

Catalina mooring, 318-21

Chafing: bow roller, 29; chain riding
stopper, 137-38; materials, 138;
means of avoiding, 287, protection
devised by Houston Yacht Club, 287,
288; prevention during storm, 297-
98; mooring pendant, 311

Chain: strength of weakest link, 11;
shot, 101; BBB, 101, 103; Proof Coil,
101, 103; stud link, 101, 103, 104,
318; elongation, 102; oversize end
links, 102; strength of, 102, 103; high
strength, 103-5; hook, 116, 117;
mooring, 307, 310, 311

Chain lead: defined, 128; size matched
to rope, 129; length, 129-30; selection, 196

Chain locker: cruising boat, 43-45;
design, 48-49; chain chute, 48, 50,
51; deck pipe, 49, 50-52; volume, 50

Chain rode: connectors, 106-10,
111; swivels, 108-9, 110, 287, 318;
catenary, 110-15; bitter end attachment, 111; Coast Guard cutter *General Greene*, 115; failure of, 114, 286;
riding stopper, 115-18, 119; length
markers, 118-19, 120; care of, 119-21;
inspection guide, 121; selection of,
194; riding stoppers, 301

About the Author

Earl R. Hinz, a former aeronautical engineer and inveterate Pacific ocean sailor (over 40,000 miles logged), retired in 1975 to devote his time to sailing and writing about boats and boating. From 1976 to 1981 he was Technical Editor of *Sea*, pioneering instrumentation and techniques for evaluating the performance of power and sailboats. He personally conducted sea trials on 104 recreational vessels. In 1979 he won the prestigious Boating Writer's International Award for his magazine report on a test program he conducted on boating equipment. In 1980 he started a monthly column on Pacific cruising for *Sea*; this column became a bimonthly feature of *Cruising World* for which he is currently a contributing editor.

Now a resident of Honolulu, he lives aboard his boat. He is also the author of *The Offshore Log, Understanding Sea Anchors and Drogues, Landfalls of Paradise,* and *Pacific Wanderer.*

Richard R. Rhodes is a graphic designer and technical artist retired from the University of Hawaii's Institute of Geophysics. An avid sailor himself, he was responsible for drawing the lines of the museum ship *Falls of Clyde* and for the design and specifications of the Hawaiian Koa racing canoe. This is the third book on which Rhodes and Hinz have collaborated.